The author bears sole responsibility for the content. The publisher accepts no liability.

First published in 2026 by PRESS DIONYSUS LTD in the UK, 167 Portland Road, W11 4LZ, London.

www.pressdionysus.com

Paperback

ISBN: 978-1-913461-49-0

© Printed 2026 by PRESS DIONYSUS

PRESS DIONYSUS

All rights reserved. Printed in the UK. No part of this book may be used or reproduced in any manner whatsoever without written permission except in the case of brief quotations embodied in critical articles or reviews.

The author bears sole responsibility for the content. The publisher accepts no liability.

First published in 2025 by PRESS DIONYSUS LTD in the UK, 167, Portland Road, N15 4SZ, London.

www.pressdionysus.com

Paperback

ISBN: 978-1-913961-48-0
Copyright © 2025 by PRESS DIONYSUS.

THE SECRETS OF FATIMA

AND

THE PAPAL ASSASSINATION

Mustafa Demirbağ

DIONYSUS

ISBN- 978-1-913961-48-0
© Press Dionysus 2025

Translated by Timur Öztürk

Cover design: Tuğrul M. Öztürk

Press Dionysus LTD, 167, Portland Road, N15 4SZ, London
• e-mail: info@pressdionysus.com
• web: www.pressdionysus.com

A TIME SEALED WITH BLOOD

"The Three Secrets of Fatima and the Vatican: A Study on

History, Faith, and Politics"

Preface

History is not merely a stage upon which wars, victories, and defeats are played out. It is also a labyrinth woven with secrets, prophecies, and truths hidden in the shadows.

In 1917, during the event known as the Miracle of Fatima, witnessed by three shepherd children in a small Portuguese village, three divine secrets were revealed to the children. For many years, these secrets remained buried within the Vatican's secret archives. Known to only a handful of Cardinals, the content of the secrets struck terror into the hearts of the Popes who read them.

The 1981 assassination attempt in St. Peter's Square was not just an attack on a single individual. It became part of a larger chain of events shaping world history. In that moment when Mehmet Ali Ağca pulled the trigger, the veil was lifted not only on one man's fate, but also on the shadowy face of global politics.

Was the assassination backed by the intelligence games of the Cold War—the KGB, CIA, Eastern Bloc states, and the Vatican? Or was it to be seen as a divine sign confirming the realization of the Fatima prophecies? Was Ağca merely a hitman in a deeper conspiracy born from the dark undercurrents of the Cold War? Or is there an even greater mystery still unfolding—one deeply entwined with the Fatima revelations?

The Fatima prophecies, the papal assassination, the Roman trials, Cold War intrigues, religious mysticism, and covert intelligence operations are explored in this book with supporting documents and evidence.

The power struggle between the KGB and CIA, the collapse of the Soviet Union, the fall of the Berlin Wall, the hidden history of the Vatican, and the fulfilment of prophecies—all form the backdrop of a gripping narrative. The Pope, who survived the assassination, later said, "The Virgin Mary saved me," and would, years later, reveal the secret.

Why did the Vatican conceal the Third Secret for so long? What was Ağca's connection to this hidden prophecy?

For readers who seek to illuminate the hidden details of the past and uncover the truths buried between the lines of history, this book is not only a work of investigation, but also a profound journey of questioning.

History recounts what has happened; yet some secrets wait patiently for their appointed time to be revealed. Perhaps the Third Secret of Fatima had simply been waiting... for its time.

Are you ready to face the truth?

Wishing you an insightful read.

"The assassination attempt on Pope John Paul II by Ağca is filled with complex political theories and allegations of conspiracy, closely tied to the Cold War era. This book aims to shed light on the motivations behind the attack, Ağca's life story, the judicial process, and its aftermath. By comprehensively examining Ağca's life and the assassination attempt, the book offers readers a unique and in-depth perspective on a pivotal moment in modern history."

Mustafa Demirbağ

About the Author

Mustafa Demirbağ (b. 1971) is a graduate of Marmara University Faculty of Law and currently practices as an independent attorney. Specializing in criminal law, he is recognized for carrying his legal expertise into both literature and academic writing.

His articles have appeared in various journals and newspapers, and he is the author of the significant study The History of Political Trials in Turkey, regarded as a reference work in the fields of politics and law. Bridging history, law, and politics, Demirbağ reflects his perspective in both academic and literary form.

What is Eschatology (The Science of the End Times)?

Eschatology, a term unique to Western theological literature, derives from the Greek words *"ἔσχατος"* (*eschatos*, "last") and *"λόγος"* (*logos*, "doctrine" or "science"). It is a theological discipline that examines beliefs and teachings about the "last things," such as the end of the world, death, the afterlife, final judgment, heaven, and hell.

The core concepts of eschatology include the apocalypse, resurrection, heaven, and hell. These concepts hold significant places in both Islamic and Western thought and captivate the deep interest of people. The apocalypse refers to the time when the world comes to an end and the Day of Judgment begins, while the resurrection denotes the place where this judgment takes place. Heaven and hell describe the destinations where souls will dwell after death. These concepts play crucial roles in belief systems and social life. Eschatology also suggests that humanity may play a part in hastening this end.

Beyond religion, the concept is addressed in philosophical and cultural contexts as well. Eschatology offers an important perspective for understanding the meaning of human life, life after death, and the end of the universe. Due to its embedded beliefs and symbolism, it holds great significance for religious communities and profoundly influences how people shape their lives.

The Subject of Eschatology

Eschatology deals with both the end of individual existence (personal death) and the end of universal history (the end of the world). Its key topics include:

- **Death**: The fate of the soul and the cessation of physical life.
- **Afterlife**: Beliefs such as resurrection and the soul's journey to heaven or hell.
- **End of the World**: Cosmic destruction or transformation and humanity's collective judgment.
- **Signs of the End Times**: Events believed to occur at the end of history (e.g., the coming of the Messiah, Antichrist, Mahdi, etc.).
- **Final Judgment**: The ultimate judgment where people are judged based on their deeds and sent to their eternal destinies.

Types of Eschatology

Eschatology varies across different religions and cultures:

Christian Eschatology

Christian eschatology focuses on the return of Jesus, the Day of Judgment, and beliefs about heaven and hell. It begins with Jesus's death and resurrection, which shape Christian beliefs about salvation, judgment, and the afterlife.

A key figure in Christian eschatology is the messianic saviour, Jesus Christ, whose crucifixion is seen as an interruption in God's divine plan. According to this eschatological expectation, Christ will return at the end of time to complete God's unfinished work. The Second Coming of Christ (*Parousia*)[1] will herald the resurrection of the dead and final judgment. Different denominations — Catholic, Orthodox, and Protestant — interpret these teachings differently.

Catholic Eschatology

Catholic eschatology is based on the teachings of the Catholic Church and concerns both the end of the world and humanity's ultimate fate. Key elements include:

1. **Resurrection of the Dead**: Both the righteous and the wicked will rise bodily.
2. **Individual Judgment**: After death, the soul is sent to heaven, hell, or purgatory for purification.
3. **Second Coming of Christ (Parousia)**: Christ returns to enact universal judgment.
4. **Final Judgment**: All humanity is judged before God.
5. **New Heaven and New Earth**: A renewed creation initiated by God at the end of time.

Islamic Eschatology

Islamic eschatology is based on the teachings in the Qur'an and Hadith, and it includes the Day of Judgment

---

[1] The "End Times" Phenomenon and Eschatology Myths Prof. Dr. Işıl ALTUN** Menderes ÇINAROĞLUMillî Folklor, 2020, Yıl 32, Cilt 16, Sayı 128

(*Yawm al-Qiyamah*) and the events that follow. Core concepts include the end of the world, the afterlife, and death.

According to Islam, the Day of Judgment will occur after all living beings have died, and all people will be resurrected to give an account of their deeds before God. The afterlife is seen as a permanent abode after this world. These teachings form a fundamental pillar of Islamic belief and provide moral guidance for how life should be lived.

Key Concepts in Islamic Eschatology:

- **Death and Barzakh**: The soul enters an intermediate realm called *Barzakh* until the Day of Resurrection.
- **Signs of the Last Day**: Major signs include the coming of the Mahdi, the emergence of the Dajjal (Antichrist), the descent of Jesus (Isa), and the corruption of the earth by Gog and Magog (*Ya'juj and Ma'juj*).
- **The Blowing of the Trumpet**: The Angel Israfil blows the trumpet twice, signalling the end of time and resurrection.
- **Resurrection and Judgment**: All humans gather before God for reckoning.
- **Heaven and Hell**: The righteous enter paradise; the wicked are sent to hell.

Jewish Eschatology

Jewish eschatology focuses on the coming of the Messiah, resurrection of the dead, and the establishment of God's kingdom on earth. Prophetic texts, especially the Book of Daniel, contain many eschatological elements.

Hindu and Buddhist Eschatology

In Hinduism and Buddhism, time is cyclical — worlds are created and destroyed repeatedly.

- In **Hinduism**, *Moksha* is liberation from the cycle of rebirth.
- In **Buddhism**, *Nirvana* represents the release from this endless cycle.

Functions of Eschatology

Eschatology serves several roles within belief systems:

1. **Moral Guidance**: Encourages righteous behaviour by emphasizing accountability.
2. **Consolation**: Offers hope and meaning in the face of death and uncertainty.
3. **Social Cohesion**: Provides a shared sense of destiny and strengthens unity.
4. **Deepening Faith**: Reinforces belief in God's divine plan.

Modern Perspectives

Eschatology has been interpreted both religiously and philosophically throughout history. Today, it also encompasses scientific scenarios for the end of the world — such as climate change, nuclear war, or asteroid impact. In theology, eschatology seeks to balance individual and collective salvation.

There are some parallels between Catholic and Islamic eschatology regarding the end of the world, humanity's ultimate fate, and God's plan.

Comparative Points: Catholic and Islamic Eschatology

Similarities:

- **Divine Justice and Judgment**:
  Both believe God will judge individuals based on their deeds, leading to either salvation (heaven) or punishment (hell).

- **Resurrection of the Dead**:
  In both, the dead will be bodily resurrected, with souls reunited with bodies.

- **Role of the Messiah**:
  In Catholicism, Jesus Christ returns to enact final judgment.
  In Islam, Jesus (Isa) returns to defeat the Dajjal and re-establish justice.

- **Prayer and Repentance**:
  Both traditions emphasize repentance and divine forgiveness.

Differences:

- **Nature and Identity of the Messiah**:
  Catholics see Jesus as the Son of God and final judge.
  Islam views Jesus (Isa ibn Maryam) as a prophet, returning to serve God's justice.

- **Purgatory and Barzakh**:
  Catholics believe in purgatory as a place of purification.
  Islam describes *Barzakh*, an intermediate realm where souls await the resurrection.

- **Signs of the End**:
  Islam provides detailed signs before the end (Dajjal, Gog and Magog, Mahdi, etc.).
  Catholicism focuses more on Christ's return and general end-time themes.

- **Theological Viewpoint**:
  Catholicism emphasizes the Trinity (Father, Son, Holy Spirit).
  Islam upholds the oneness of God (*Tawhid*).

Christianity vs. Islam: Eschatological Comparison

When comparing Christian and Islamic eschatology, both systems share beliefs in the apocalypse, heaven and hell, the soul's fate, and end-time events. Each tradition sees these events as unfolding through divine intervention.

However, in Christianity, the end is closely tied to Jesus's Second Coming. In Islam, it involves the emergence of the Mahdi and Jesus's return as a supporter. Both religions describe heaven and hell, though in Christianity heaven is eternal joy in God's presence, while in Islam it is seen as a reward beyond this world.

Understanding the **Three Secrets of Fatima** from a Catholic Christian perspective requires familiarity with the discipline of eschatology.

It is especially beneficial for Turkish society — predominantly Muslim — to understand the belief systems of the West and the forces that shaped them. To grasp the background of Western religiously driven political strategies throughout history, one must understand how eschatological thinking has been applied. The **Third Secret of Fatima** was long kept hidden by the Vatican and was only publicly revealed in the year 2000.

Such events show that religious prophecies are not solely theological concerns — they often directly serve the worlds of global politics and intelligence. Understanding how Western religious discourse is intertwined with political decisions is particularly useful when interpreting international relations and current events.

Moreover, eschatological concepts help illuminate how religion and politics are intertwined and provide insight into popular culture's fascination with "apocalyptic prophecies." Knowing the core ideas of eschatology aids not only in understanding religious matters but also the political and cultural dynamics of the West.

The **Third Secret of Fatima** is not merely a prophecy — it is a phenomenon deeply intertwined with Western belief systems and political options.

In conclusion, the Third Secret of Fatima and the concept of eschatology provide a vital key to understanding how religion, politics, and culture intersect in the Western world.

> "The history of mankind is a theater of the coexistence of good and evil."
> — *Pope John Paul II*

THE SECRETS OF FATIMA

Picture 1. In 1917, a small town became the center of a great secret... On this land, where the Holy Virgin appeared, history witnessed a sealed prophecy. In Fatima, the sky opened, and a message was delivered to three shepherd children. Today, these sacred lands are not only a place of pilgrimage but also a witness to one of history's sealed prophecies.

Fatima and Her Miracle: Holy Secrets, Prophecies, and Divine Apparitions

The Mysterious Origins of the Town of Fatima

The lands of Portugal have been shaped for centuries by a rich blend of history and legend. From the 700s to the 1250s, Muslim kingdoms or sultanates had conquered the southern half of Portugal. From the 8th to the 13th century, these lands bore deep traces of Islamic civilization and were shaken by Christian kingdoms' efforts of reconquest. The cultural heritage rising in the shadow of Andalusia permeated the soul of Portugal.

One part of this heritage is the town of Fatima, named after Fatima, the daughter of the Islamic prophet Muhammad. However, there is also another legend associated with the region's name: it is said that a Moorish princess named Fatima was kidnapped and baptized by a Christian knight, taking the name Oriana. This tragic tale, where love and religion intersect, immortalized the town's name.

Until the story of the three shepherd children emerged at the beginning of the 20th century, Fatima—located in central Portugal—was an ordinary town. In fact, until the miracle that occurred in 1917, neither Portuguese history nor the Catholic Church had given any significance to this small town. After the event, however, it became the country's most important religious center from the early 20th century onward.

The Shepherd Children and the Miracle of Fatima

Picture 2, Three little shepherds, bearers of a great secret... Lucia, Francisco, and Jacinta were still children when they heard the message from the sky in Fatima. But was what they saw a sign given not only to them, but to all of humanity?

May 13, 1917 – Town of Fatima, Portugal

History is full of turning points that shape the destiny of humanity. But there are certain days on which not only events change but history itself shifts course. One such day occurred on May 13, 1917, in Fatima.

As the first rays of sunlight illuminated the barren lands of Fatima, three small shepherd children—10-year-old Lucia dos Santos, 9-year-old Francisco Marto, and 7-year-old Jacinta Marto—were herding their sheep.

The day began like any other, but soon an extraordinary event unfolded.

Suddenly, a bright flash of light from the sky startled them. The children were shaken by a sound like thunder. When they looked up, they saw a woman in radiant white clothing surrounded by light. This elegant figure told them not to be afraid and asked them to come to the same place on the 13th of each month to pray and speak with her.

When the children recounted this extraordinary encounter to their families, no one believed them at first. However, when the mysterious woman reappeared the following month, she told the children she would perform a miracle to convince the nonbelievers. She instructed the children to tell people to come on October 13 and look at the sun.

The news spread rapidly by word of mouth and soon made headlines in local newspapers. The extraordinary event expected to take place in Fatima drew immense interest from the Portuguese people. On the appointed day, thousands flocked to Fatima. Together with the three children, the crowds looked skyward, preparing to witness history.

The sun appeared to dance—or at least that's what the thousands standing there claimed to have seen.

The young Lucia and the two other shepherd children watched in awe. The sky trembled. People fell to their knees. Some prayed; others thought the end of the world had come.

Thousands who looked at the sun later claimed, "We saw the sun move from its place, zigzag, and dance as if alive." Thousands truly believed they had witnessed a miracle. Strangely, only the three children could see or hear the woman, yet thousands present experienced an unexplainable state of awe.

Was a voice heard at that moment, or was it all an illusion? The children claimed the woman gave them three secrets. These secrets remained hidden for years and would eventually alter global balances. The first two secrets were revealed soon after, but the third would remain undisclosed for decades, protected in the Vatican's Secret Archives.

Years later, when the Vatican announced it would reveal the final secret, the entire world waited in anticipation.

The Miracle of the Sun (Milagre do Sol)

Picture 3. 1917, Fatima... Thousands of eyes turned to the sky, the sun danced, and a miracle took place. Was that moment merely a divine sign, or a mysterious warning given to humanity?

The woman who spoke to the shepherd children and appeared only to them was believed to be none other than the Virgin Mary. According to the belief, the Virgin Mary gave the children what came to be known as "The Three Secrets of Fatima" and told them that she would soon take two of the children with her. Church records confirm that the Virgin Mary first appeared to the children on May 13, 1917.

During the final apparition on October 13, 1917, thousands (some sources claim 70,000) gathered in Fatima and reported seeing the sun dance. However, at that time, the Church did not take these claims seriously.

Yet, in the devastation and uncertainty caused by World War I, the Fatima miracle served as a divine light of hope and calling for many people.

Eventually, the Church could no longer ignore the growing rumors and prophecies. The local bishop ordered an investigation. All those who claimed to have been present that day were interviewed.

Many eyewitnesses stated that "the clouds suddenly parted, and the sun danced in the sky, spun, and changed colors." Some claimed that "the sun approached the earth and then returned to its place," and others reported that people were miraculously healed during and after the event. Furthermore, despite the rainy day, several witnesses claimed that after the miracle, "their soaked clothes and the ground were completely dry."

Based on these testimonies, the Bishop of Leiria declared the apparition of the Virgin Mary to the children to be credible and miraculous. Later, with Vatican approval, the Archbishop of Portugal officially recognized the event as a true miracle. Newspapers of the time gave extensive coverage to the story and published reports from the event.

This miraculous occurrence was named the "Miracle of the Sun" (Milagre do Sol). According to belief, the spirit of the Virgin Mary appeared to call wayward souls to repentance, prayer, and peace. A warning message was delivered to all humanity, beginning with the people of Portugal. Catholic Christians believe that Mary appeared in Fatima to guide humanity to the right path, and the Catholic Church interprets the event as a message and sign from the Virgin to the faithful. Mary gave the three secrets, to be revealed one by one, through the Church's hierarchy.

Jacinta and Francisco, two of the shepherd children who witnessed the miracle, died a few years later during the Spanish flu pandemic that spread rapidly across Europe. This fulfilled the Virgin Mary's prophecy about the children. Lucia, the surviving child, revealed the three secrets to the Vatican, but the Church kept them hidden for many years.

Some scientists and secular circles suggested the event could have been "a kind of optical illusion, mass hysteria, or atmospheric phenomenon." Nevertheless, the scale and impact of the event remained largely unexplained.

According to Church records, the town of Fatima had a population of only 10,000 at the time. After the news spread, hundreds of thousands of Catholics began visiting the town each year in hopes of making a pilgrimage. Fatima became a site of historical importance because of the Virgin Mary's reported appearance to three shepherd children in 1917. Due to its religious and historical significance, the town was included in the UNESCO World Heritage List in 2017.

Picture 4-5. In the Portuguese press at that time, the headline "O Milagre de Fátima" drew attention. This Portuguese title means "The Miracle of Fatima." News about the event reflected the scenes of the gathered crowd in prayer, how the children were received by the public afterward, and the atmosphere of the period. The newspapers conveyed both the event itself and the religious fervor that followed.

A Search for Hope in the Shadow of War and Uncertainty

Picture 6. The so-called Miracle of the Sun, claimed to have occurred in 1917 in the village of Fatima, Portugal, was interpreted by hundreds of awestruck witnesses as a divine sign and has been recorded as one of the most mysterious events in history.

During World War I (1914–1918), Portugal sided with the Allied Powers and fought against Germany. Portugal participated in conflicts on both the Western Front and in its African colonies.

In 1917, Portugal was not only dealing with the Miracle of the Sun but also grappling with a deep crisis caused by war, poverty, and political uncertainty. As World War I ravaged Europe, Portugal sent thousands of young soldiers to the front. The country faced economic hardship, famine, and widespread social unrest. Amidst the destruction and daily struggles, the people desperately sought hope.

This atmosphere amplified the impact of the events in Fatima. The people, living under the shadow of war and poverty, interpreted the "Miracle of the Sun" as a divine intervention. For the suffering Portuguese people during this dark time, the miracle became a spiritual beacon of hope. People saw it as a sign of comfort and salvation.

At the time, tensions between the newly established Republic and the Catholic Church were high in Portugal. The secular government sought to diminish the Church's influence and was dismissive of religious phenomena and miracle claims. However, the events in Fatima resonated so deeply with the public that political authorities could not ignore them.

In the brutal environment of World War I, the Fatima Miracle planted a seed of hope in the hearts of the desperate and impoverished Portuguese. It became not just a religious phenomenon but also a symbolic reflection of a period shaped by war and social upheaval. The suffering brought by war heightened people's longing for a divine savior, making Fatima the focal point of this yearning.

Picture 7. The heavens parted, and light descended to the earth... Three little shepherds, guided by the whispers they heard in Fatima, became witnesses to one of history's greatest secrets. But was what was revealed the whole truth, or is there still a prophecy being kept hidden?

The Fatima Miracle has inspired many branches of art in the Catholic world. In painting and iconography, the Virgin Mary's appearance to the three children is frequently depicted. In sculpture, monumental Fatima statues stand in churchyards and squares. Literature has captured the event through poems, memoirs, and novels. In music, hymns and compositions have been dedicated to Fatima. Numerous films and documentaries dramatizing the event have been made. Theaters present religious performances of the miracle, while Fatima figures appear in embroidery and figurine design. The Fatima Miracle has left a lasting impact on Catholic art.

The Vatican's Blessing and the Shrine of the Virgin Mary

Over time, the Fatima miracle has been interpreted through various perspectives. Debates continued for years; for believers, it was a divine sign; for scientists, possibly mass hysteria or an atmospheric phenomenon. Yet the enthusiasm of witnesses and the widespread impact of the event ensured it was viewed not only as a religious story but also a sociological and historical phenomenon.

Despite the debates, Fatima is regarded as a sacred site in the Catholic world, attracting thousands each year to the location where the miracle supposedly occurred.

Many Christian pilgrims visit the shrine in Fatima on May 13 and October 13—anniversaries of the Virgin Mary's first and final appearances—to celebrate the Day of the Virgin Mary. Pilgrims receive special blessings and pray there. A church was later built on the site where the Virgin Mary reportedly appeared to the children, and images of the two deceased shepherd children were placed inside. In later years, Vatican representatives began officiating ceremonies in Fatima on the miracle's anniversaries. Regardless of the truth behind the Miracle of the Sun, it remains etched in human history as a profound mystery.

Picture 8. The silent witness and guardian of the secrets… Sister Lucia, the last person to bear the prophecies of Fatima hidden in the shadows. She knew the truth, but chose to remain silent until the time was right. So, which secrets were still waiting in the dark?

The Silent Witness of Secrets

The Bishop of Leiria gave the surviving and most prominent witness, Lucia, a sacred mission—to record her experiences in writing. Lucia chose to become a nun. In the legendary land of Fatima, under the shadow of secrets hidden for centuries, Lucia's presence took on profound meaning—she became the guardian of divine secrets and their silent witness.

Lucia, having witnessed the miracle at a young age, devoted her life to prayer and meditation. The secrets she carried became a spiritual burden.

With great wisdom, Lucia safeguarded Fatima's secrets. In doing so, she didn't just preserve a historical event but also a divine invitation to humanity's inner transformation. Each secret held both a warning and a message of hope. Her lifelong meditative devotion deepened the meaning of these messages, turning the act of guarding them into a form of worship and surrender.

To Sister Lucia, the secrets were not just unseen truths but a sacred heritage passed from heart to heart. Her life was woven with the duty of protection—sometimes marked by inner solitude, sometimes by indescribable peace.

The secrets Lucia preserved were meant to guide future generations like a beacon rising from Fatima's soil. Her quiet effort continued with the belief that, one day, the right hearts would understand and embrace them. To her, each secret wasn't merely to be hidden—but awaited the day it would be shared as a divine truth.

As the guardian of Fatima's secrets, Sister Lucia carried the marks of this divine mystery in every moment of her life. Her gaze reflected sorrow and hope interwoven through the years; her hands, like a solemn vow born of prayer, showed unwavering dedication to protecting the sacred. Lucia's story speaks not only of hiding secrets but of the purest form of faith and surrender touching the depths of the human soul.

Thus, until the day the divine secrets hidden in Fatima would be revealed, Sister Lucia bore them with the same deep silence as the first day.

Who Wrote the Secrets?

The duty of bringing the messages of the Virgin Mary to the world fell solely to the surviving child, Lucia dos

Santos. After experiencing these extraordinary events in her childhood, Lucia, the only one to live on, devoted her life entirely to God and the Church. In 1948, under the supervision of the Vatican, she became a Carmelite nun and passed away in 2005 at the age of 97, five years after the revelation of the Third Secret.

Sister Lucia was born in 1907 in Aljustrel, and her life was deeply shaped by the prophecies of the Virgin Mary she witnessed in Fatima. She made great efforts to convey the messages she had received from the Virgin Mary to humanity, living in various places in Portugal during this time. She never spoke about the secrets without the Church's permission, and she spent her life within the privacy, worship, and seclusion of the monastery. Later, under the name Sister Lucia, she wrote three memoirs.

At the request of the Vatican, Lucia finally wrote down the Third Secret of Fatima, which she had kept hidden for a long time, and was recognized by the Church as the "Silent Witness of the Secrets." After her death, the process of declaring her a saint, like the other shepherd children who witnessed the miracle, was initiated.

Lucia's mission was to remain faithful to Catholic Christianity and to guide people toward goodness through prayer. Her memories, eyewitness accounts, and writings still retain their importance today, serving as a guide and inspiration for many Catholics. Through the messages she carried, she managed to shed light on the complex social and political realities of her time and worked tirelessly to spread the sacred teachings entrusted to her.

The mystical truths behind Sister Lucia and the secrets of Fatima have left a deep mark on the history of Christianity, prompting reflection and questioning of the depths of Catholic faith. In 1917, at the very center of the miraculous events in the village of Fatima, Lucia passionately guarded these secrets, believing they carried messages that transcended the ages.

The Three Secrets of Fatima remained hidden in the shadows until the 1940s—until Sister Lucia wrote her memoirs and revealed the first two secrets to the world. But the Third Secret held an even greater mystery. Recorded under the heading "By Order of the Bishop of Leiria and the Most Holy Mother", this secret was committed to sacred lines by Sister Lucia's trembling hand on January 3, 1944.

And in those lines, the sealed prophecy of destiny seemed to echo: "A man dressed in white will be struck down by weapons and will fall to the ground, covered in blood…"

Sister Lucia inscribed these sacred secrets on parchment, which was then placed inside a sealed envelope, locked away in the darkness of the unknown. Initially kept under the care of the Bishop of Leiria, this envelope sought a safer haven in the hands of time and fate. Finally, on April 4, 1957, it was delivered to the Vatican and placed in the Secret Archives of the Holy Office—that ancient vault where the secrets slept in shadow. The Bishop of Leiria informed Sister Lucia of the transfer of the secrets. Thus, the sealed lines of the prophecy sank into a new silence in the depths of the Vatican.

The Third Secret remained undisclosed until the papacy of John Paul II, becoming the subject of many prophecies and mystical interpretations. At last, in the year 2000, the Vatican revealed its full contents, causing a global stir. The prophecies concerning the Pope and the symbols reflecting the upheavals in the Church's history were received as both frightening and thought-provoking. Containing Sister Lucia's profound insights into God's will and the future of the Church, the secrets were interpreted by Catholics as a call to hope and awakening, forming a spiritual shield against the challenges of the modern world.

The First and Second Secrets of Fatima Revealed:
The Spread of Sister Lucia's Testimony

Sister Lucia, one of the most important witnesses of the Fatima events, had delivered these secrets to the Vatican in written form. However, the letters she wrote in the 1940s began to attract great public attention, and curiosity about the secrets grew stronger. Under such pressure, it became increasingly difficult for the Vatican to keep the secrets hidden. Sister Lucia had stated that certain conditions needed to be met for the secrets to be revealed. The Vatican, however, chose to release the information gradually to avoid panic and speculation. Finally, in 1941, the Vatican was compelled to announce the first two secrets of Fatima.

Sister Lucia's Letters Regarding the Secrets of Fatima

Sister Lucia dos Santos, who documented the mysterious prophecies of Fatima, detailed the messages contained in these secrets and her correspondence with the Vatican in various letters. The letters she wrote specifically about the secrets have attracted great interest not only in religious circles but also among historians and researchers.

In 1941, Sister Lucia wrote letters revealing the first two secrets, but the Third Secret was penned in a special letter in 1944. This letter was first sent to the Bishop of Leiria and later, in 1957, delivered to the Vatican, where it was placed in the secret archives. Although Lucia requested the secret to be revealed in 1960, the Vatican declined this request, and the letter remained hidden for many years.

Lucia's letters created a significant stir in the Catholic world, and the Vatican's stance on these secrets has frequently been criticized.

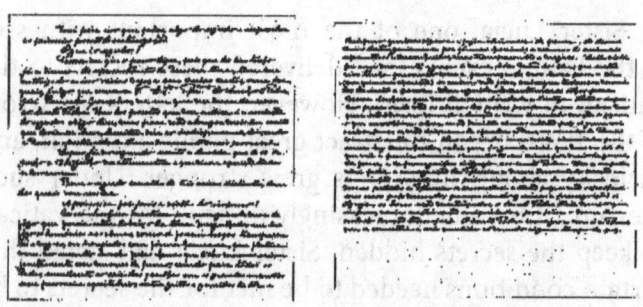

*Picture 9- 10. **The First and Second Parts of the Secret Presented by Sister Lucia to the Bishop of Leiria-Fatima on August 31, 1941 (Original Text)** A handwritten script, a prophecy, a sealed secret... This text, flowing from the pen of Sister Lucia, carries the unknown truths of Fatima. Was it a concealed warning, or an inevitable roadmap written into the destiny of humanity?*

First Secret: Cries Rising from the Depths of Hell

According to Sister Lucia dos Santos' writings, at that sacred moment in Fatima, the Virgin Mary opened the gates of hell before the children's eyes. In the first secret, described in Lucia's own words, an indescribable and terrifying scene of torment was depicted:

"A sea of fire appeared before us. In this fire, demons and damned souls were writhing in endless agony. As the flickering sparks rose to the sky, human screams shook the earth. The demons, in horrifying forms, wandered about like dark shadows. We trembled with fear, unable to resist the terror rising within us."[2]

During this vision in 1917, as the children's hearts trembled with dread at the horrific scene, the Virgin Mary gave them a warning: the world was tainted with sins, and if humanity did not repent, greater disasters would ravage the earth. This secret was rooted in the traditional Christian doctrine concerning the damnation of sinful souls to hell. The devastating impact of the First World War had already led to the deaths of millions of people of all religions and nations across the globe. Empires had collapsed, and the world was heading toward an even greater war.

Indeed, in 1939, the Second World War began with Adolf Hitler's invasion of Poland. With the outbreak of war, the Vatican believed the Fatima prophecies were being fulfilled. Therefore, in 1941, the Vatican revealed the first two secrets, aiming both to reinforce the Catholic faith and to encourage people to turn to religion. At the time, the Church was spreading the belief that the war was a punishment from God and was calling people to repentance.

Second Secret: Prophecy on Russia and World Wars

In the first secret of Fatima, the Virgin Mary had shown the children terrifying images of hell and the

[2] https://www.vatican.va/roman_curia/congregations/cfaith/documents/rc_con_cfaith_doc_20000626_message-fatima_en.html

torment of sinful souls. The second secret, on the other hand, served as a warning of what those sins would cause in the world. If people did not repent and cleanse themselves of sin, wars and disasters would occur—not just in the afterlife, but in this world as well. In this context, the second secret was a continuation of the first and pointed to great events that would shape the fate of humanity.

The second secret of Fatima, also written by Sister Lucia dos Santos, was reported to be a prophecy foretelling events that would deeply impact human history. This secret included messages about the First and Second World Wars, the secularization of Russia, and world peace.

According to what the Virgin Mary conveyed to the children, the First World War would come to an end, but if humanity did not repent, an even greater war would break out. If Russia continued to turn away from God, the world would be dragged into great calamities, wars would erupt, and the Church would be persecuted. However, if the Pope consecrated Russia and humanity repented, peace would be restored.

The Soviet Union and the Rise of Communism

In 1917, the Russian Revolution took place, and the Soviet Union was born. The official ideology of the Soviets rapidly began to influence the world. Communism was seen as a major threat to the Catholic Church. In the 1940s, Stalin's policies and the spread of socialist ideology throughout Europe caused great concern in the Vatican. At this point, the Fatima prophecies would become a powerful propaganda tool for the Vatican. The Church used these prophecies in the struggle against communism, inviting people to return to religion and encouraging prayers for Russia's return to faith.

Sister Lucia wrote this secret with the following words:

"If there is no repentance, Russia will spread its errors throughout the world, causing wars and persecutions. The Church will suffer, the good will be martyred, the Holy Father will suffer greatly, and many nations will be annihilated."

Historical Events and the Revelation of the Prophecy

Interestingly, the date when Lucia revealed this second secret coincided with the middle of the Second World War. Moreover, the prophecy mentioned that a great war would begin during the pontificate of Pope Pius XI, and indeed, the Second World War began in 1939, shortly after the death of Pope Pius XI.

However, some historians have suggested that Lucia's revelation of this prophecy in 1942 is questionable and may have been modified or added after the war had already started. Likewise, claims have been made that the emphasis on Russia in the prophecy was used by the Church to rally support against communism.

The Vatican's Response and the Consecration of Russia

While the Second World War was ongoing, the Vatican decided in 1942 to make these prophecies public. That same year, Pope Pius XII held a special ceremony to consecrate Russia. However, as the prophecy had foreseen, Russia did not immediately return to religion, nor was world peace established. Nevertheless, the Church believed that these prophecies were a vital tool to unite faith communities and to take a stand against communism—and would continue to use them as such.

Pope Pius XII, in his apostolic letter Sacro Vergente Anno published on July 7, 1952, performed a special consecration of Russia to the Virgin Mary. In this letter, he explained that he prayed for the protection of Russia and its return to God. This act was in line with the request for the consecration of Russia mentioned in the second secret of Fatima. However, the Soviet Union, by continuing to spread communist ideology throughout the 20th century, seemed to mock the Vatican's prophecies.[3]

Picture 11 – 12. A holy call to atheist Russia… With hands raised to the sky, Pope Pius called for the soul of a nation to be reclaimed. But was this merely a prayer, or was it a destiny written in the secrets of Fatima?

On October 31, 1942, during a radio broadcast to Portugal, Pope Pius XII also stated that he consecrated the Church and all humanity to the Immaculate Heart of Mary. This was linked to the request for the consecration of Russia mentioned in Fatima's second secret.

---

3 **Apostolic Letter:** A type of official document issued by the Pope.

The Second Secret and Soviet Expansionism

After Hitler was eliminated in the Second World War, the U.S. and the West believed they could breathe a sigh of relief—only to find themselves facing the communist threat after the fascists. On one side was Russia's expansionist tendency; on the other was the communist ideology, which had been spreading among Western populations since the 1917 revolution, creating widespread fear in the capitalist world. For example, in Italy, due to fear of the communists, everyone was expecting the Russians to arrive. It was believed that in the event of a Russian invasion, communist sympathizers would assist the Russian armies.

In response, on[4] March 1946, during a conference in Fulton, USA, Winston Churchill stated that an "Iron Curtain" had been erected across Europe. This statement had a strong impact, and in the West, communist countries came to be referred to by this term. The Western nations began to call themselves the "free world." On[5] March 12, 1947, the U.S. Congress approved the Truman Doctrine, publicly declaring it to the world. The Truman Doctrine also marked the official declaration of the Cold War. From then on, NATO countries would be designed according to the U.S.'s war strategy. The Vatican was crucial at this point.

The second secret was directly linked to the most important developments of the 20th century, especially the threat of communism, the rise of the Soviet Union, and

---

[4] **The World's Largest Intelligence Agencies: MIT - Mossad - CIA - Gladio, Operations - Assassinations - Secret Reports** Ali Kuzu, Bilge Karınca, 2007, p. 81

[5] **A Short History of the 20th Century** Sina Akşin, Türkiye İş Bankası Publications, 2015 edition, p. 283

the Vatican's global role. This prophecy coincided exactly with Russia's efforts to spread communism worldwide during the Cold War. The revelations of the Fatima secrets became part of the ideological struggle between the Vatican and the Soviet Union, pitting religion against ideology. The disclosure of these secrets was a clear indication of the ideological battle between the Vatican and the USSR. This tension between religious belief and communist ideology amounted to a kind of "spiritual war." The Vatican formed the most important front in this war.

The Third Secret, Hidden for Years in the Archives of the Holy Office

August 17, 1959

Sister Lucia was reluctant to share the third secret with the public for a long time. Although she had written down the first two secrets on August 31, 1941, she hesitated due to the gravity of the third. The secret, which Sister Lucia had written in 1944, was first handed over to Catholic Church authorities in Portugal, and later in 1957 delivered to the Vatican in a sealed envelope. On April 4, 1957, the document was placed in the Secret Archives of the Vatican's Congregation for Religious Orders and remained sealed until the year 2000.

Father Pierre Paul Philip, O.P., Commissioner of the Vatican's Holy Office, carefully carried the small sealed envelope. With Cardinal Alfredo Ottaviani's approval, the document was delivered to Pope John XXIII—the final act of a prophecy hidden for centuries.

The Pope gazed long at the envelope. His fingers moved over the sealed wax. A deep silence fell for a moment. The cardinals held their breath. The room was filled with a tension that even the thick stone walls of the Vatican could not contain. Finally, Pope John XXIII spoke slowly, averting his eyes:

"We will wait... I will pray... I will let you know my decision."

And he waited. He thought for days and weeks. However, he decided not to reveal it. The sealed envelope was once again sent back to the dark archives of the Holy Office.

March 27, 1965

Pope Paul VI, together with Substitute Archbishop Angelo Dell'Acqua, read the contents of the envelope—and his face turned pale. What was written inside was terrifying. Only he knew the contents. For several minutes, no one spoke. Only the flicker of a candle flame disturbed the heavy air in the room.

Finally, the Pope took a trembling breath and ordered the seal to be closed again. He told those beside him:

"We cannot reveal this to the world."

And once again, the secret was doomed to be forgotten.

May 13, 1981

St. Peter's Square... A gunshot rang out.

Pope John Paul II collapsed to the ground, covered in blood. The bullets from the assassin's gun had exploded right in the middle of a historical prophecy.

When he regained consciousness in the hospital bed, the first thing he asked for was the envelope containing the Third Secret of Fatima. On July 18, 1981, Cardinal

Franjo Šeper handed over two envelopes to Substitute Secretary of State Archbishop Eduardo Martínez Somalo. The first envelope was white and contained the original Portuguese text handwritten by Sister Lucia. The second envelope was orange and contained the Italian translation of the secret.

On August 11, Archbishop Martínez returned both envelopes to the Archives of the Holy Office.

But there was a problem...

Were the original text in the white envelope and the translation in the orange envelope truly identical?

Or was someone still trying to hide the truth inside the Vatican?

The Third Secret: A Prophecy of the Apocalypse?

The third secret of Fatima was considered one of the most mysterious and most speculated-about prophecies in history. Despite Sister Lucia's wishes, it was not revealed in 1960 and was kept hidden by the Vatican for many years.

This secrecy fueled speculation that the secret contained a terrifying prophecy about the apocalypse, extraterrestrial life, or a global catastrophe. The Vatican's reluctance to disclose the secret strengthened the belief that it contained extraordinary and perhaps deeply significant truths about humanity's fate. The third secret, known only to a limited number of cardinals, was the subject of debate for years in both religious and academic circles.

The third secret was not merely a religious text but also seen as a prophecy deeply intertwined with the political and ideological turmoil of the 20th century. Shaped under the shadow of the Cold War, this mystical secret added a new dimension to the ideological battle between the Vatican and the Soviet Union, becoming one of the elements reinforcing the power of religion on the global stage.

Picture 13. A name buried in the shadows: Cardinal Ottaviani... Secret documents, whispered prophecies, and the deep secrets of the Vatican... Was he hiding the truth, or protecting it?

Cardinal Alfredo Ottaviani and the Secrets

Cardinal Ottaviani[6] was one of the few clergymen who read Fatima's third secret. He was a significant figure in preserving the secrets of Fatima and the doctrines of the Catholic Church. He was particularly known for his efforts to maintain the Church's traditional structure. His role in presenting the third secret of Fatima in diplomatic language revealed his influence in both religious and political matters.

Cardinal Ottaviani assumed leadership of the Vatican Holy Office in 1959 and continued in this role until 1966. This office was responsible for safeguarding the doctrines of the Roman Catholic Church and combating heresy. Ottaviani was one of the leading figures of the conservative wing that opposed the modernization efforts during the Second Vatican Council held between 1962 and 1965. He fought to preserve Catholic teachings and keep them distant from modernizing influences.

Cardinal Ottaviani's Statements About the Secrets

In 1963, Cardinal Ottaviani made a significant statement regarding Fatima's third secret at the Pontifical Marian Academy and issued an important warning to the Catholic world.

He strongly emphasized that the Church would face "very difficult days" and that more prayers were needed.

---

6 (1890–1979), an important clergyman of the Roman Catholic Church and an influential figure in the Vatican during the mid-20th century. He was known as a conservative theologian defending the Church's traditional teachings. He opposed the modernization process of the Roman Catholic Church.

The Cardinal expressed concern over the decline in religious values by saying he hoped "the number of those who abandon the faith would not be high."

With this statement, the veil over the secret was partially lifted. The potential challenges the Church might face—loss of faith, religious corruption, and global chaos—were associated with the secrets.

The Cardinal's words indicated that this secret was not merely an individual spiritual warning but a message with global implications.

Publication in the Santa Rita Magazine

Santa Rita magazine was a widely read publication in the Catholic world. For that reason, the Vatican decided to publish part of the secret in Santa Rita using diplomatic language to reach a broader audience. This selective release strategy reflected the Vatican's intention to disclose the secret in a controlled manner.

A Warning Instead of a Direct Revelation

The publication was more of a call for humanity to pray more, work for peace, and turn toward spiritual values than a clear prophetic declaration.

There were criticisms that the portion published in Santa Rita did not reflect the full content of Fatima's Third Secret. Critics claimed the Vatican concealed the complete secret from the public and only revealed the parts it deemed appropriate.

For this reason, the incomplete disclosure of the secret has led to various speculations and distortions of the prophecies.

Why Were the Secrets Sent to Cold War Leaders?

During the Cold War, Pope John XXIII (Roncalli) sent Fatima's third secret as a diplomatic gesture in 1960 to U.S. President John F. Kennedy and Soviet leader Nikita Khrushchev. The transmission of the secret to political leaders served as a warning regarding nuclear war or global catastrophe. This demonstrated that the secret was not merely a religious issue, but also intertwined with the political and international affairs of the time. The Vatican aimed to highlight not only spiritual values but also international peace and diplomatic dialogue among world leaders.

The secret, alongside religious teachings, carried warnings about a new world order, referencing the political atmosphere of the time.

The Secret's Publication and Political Effects

Following its publication in Santa Rita and its delivery to world leaders, the Vatican's spiritual and diplomatic role in international relations was underscored.

Warning About Abandoning the Faith

Cardinal Ottaviani's statement, "I hope the number of those who abandon the faith will not be high," reflected concerns over the diminishing influence of religion and increasing secularization in modern times.

After Pope John XXIII (Roncalli) sent Fatima's Third Secret to U.S. President John F. Kennedy[7] and Soviet leader Nikita Khrushchev,[8] the reactions and general approaches of these leaders remain largely undisclosed.

However, Kennedy, being the first Catholic president of the U.S., managed his relationship with the Vatican with great care. It is likely that he approached the Pope's messages with sensitivity. There is no official record of Kennedy making a direct statement about the message, but many of his speeches during the Cold War that emphasized world peace reflect a cooperative stance with the Vatican.

Given the belief that the Third Secret of Fatima warned against nuclear war, Kennedy may have interpreted the message as a call for peace. Indeed, in 1963, the Partial Nuclear Test Ban Treaty was signed, and the Vatican supported this process. With this agreement, the world breathed a temporary sigh of relief.

---

7 John F. Kennedy (1917–1963), the United States' first and only Catholic president. Kennedy's Catholic identity sparked significant controversy both during his election campaign and throughout his presidency. There were concerns in the U.S. that a Catholic president might be influenced by the Pope. The Protestant majority raised claims that the Vatican would extend its influence over the United States. Kennedy responded to these debates by saying, "I am not a Catholic president; I am a Catholic who is president of the United States."

8 Nikita Khrushchev (1894–1971) served as the leader of the Soviet Union from 1953 to 1964. He initiated the process of "de-Stalinization" after Stalin's death and led during some of the Cold War's most critical moments. His tenure is marked by events such as the construction of the Berlin Wall, the Cuban Missile Crisis, and Soviet achievements in the space race. However, due to failures in economic reforms and the weakening of the Communist Party, he was removed from office in 1964 and replaced by Leonid Brezhnev.

Nikita Khrushchev's Reaction

Khrushchev led the Soviet Union during a period when it adopted an atheist ideology and pursued anti-religious policies. Therefore, it would have been difficult to expect him to take such a religious message from the Vatican seriously. There is no definite record that Khrushchev received or officially responded to the message.

Still, if the Pope's message emphasized peace and the threat of nuclear war, could Khrushchev have seen it as a political opportunity to ease Cold War tensions?

Peace Efforts on the Brink of World War III

Both Kennedy and Khrushchev began taking steps to reduce Cold War tensions following the 1962 Cuban Missile Crisis. If Fatima's Third Secret contained a message of peace, it's conceivable that both leaders were influenced by it. Since this diplomatic communication from the Vatican was kept highly secret, only limited information is available regarding the reactions and content of the message.

Fatima's Contribution to World Peace

In 1963, the Vatican supported diplomatic relations between the U.S. and the Soviet Union that began over nuclear armament. The Vatican's messages and Pope John XXIII's peace efforts became a significant moral force for peace during the most intense period of the Cold War.

Relations Between the Vatican and Eastern Bloc Countries (Cold War Period)

During the Cold War (1947–1991), relations between the Vatican and Eastern Bloc countries were shaped by ideological conflict, diplomatic maneuvering, and secret meetings. During this period, the Vatican openly adopted both a religious and political stance against the atheist and communist policies of the Eastern Bloc.

Eastern Bloc Countries and Atheism

Under the leadership of the Soviet Union, the Eastern Bloc adopted atheist state policies. Religions were seen as threats to communist ideology. The Catholic Church and other religious groups were subjected to pressure in these countries—church properties were confiscated, and clergy were imprisoned. These pressures were particularly noticeable in countries such as Poland, Czechoslovakia, and Hungary.

The Vatican's Strategy

Ostpolitik:[9] Initiated in 1963 by Pope Paul VI, the Vatican's Ostpolitik policy aimed to establish dialogue with Eastern Bloc countries. Through diplomatic channels, this policy sought to protect the rights of the Catholic Church in Eastern Europe. The Vatican's goal was to preserve the Church's presence, defend religious freedom, and at the same time, undermine the Eastern Bloc during the Cold War. The Vatican opened dialogue chan-

---

9 **Ostpolitik**, meaning "Eastern Policy" in German, refers to the foreign policy doctrine of West Germany from 1969 to 1974 aimed at normalizing relations with East Germany, the Soviet Union, and Eastern European countries. Under West German Chancellor Willy Brandt, this policy helped ease East-West tensions during the Cold War and paved the way for German reunification.

nels and established official contact with countries like Poland, Hungary, and Yugoslavia under Soviet influence.

Despite the pressures in Eastern Bloc countries, the Vatican made efforts to maintain communication and diplomatic relations. Through local churches in Eastern Europe, the Catholic Church tried to maintain religious practices and faith. The Church carried out an ideological struggle against communism by emphasizing the preservation of spiritual values.

Picture 14 – 15. White smoke rising from the dome of the Sistine Chapel... A new pope has been elected, and history turns a new page. Ancient rituals echoing through the Vatican herald the decision that will shape the fate of the world.

White Smoke Rising from the Sistine Chapel

On October 16, 1978, when white smoke rose from the Sistine Chapel[10] in the Vatican, the world welcomed a new Pope. The news that a 58-year-old had been elected to lead the Catholic Church shook the world. For the first time in 455 years, a non-Italian—this time a Pole—had ascended to the head of the Catholic Church. Rather than the usual choice of an elderly Pope, this time a new figure emerged: a young and energetic leader who would strengthen the Church and stand against communism. This election was not just a religious change but a major event with global implications. By choosing a Polish Pope, the Vatican was declaring to the world that Catholicism was a global power.

---

10 The Sistine Chapel is one of the most important religious and artistic structures in the Vatican, especially significant as the site where papal elections (the Conclave) take place. The Pope, who holds the highest office in the Catholic Church, is elected through secret ballots conducted by the cardinals gathered in the Sistine Chapel. Adorned with Michelangelo's unparalleled frescoes, the chapel is one of the most important centers of the Catholic world both religiously and regionally. The smoke rising from the Sistine Chapel is a traditional signal used to announce the result of the papal election process. Black smoke (Fumata Nera) indicates that the cardinals have not yet chosen a new Pope, while white smoke (Fumata Bianca) signals that a new Pope has been elected. Following the appearance of white smoke, the announcement "Habemus Papam" ("We have a Pope") is made from St. Peter's Basilica.

Picture 16. The voice that came after the Iron Curtain... A leader rising from Poland, who would change not only faith but history itself. Pope John Paul II: the architect of a journey woven with diplomacy, resistance, and secrets.

That evening, on October 16, the man who stepped onto the balcony of St. Peter's Basilica to greet the people of Rome and the pilgrims gathered in the piazza waiting for the decision of the College of Cardinals was Karol Wojtyła. As the enthusiastic crowd responded with applause, the new Pope humbly greeted the people and gave a brief speech. In his speech, he stated that he came from "a distant country" and submitted himself to the will of God.[11] By using the phrase "from a distant coun-

---

11 Memory and Identity, Pope John Paul II, Why This Book August 2005, p. 159

try," Pope John Paul II was referring to his birthplace, Poland—a surprise to the world that someone from Eastern Europe would become Pope.

With these words, the Pope implied both his geographical distance from the Vatican and the fact that Poland was under Soviet influence at the time, hinting at the Iron Curtain. This later connected with his strong stance against communism during his papacy.

The newly elected Pope made a great impact not only in religious terms but also politically and socially. This election symbolized far more than a routine change. One of the longest and most influential papacies in modern history—lasting 26 years (1978–2005)—was about to begin.

A key figure in his election was Zbigniew Brzezinski,[12] an important name in the American deep state and also of Polish origin. The previous Pope had held office for only 33 days before his death, which some alleged was due to poisoning. His successor, John Paul II, took part in Reagan's famous democracy project. His mission was to fulfill the requirements of the Cold War. Religion would be used to bring down the Eastern Bloc.[13]

---

12 Zbigniew Brzezinski (1928–2017) was a Polish-American political scientist, diplomat, and geostrategist. He played an important role in American foreign policy during the Cold War. From 1977 to 1981, he served as National Security Advisor to U.S. President Jimmy Carter. Brzezinski was influential in Cold War American foreign policy, particularly in strategies opposing the Soviet Union. He is known as one of the proponents supporting the Mujahideen against the Soviet invasion of Afghanistan. He is also known for his work *The Grand Chessboard*.

13 Which Europe? Banu Avar, Remzi Publishing House, 7th Edition, p. 295

Karol Józef Wojtyła, who came from a small town in Poland, would later become one of the Vatican's most influential leaders and change the course of history. Under the new name Pope John Paul II, he became a figure directly linked with the collapse of communism, the modernization of the Catholic Church, and the Third Secret of Fatima. For these reasons, he is considered one of the most beloved and influential popes in Church history.

Throughout history, many Popes were associated with the sacred texts and mysteries of the Catholic faith. But none would be as closely linked to them as John Paul II. In the years to come, intriguing events would unfold in both the Vatican and the world.

Was his life directly connected with the fate of the "white-robed Pope" mentioned in the Third Secret of Fatima?

Was the assassination attempt he survived in 1981 one of the prophecies of the Third Secret?

Did Pope John Paul II view his survival as a miracle? And would he dedicate himself to spreading Fatima's message around the world?

Was he the "Pope of the Secret"?

Pope John Paul II, the CIA, and Conspiracy Theories

There were various claims that the Pope's election was supported by covert U.S. operations. According to these claims, the CIA collaborated secretly with the Vatican to support his election, positioning John Paul II as a "spiritual weapon" against the Soviets. Zbigniew Brzezinski, one of America's most influential figures, was said to be a key architect of the collaboration between the U.S. and the Vatican.

Although these claims were never definitively proven, the evident strengthening of U.S.-Vatican relations following the Pope's election offered strong clues regarding Brzezinski's role.

From Karol to Pope: A Youth Marked by Hardship

Born in 1920 in the town of Wadowice, Poland, Karol Wojtyła lost his mother and brother at a young age and began a difficult life in poverty with his father. Like millions of others, his life was dramatically altered when the Nazis invaded Poland. Though he wished to pursue university studies, the Nazis had shut down the schools. To survive, he worked in stone quarries while secretly attending a clandestine seminary. During his country's difficult times, he also participated in underground theater groups, showing an interest in the arts. Despite Nazi oppression, he pursued his religious calling and joined a secret seminary. Amidst the chaos of World War II, he continued with theater but gradually dedicated himself entirely to the Christian faith.

His appointment as a priest in 1946 marked the first major turning point in his life. But for him, the priesthood was not only about worship—it was also about offering hope and promoting social change. John Paul II's youth and upbringing took place in a Poland scarred by occupation and, later, by an oppressive communist regime. These experiences left deep wounds but also nurtured an unshakable commitment to freedom and the power of faith. These were the roots of his later focus on opposing communism and promoting freedom during his papacy.

Poland's painful historical trajectory—Nazi occupation followed by communist repression—left deep marks on young Wojtyła's heart. Like all authoritarian regimes, this era saw the suppression of human values, restriction of freedoms, and near-erasure of faith. Witnessing these injustices, Karol came to understand how fragile societal and spiritual freedom really was.Raised with Christian faith and Catholic traditions from childhood, Karol came to believe that religion could be not only a path to personal salvation but also a symbol of social resistance. Thus, standing against the spiritual erosion of communism became not only a political act for him but a sacred mission for life.

The Fatima Secrets and Divine Warnings

The miracles said to have occurred in Fatima and especially the Fatima secrets were, for many Catholics, warnings against the moral decay and spiritual darkness brought by communism. John Paul II deeply embraced these divine messages. Believing that the Fatima secrets were a call to awakening and repentance, Wojtyła saw them as a symbol of the spiritual devastation communism had caused. The Fatima revelations offered him a divine guidance that exposed the harmful aspects of communist ideology.

The struggles he experienced at a young age and the psychological collapse caused by oppressive regimes led him to interpret the fight against communism not just as political resistance, but as a divine battle for the salvation of the human soul. This perspective laid the foundation for his later emphasis on universal values such as freedom, human rights, and interfaith dialogue.

The world in which John Paul II was raised gave him lessons of both pain and hope. The historical oppression of his youth filled him with deep spiritual sensitivity, and the divine messages of Fatima gave his fight against communism a sacred meaning. Thus, he entered history not only as a political figure but also as a spiritual leader fighting for humanity and faith.

Picture 17. At the tip of faith's staff, there was not only prayer but also the burden of the unseen war between East and West. The Pope's steps were heading toward the temple; yet his shadow fell upon a global chessboard where ideologies clashed.

Silent Resistance Against Communism

After becoming a priest, he served in Poland under the oppressive Soviet regime. The communists shut down churches, restricted religious freedoms, and attempted to destroy faith.

Karol organized secret religious services, inspired hope in his people, and brought together the youth. As Poland came under Soviet influence after World War II, Karol Wojtyła began to stand out for his resistance to religious repression. Despite Soviet policies, he continued to give moral support and encouraged people to practice their faith freely.

He was appointed Archbishop of Krakow in 1964 and became a Cardinal in 1967. Though he did not engage in direct conflict with the communist regime, he became a symbol of indirect resistance by advocating for religious freedoms and raising awareness among the people. He was the leader of a silent resistance, and soon the whole world would hear his voice.

He came not just to change the Catholic Church, but the world itself. When he said, "Do not be afraid!" it wasn't just a message for Catholics, but for the millions suffering under communist regimes.

His election was a major threat to the Soviets and turned him into one of the key figures of the Cold War. He became the greatest source of inspiration for Poland's anti-regime Solidarity Movement (Solidarność). With his sermons, Catholics began to fight for freedom more bravely. His election was the beginning of a chain of events that would eventually lead to the end of the Cold War. Years later, the bullets that struck his body would ignite the fire of rebellion.

Picture 18 – 19. Two Poles, one destiny: One, the spiritual leader of faith; the other, the voice of freedom. Pope John Paul II and Lech Walesa came together as two figures who changed the course of Poland's history.

This difficult struggle would lead to the fall of the Berlin Wall in 1989. The Pope welcomed this with great joy and saw the collapse of communism as a victory. He was not wrong—he played the most critical role in that victory.

Pope John Paul II and Poland's Solidarity Movement (Solidarność)

After World War II, Poland fell under the influence of the Soviet Union. The regime not only restricted religious freedoms to weaken the power of the Church but also banned trade unions and independent civil movements.

But the Polish people and the Catholic Church did not bow to these pressures. In 1980, with a workers' strike in Gdańsk, the Solidarity Movement was born—the first major civil resistance against the communist regime in Poland. Led by Lech Wałęsa,[14] the movement demanded workers' rights, freedom, and democracy. In response, the communist government declared martial law and tried to suppress the movement. At this critical moment, support from Polish-born Pope John Paul II became its greatest strength.

From the papal throne, John Paul II sent this message to Poles:

"Pray for the Son of God."

Though it seemed like a simple religious expression, it carried a major political message. Praying for the Son of God became the voice of people resisting the communist regime. The Catholic Church became one of the biggest supporters of Poland's freedom struggle. His speeches were not just religious texts but global messages.

In 1979, Pope John Paul II decided to make a historic visit to Poland. This visit was highly significant for both him and the world because it was the first major papal visit to a communist country during the Cold War. Hundreds of thousands took to the streets to see the Pope. In his historic speech at Victory Square in Warsaw, the Pope said:

"Let the spirit of God descend and change this land."

---

14 Lech Walesa (b. 1943) is a Polish trade union leader, human rights advocate, and politician. In the 1980s, as the leader of the Solidarity (Solidarność) Union, he became a symbol of peaceful resistance against the communist regime. He served as the President of Poland from 1990 to 1995. In 1983, he was awarded the Nobel Peace Prize.

These words were perceived as a challenge to the communist regime and became a major source of hope for millions of Poles. The Pope reignited his people's belief in freedom and independence.

Communist officials were deeply alarmed by the public's enthusiastic reception of the Pope but couldn't prevent the visit. This visit directly inspired the Solidarity Movement and launched the largest public resistance against Poland's communist regime. The strikes that began in 1980 grew, and under the leadership of Lech Wałęsa, the independent Solidarity trade union was established.

In response, the government declared martial law in 1981, banned the opposition movement, and imprisoned its leaders. But this step marked the beginning of the end. Pope John Paul II decided to continue supporting the movement covertly.

The Vatican, in cooperation with the U.S., provided financial and spiritual support to Solidarity. Through secret diplomatic talks, U.S. President Ronald Reagan and the Western world were encouraged to support the movement. This was one of the key moments when the West and the Vatican united against communism during the Cold War. The Vatican could not afford to lose this front.

This movement is considered one of the most critical events that triggered the collapse of communism in Eastern Europe. The Pope's support not only gave the Polish people courage but also set off a chain of events that would shake the Soviet Union.

The Fall of Communism and the Pope's Victory

1989: The Fall of Communism in Poland and the Solidarity Movement

The year 1989 was a critical turning point in the history of Poland and Eastern Europe. Faced with intense public pressure, the communist government was forced to negotiate with the Solidarity Movement, which had grown into the most powerful social force in Poland since the 1980s.

Following prolonged protests, strikes, and growing public support, free elections were held in Poland. The communist regime collapsed as a result of these democratic elections, and the Solidarity Movement achieved a major victory. Its leader, Lech Wałęsa, became Poland's first democratic leader. This event triggered the collapse of communist regimes not only in Poland but across Eastern Europe.

This democratic transformation in Poland inspired other historic events such as the fall of the Berlin Wall in 1989 and the collapse of the Eastern Bloc. In an era that remembered great leaders like Churchill, Gandhi, Mao, and Roosevelt, Pope John Paul II emerged as one of the most significant figures on the international stage. What set him apart from politicians was his emphasis not on diplomacy, but on words, drama, and symbols.

Picture 20. Pope John Paul II: the invisible hero of the Cold War, the silent architect of history. Weapons fired, walls rose, the world was divided in two...But he was neither toppled by assassination attempts nor silenced by threats. With his diplomacy, he shaped wars; with his words, he shook walls. Pope John Paul II was not just a religious leader—he was a figure who changed history in the shadow of the Cold War.

Pope John Paul II and His Impact on the Collapse of Communism

Pope John Paul II, of Polish origin, played a major role as a spiritual leader in the collapse of communism. By supporting the faith of the people and the Solidarity Movement in Poland, he contributed to the weakening of the communist regime. The Pope's messages and visits strengthened the Polish people's quest for democracy and freedom.

Pope John Paul II's influence was not limited to Poland; he also defended spirituality against the wave of Marxism and revolution in Latin America. By affecting diplomatic relations between the Western and Eastern Blocs, he also weakened the Soviet Union. He played an indirect but significant role in the fall of the Berlin Wall in 1989 and the dissolution of the Soviet Union in 1991.

Picture 21 – 22. ***The Holy See Flag:*** *The key on the left, made of gold, represents the power of Heaven, while the key on the right, made of silver, symbolizes earthly power. The flag is displayed in many Catholic Churches around the world.*

As a result, the events that took place in Poland in 1989 radically changed the political structure not only of one country but of all of Eastern Europe. The Solidarity Movement led by Lech Walesa and the spiritual leadership of Pope John Paul II were among the most important factors that brought an end to communist regimes.

The Vatican: Capital of Faith or Center of Hidden Power?

A Small State with Great Influence

The Vatican State is the world's smallest independent state and was officially established in 1929 with the Lateran Treaty signed with Italy. The structure of the state includes both religious and administrative elements. It has a government that manages its internal affairs and a Ministry of Foreign Affairs that conducts diplomatic relations. Additionally, the Vatican City State Council, chaired by the Pope, plays an active role in the administration. The territory of Vatican State spans only 44 hectares and includes many religious and historical structures.

The Vatican is an important religious and cultural center for the Catholic Church. Recognized as the heart of Christianity, it is a sacred place for millions of Catholics worldwide. Moreover, structures like St. Peter's Basilica located in the Vatican are also considered pilgrimage sites for Catholics. Culturally, the Vatican's art collections and museums attract significant international interest and visitors. Therefore, the Vatican holds great global importance in both religious and cultural terms.

A Brief History of the Vatican

The founding of the Vatican has roots in Christian belief and dates back to the time of Saint Peter. Considered one of the most important figures in Christianity and one of Jesus's apostles, Saint Peter played a crucial role in spreading the Christian faith and came to Rome, where he established churches. After Saint Peter was martyred in Rome, his tomb became a sacred site for Christians, and the area was called the Vatican. Thus, Saint Peter played an essential role in the foundation of the Vatican and the spread of Christianity.

Saint Peter's arrival in Rome, his dissemination of the Christian faith, and his assumption of the title of Pope laid the foundations of the Vatican. After his execution, the sanctification of his burial site and the construction of a temple on it led to the Vatican becoming the center of Christianity. The foundation of the Vatican dates back to the 4th century AD and is closely related to the spread of Christianity in the Roman Empire. The acceptance of Christianity as the official religion and its rapid spread within the Roman Empire had a profound effect on the early period of the Vatican. These early periods were crucial in the organization of the Christian community, the formation of the papacy, and the establishment of Rome as the religious center.

The spread of Christianity played a significant role in the transformation of the Roman Empire. When Christianity was declared the official religion in the 4th century, it deeply affected the religious and cultural structure of the empire. The acceptance of Christianity caused fundamental changes in Roman society and politics. During this time, the Vatican became the center of the Christian world and was considered a key factor in the transformation of the Roman Empire.

In the Middle Ages, the power of the Vatican grew under the religious and political leadership of the Pope and the influence of Canon Law. The Pope held both spiritual and worldly authority, intervening in both religious and state affairs. The Pope's powers were defined by Canon Law, and their implementation significantly influenced religious doctrine and social life. The Church guided the daily lives, moral values, and social order of the people, making the Vatican a defining force in medieval Europe.

The Pope and Canon Law profoundly influenced the political and social structure of medieval Europe. As a spiritual leader, the Pope held great authority over statesmen and kings, reinforced by the rules of Canon Law. Canon Law set legal standards in areas such as marriage, inheritance, crime, and punishment, contributing to the formation of a stable social order in Europe. The Pope's religious and political power, supported by the fundamental principles of Canon Law, established the Vatican as a decisive force in medieval Europe.

The Vatican's Role in the Modern Era

The Vatican's modern role has increasingly influenced international relations, diplomacy, and issues such as religious freedom. As the leader of the Catholic Church, the Pope has assumed a mediating role in international relations, contributed to peace processes, and supported the resolution of various conflicts. Additionally, the Vatican has gained a significant position in global politics through diplomatic relations with various states and its membership or observer status in international organizations.

Historically, the Vatican's political influence has been diverse. The Church's influence on political authority was quite pronounced throughout the Middle Ages. Particularly in Europe, the Vatican's political intervention and authority had a direct effect on the governance of states. Furthermore, due to the political power of religion, the Vatican's societal impact was also profound. These societal influences are related to the role of religious teachings and ethical values in shaping society. The Church's impact has often been evident in areas such as education, health, and social assistance.

Economic Power and Assets

The Vatican's economic power and assets have historically been significant. Its assets are generally gathered under the title of the Holy See and include properties, investments, and financial holdings. The Vatican's economic status and assets are closely linked with the role of the Vatican Bank and should be examined alongside its religious, political, and social influence.

The Vatican Bank

Officially named the Istituto per le Opere di Religione (Institute for Works of Religion), the Vatican Bank manages the Vatican's economic assets and conducts its financial transactions. Established in 1942, this bank is the central institution of the Vatican's financial power. While managing the Vatican's properties, investments, and other resources, the bank also plays a role in international financial relations. It ensures the security of the Vatican's assets while also supporting the financial needs of Catholic institutions worldwide.

Modern Reflections of the Vatican's Historical Power

The Vatican's role in international diplomacy is deeply tied to the historical and cultural wealth of the Catholic Church. The Vatican maintains representations in various regions of the world to establish and sustain diplomatic relations.

The Vatican's historical power continues to influence international diplomacy today. It plays a significant role in relations with other states and remains an important factor in the international community. Today, its influence in diplomacy still persists based on its historical roots, making it a significant factor in international relations.

Looking at the Vatican's political role with historical and contemporary examples, its neutrality policy during World War II and its stance on the Holocaust stand out. Additionally, its role in relations with Eastern Bloc countries in 1984 and its anti-communist position are also noteworthy from a historical perspective.

The Pope is the spiritual leader of the Catholic Church and is regarded as the successor of Saint Peter. The papacy holds great significance in the Catholic faith, and the Pope's powers are extensive. He is the final authority in the Church's religious, moral, and disciplinary matters and has the authority to define theological positions. Furthermore, the Pope has the power to revise divine doctrines and the teachings of the Church. The authority of the papacy is based on the belief that "The Pope is God's representative on Earth."[15] According to this belief, all spiritual and temporal, political powers belonged to him. Everyone, from kings to serfs, had to submit to

---

15 Renaissance Europe: Turkey's Process of Identifying with Western Civilization Halil İnalcık, Türkiye İş Bankası Publications, 15th Edition, 2021, p. 14

the Pope for salvation in the afterlife. The Church was considered the sole intermediary between God and mankind. However, throughout history, this absolute authority was questioned, weakened for political reasons, and at times suffered serious losses of power. Despite this, the papacy continues to exist today as a powerful authority.

The Pope's powers include doctrinal authority as the Church's religious leader, the authority to provide spiritual and ethical guidance, to determine church discipline, to canonize saints, to announce theological positions, and to grant indulgences to the faithful. These powers make the Pope a significant leader and authority figure in the Catholic Church.

The Vatican: Land of Faith, History, and Secrets

Throughout history, the Vatican has been a center of international power struggles. During the Cold War, the Vatican was targeted by both Eastern and Western Blocs, and today it continues to attract the attention of intelligence services from countries such as China, the U.S., and Russia. The Vatican is not merely a religious center but a strategic and geopolitical intelligence battleground full of intrigue.

From the depths of history, the Vatican has played a crucial role as a religious authority, shaped in part by various intelligence activities. In the Middle Ages, the Catholic Church engaged in many covert actions to preserve and expand papal power. During this time, popes carefully evaluated information from their clerics and diplomats to maintain a balance between religion and politics. In the Reformation and Renaissance periods, the Vatican evolved into not only a religious center but also an organization that gathered intelligence and made strategic decisions.

Despite its small geographical size, the Vatican maintains a wide diplomatic network around the world. The papacy holds representations in 183 countries and sustains diplomatic relations with them. Diplomacy has become a means for the Vatican to play an active role in international affairs beyond its religious leadership position. The Pope's frequent international visits and diplomatic meetings create both religious and political impacts, increasing the global influence of the Catholic Church. Diplomatic relations also allow the Vatican to engage directly in information exchange on the international stage.

Picture 23. The Silent Guardians of the Vatican: The Secret Beneath the Armor

For five centuries, the Swiss Guards have moved silently like the shadow of the Pope, known as the protectors of the Vatican's oldest secrets. Tasked with ensuring the Pope's security, the Swiss Guards are recognized as the world's oldest and smallest standing army. Behind their colorful and magnificent uniforms lie elite warriors trained against assassinations, intrigues, and unknown threats.

Only Catholic men born in Switzerland are accepted into the fixed unit of 135 soldiers. After the assassination attempt on Pope John Paul II in 1981, this sacred protective corps blended ancient traditions with modern security techniques, transforming into an even more mysterious force.

Vatican Security Units

The Vatican's security units primarily consist of two main bodies: the Swiss Guard and the Gendarmerie Corps. The Swiss Guards are the Pope's official bodyguards and are responsible for ensuring high-level security during Vatican events. This elite unit, established by Pope Julius II in the 16th century, is composed of select soldiers who undergo rigorous military training. Despite their Renaissance-era uniforms, the Vatican's famous Swiss Guards are not merely decorative. They carry halberds (a type of pole weapon), but machine guns are always within close reach. Behind the ornate uniforms where tourists take photos at the bronze gate of St. Peter's Basilica, weapons are hidden inside a brass umbrella stand.

Vatican security is a blend of modern and medieval elements: Swiss Guards in civilian clothes and papal gendarmes move alongside the Pope's vehicle. This resembles the protection provided by the U.S. Secret Service to the President. However, guards in the Vatican must never turn their backs on the Pope, even when responding to threats. Pope Paul VI stated that turning one's back on the Pope would be disrespectful. On the other hand, the Vatican Gendarmerie Corps is responsible for maintaining daily order, ensuring security, and investigating crimes within Vatican borders. These units play a key role in maintaining the Vatican's safety through their disciplined structure and tight operational coordination.

Vatican Intelligence Activities

The Vatican's security and intelligence entities work in coordination under papal administration to provide effective protection against both internal and external threats. In this context, Vatican intelligence activities are generally conducted in line with religious values, focusing mainly on identifying security risks in advance and protecting the interests of the Vatican State.

Although the Vatican does not have an official intelligence agency like traditional nation-states, history contains many examples of intelligence activities. These efforts are usually conducted through the Vatican's vast diplomatic network and church mechanisms. The Pope's continuous communication with church leaders around the world enables the regular collection of information related to global events and political developments.

Many scholars argue that the Vatican uses this information flow primarily to strengthen its spiritual and cultural leadership role. Thus, rather than the existence of a structured Vatican Intelligence Service, it might be more accurate to perceive it as a legendary institution. Since the Middle Ages, the Papacy has employed spies, intelligence networks, and covert diplomatic missions both to protect itself and to spread the faith. The Jesuit Order was at the center of these covert operations, acting as the eyes and ears of the Vatican.

Facts and Legends: Myths About Vatican Intelligence

The myths and rumors surrounding the Vatican's intelligence networks have often been exaggerated due to the Church's religious and political influence over the years. These legends stem from the belief that the Vatican has been involved in covert accusations or espionage since the Middle Ages in order to protect the Catholic Church and maintain its influence over Christendom. In reality, the Vatican's intelligence structure includes some official and diplomatic activities aimed at protecting its diplomatic relations and religious priorities; however, it does not function as a comprehensive and systematic agency like modern intelligence organizations. The Vatican's Secret Archives are one of the elements that fuel the mystery surrounding its intelligence-gathering.

Picture 24. The shadow behind the Iron Curtain... Spies, assassinations, and secrets that were never leaked... The KGB is not merely an intelligence agency, but one of the greatest mysteries in history.

The Perception of the Vatican as a Secret Intelligence Organization

The perception of the Vatican as a secret intelligence agency is largely a misconception rooted in historical myths and exaggerated novels. While the Vatican may occasionally gain access to confidential information due to its connections with many states and religious institutions, this cannot be compared with the operations of modern intelligence organizations.

Furthermore, widespread theories suggesting that the Pope employs personal intelligence services often lack any concrete evidence. In truth, the Vatican's information-gathering and security policies are mostly developed within the framework of diplomatic relations and operate in accordance with official state policies on an international level.

The information available regarding the Vatican Intelligence Service lies on a fine line between myth and reality. While there is no clear evidence that the Vatican possesses an official intelligence agency, considering its historical and diplomatic role, it is believed that the Vatican is involved in various intelligence-gathering activities. In addition to its religious influence, the Vatican holds strategic importance in terms of preserving history, art, and knowledge, making involvement in intelligence activities plausible for effective diplomacy. However, concrete data about the nature and scope of such activities remains scarce. Shrouded in myths, the Vatican continues to maintain its mystique and captivate interest around the world.

Cold War: The Vatican and the KGB

The KGB, or "Komitet Gosudarstvennoy Bezopasnosti," was established in 1954 as the security and intelligence agency of the Soviet Union. The KGB's primary duties were to protect the Soviet state against internal and external threats, monitor and control foreign intelligence activities, maintain internal security, and neutralize regime opponents.

In this context, espionage and counterespionage, political pressure, and the promotion of Soviet ideology were among the KGB's main responsibilities. During the Cold War, the KGB formed a broad intelligence network both domestically and internationally to serve the Soviet Union's foreign policy goals.

At that time, the KGB conducted numerous global operations. In addition to targeting the U.S. and NATO countries, ideologically influential structures were also within its scope. After World War II, the Catholic Church and the Vatican adopted an anti-communist stance, posing a threat to the Soviet Union's internal politics and influence in the Eastern Bloc.

For this reason, the Soviet Union saw the Vatican as one of the greatest threats to communism. The KGB attempted to infiltrate the Vatican with agents to obstruct the Church's anti-Soviet activities. Pope John Paul II played a pivotal role in the Cold War by supporting the anti-communist movement in Poland. Allegedly, the KGB attempted to assassinate Pope John Paul II in an effort to diminish the Vatican's influence. In response, the Vatican, in cooperation with the Western Bloc, carried out both covert and overt operations to counter Soviet influence.

In a book published in the U.S. in 2006, it was claimed that the Soviet Union had spies within the Vatican monitoring the Pope. The book, titled Spies in the Vatican, was authored by experienced former CIA operative John Koehler.

The book alleged that during the Cold War, Polish Pope John Paul II was being monitored by Polish priest-spies inside the Vatican on behalf of the KGB and the Stasi. Koehler also suggested that the East German secret service Stasi might have abetted Mehmet Ali Ağca, the would-be assassin of the Pope. However, these claims could not be proven in court during the investigation into the assassination attempt.

According to the author, 200 boxes of documents related to the assassination are still stored in the Vatican archives. The former CIA agent also claimed that after the death of Pope John Paul II, the German-born Pope Benedict XVI, who was aware of these documents, prevented their public release.

KGB Infiltration Operations into the Vatican

Throughout the Cold War, the activities conducted by the KGB against the Vatican attracted attention for their impact on both international dynamics and religious relations. During this period, the KGB's intelligence operations played a decisive role in shaping Vatican policies. Given the Vatican's strong diplomatic ties and spiritual leadership position, it was a clear strategic target for the KGB. However, various measures taken by the Vatican and its secret intelligence networks helped it resist these threats.

The most prominent of the KGB's activities against the Vatican were efforts to reduce the Catholic Church's political and religious influence. The KGB conducted infiltration operations to control the flow of information within the Vatican. These operations aimed to silence dissenting voices within the Church and promote a pro-Moscow stance. At times, these actions strained relations between the Vatican and Western states, drawing the Vatican into a full-blown political war. Nonetheless, the Church's deep diplomatic network and the strategic measures taken by the Vatican at times limited the

KGB's influence and strengthened efforts to preserve the Church's independence.

Espionage Stories in the Shadow of the Cold War

During the Cold War, the tensions between the U.S. and the Soviet Union deepened through intelligence wars. In this process, due to the anti-communist stance of the Catholic Church—especially that of Pope John Paul II—the Soviet intelligence agency KGB accelerated its efforts to infiltrate and influence the Vatican.

Pope John Paul II's support for the Solidarity Movement in Poland and his strengthening of the anti-communist movement in Eastern Europe prompted immediate Soviet reaction, and the KGB launched its infiltration plans into the Vatican.

To penetrate the Vatican and leak information, the KGB used the following methods:

Informant Cardinals and Clergy: It was alleged that some clergy within the Vatican collaborated with the KGB, particularly priests originating from Eastern Europe.

Bulgarian and Hungarian Connections: The intelligence services of pro-Soviet Bulgaria and Hungary carried out espionage activities in the Vatican on behalf of the KGB. However, with support from Western intelligence services, especially the CIA, many KGB agents were exposed.

KGB Agents Exposed in Vatican

Monsignor Luigi Poggi: A key figure targeted by the KGB during the Vatican's diplomatic contacts with the Eastern Bloc. He was accused of leaking internal information about Soviet-Vatican diplomatic talks in the 1980s and was later subjected to internal investigation by the Vatican.

Agent Pankov: Known as an agent who leaked information to the KGB through Bulgaria and sought to weaken the Vatican's connections with Eastern European churches. It was later revealed that he reported on the Vatican's secret meetings with bishops from Eastern Europe.

Agent Gromov: Placed in the Vatican through East Germany's Stasi intelligence service. After the fall of the Berlin Wall in 1989, he was identified in Stasi archives and found to have transmitted detailed information to the KGB about papal election processes.

Michał Goleniewski: A Polish KGB agent assigned to monitor the Vatican's activities in the Eastern Bloc. In the 1960s, he defected to the CIA and exposed the KGB's espionage operations inside the Vatican. The information he provided significantly revealed the Soviet influence over the Vatican.

Bogdan Cevic: Infiltrated the Vatican through Yugoslavia and was tasked with monitoring church leaders. In the 1980s, he tried to undermine Pope John Paul II's anti-communist policies by spreading false intelligence, thereby eroding trust within the Church. His connections were exposed in 1991 with the collapse of the USSR.

Ivan Kozyrev: Known as a high-level Soviet intelligence official, he was responsible for manipulating certain clergymen within the Vatican. He was found to have passed details of the Pope's speeches to the KGB. His identity was revealed after the fall of the Soviet Union.

The Fall of the Soviet Union and the Revealed Truths

After the collapse of the Soviet Union in 1991, the testimonies of former KGB agents and Western intelligence reports revealed that the KGB had significantly infiltrated the Vatican. Following the USSR's dissolution, some agents embedded in the Vatican surrendered to Western intelligence services and provided information about the Soviet Union's operations against the Catholic Church.

Following the failed assassination attempts on Reagan and later on Pope John Paul II, the world witnessed an even more complex period within the politically tense Cold War landscape. These events showed that not only were individual leaders targeted, but also the ideological symbols they represented.

These developments created a massive global resonance and sparked renewed discussions on cooperation and diplomacy within the blocs. As distrust between the Western and Eastern blocs grew, many countries began developing new strategies to protect their political leaders and religious figures. This period also transformed perceptions of intelligence and security. After these incidents, the heightened sense of threat toward leaders once again underscored the importance of revisiting international security policies.

Picture 25. CIA: Master of shadow games... The sealed emblem of mystery and power... Covert operations, unseen wars, and enigmas written between the lines of history... Hands behind the curtain, fates scripted, and history steered... Assassinations, coups, vanished secrets... Where does truth begin, and where does the lie end?

CIA's Relations with and Influence on the Vatican

The Central Intelligence Agency (CIA), the foreign intelligence service of the United States, was established by the National Security Act signed by President Harry S. Truman in 1947. Its purpose is to gather various types of intelligence globally to protect national security. The CIA played especially active roles during the Cold War, becoming a critical instrument in determining political and military strategies. Accordingly, since its inception, it has played a key role in international espionage, covert operations, and intelligence sharing between governments. Like every intelligence organization, secrecy and operational mystery have become part of the CIA's controversial nature.

With the outbreak of the Cold War, the agency continuously expanded its strategies and operations to counter the Soviet Union and other communist countries. The CIA's main duties include gathering and analyzing intelligence for national security and presenting this information to relevant state departments. In addition, the CIA has the authority to conduct covert operations; these often involve influencing regime changes in foreign countries, counter-terrorism, and espionage. The agency also profiles foreign leaders and threats for risk assessment.

The relationship between the CIA and the Vatican during the Cold War is an important topic in understanding the global balance of power. These relations help us understand how the two institutions interacted throughout history and the global impacts of these interactions. Particularly during and after the Cold War, the types of collaborations the CIA engaged in with the Vatican in line with its strategic goals, and how these shaped political and social events, are of historical and geopolitical significance.

The Vatican, with its unique historical and diplomatic power, became a particular focus for the CIA, just as it was for the KGB. In relations that date back to the Cold War era, the Vatican's global religious and political influence contributed to expanding the CIA's operational capabilities. During this period, the CIA increasingly utilized the Vatican to monitor and engage with religious movements in Eastern Bloc countries, and the relationship intensified on various diplomatic and operational grounds.

The Cold War marked a period when CIA–Vatican relations took on a more strategic dimension. During this era, the Catholic Church's influence in Eastern Europe was considered by the CIA to be a religious and ideological counterbalance to Soviet influence. In countries like Poland, where the Church had a strong presence, it provided the CIA with a significant channel for observation and interaction. The Vatican was seen as a beacon of hope for Catholics within the Soviet bloc, and the election of Pope John Paul II contributed to a more active and effective CIA strategy.

CIA's relationship with the Vatican was developed to strengthen both parties' strategic positions on the global stage. Although these relations were mostly conducted covertly, they laid the foundation for effective international cooperation. While the Vatican used its religious influence to affect political balances in various countries, the CIA provided the Vatican with counterintelligence and expertise in exchange. This dynamic led to a natural strategic alignment between the two parties, particularly during the Cold War, in pursuit of their shared interests.

Through its vast religious network and strong communication with local communities worldwide, the Vatican had access to significant information in many countries. This information was carefully analyzed by the CIA and used in planning relevant operational processes. Special and behind-the-scenes information provided through the Vatican's diplomatic channels also held valuable strategic importance for the CIA. In turn, the Vatican strengthened its position by benefiting from the CIA's technological and logistical capabilities in support of its own strategic goals.

The CIA's relationship with the Vatican had the capacity to influence global politics and strategic balances. Throughout the Cold War, the Vatican's anti-communist stance was evaluated by the CIA as a strategic advantage, offering a useful platform for various operations. Thanks to intelligence sharing, both parties increased their ability to act in line with common strategic interests, playing a significant role in shaping the policies of Western Bloc countries. These relations, through the exchange of knowledge and power, allowed both the CIA and the Vatican to operate more effectively on the global stage.

The religious and societal impacts of the CIA's relationship with the Vatican left deep marks on a global scale—traces of which are still visible today. The Vatican's role in religious leadership intersected with the CIA's ideological goals, influencing various religious organizations and communities. While this relationship increased the Vatican's legitimacy in some communities, it caused suspicion and distrust in others. The CIA found opportunities to monitor, influence, and direct social movements by leveraging the Vatican's broad religious network. As a result, this cooperation reshaped religious loyalties and social structures and played a role in enhancing interfaith dialogue and the global influence of religious leaders. Its effect on NATO member countries like Turkey is a separate topic of investigation for historians and political scientists.

Ideological Disputes Within the Catholic Church and Pope John Paul II

The Catholic Church has gone through numerous reforms and changes throughout history. Pope John Paul II stood out during this transformation process as a leader who both preserved traditional values and sought to adapt to the modern world. However, this approach led to significant ideological divisions and debates within the Church.

Pope John Paul II was a leader attempting to redefine the Catholic Church's role in the modern world. While his strong authority inspired admiration in some, it disappointed others who felt the Church was not progressing enough. His papacy became one of the most prominent symbols of the ongoing conservative-reformist conflict within the Catholic Church. He was a leader who wished to implement deep reforms in the Church while also maintaining traditional authority.

- He supported the modernization reforms brought by the Second Vatican Council (1962–1965) but did not want to compromise on core Church doctrines.

- He took a firm stance against Marxist-influenced liberation theology and left-leaning priests.
- The Pope sought to build a strong, united, renewed, and conservative Church. He proposed initiating dialogue with the Eastern Orthodox Church, marking the first official talks between Catholics and Orthodox Christians since 1054.

This situation led to division within the Church:

- Conservative cardinals sided with the Pope against reformist groups questioning his authority.
- However, more radical reformist clergy and some theologians felt the Pope ruled the Church too authoritatively.
- Especially left-leaning Catholic priests in Latin America and intellectual theologians in parts of Europe were uneasy with the Pope's stance.

In countries like the Netherlands, he directly summoned Church officials not adhering to Rome's rules to the Vatican.

While previous Popes held regular meetings with bishops to discuss such issues, Pope John Paul II preferred direct intervention. Some clergy and academics in the Vatican criticized his overly centralized management style.

- Especially in Germany and France, some reform-minded clergy began to challenge the Pope's authority.
- The Pope imposed discipline by removing reformist scholars from positions within the Church.

These divisions made the Vatican more vulnerable to foreign intelligence services.

The Conflict Between Conservatives and Reformists

- Conservatives supported the Pope's strict defense of his authority and the Church's traditional doctrines.
- Reformists wanted a more open, liberal Church sensitive to individual rights.
- Topics such as birth control, priestly marriage, and the ordination of women sparked major debates.

THE POPE'S STANCE

- Pope John Paul II remained committed to the reforms of the Second Vatican Council (1962–65) but distanced himself from excessive modernization of the Church.
- His removal of reformist theologians like Hans Küng from Church positions drew significant backlash.
- He supported ecumenical dialogue (efforts toward unity between Catholics and other Christian denominations), but opposed reforms that might weaken the Church's central authority.

DID DIVISIONS AND INTELLIGENCE WARS MAKE THE POPE A TARGET?

This issue must also be evaluated in the context of internal divisions within the Vatican and infiltration by foreign intelligence services. In this context, three key questions arise:

- How did divisions within the Vatican pave the way for threats against the Pope?
- What influence did foreign intelligence services, especially the KGB and CIA, have on the Vatican?
- What role did this intelligence wars play in the attack on Pope John Paul II?

These divisions made the Vatican more vulnerable to foreign intelligence services. Some clergy opposed to the Pope began lobbying within the Vatican by establishing connections with external powers. Especially the Pope's support for the Solidarity Movement in Poland provoked strong reactions from Eastern Bloc countries and particularly the KGB. The internal divisions within the Vatican and the activities of foreign intelligence agencies played a significant role in the attempted assassination of Pope John Paul II. The Pope had made many enemies both inside and outside the Church. His stance against the communist regime in Poland disturbed the Soviets and Eastern Bloc countries. Reformists within the Church wanted to weaken his authority, while conservatives aimed to protect his leadership. In this environment, foreign services easily infiltrated the Vatican. The KGB and Bulgarian intelligence conducted operations to undermine the Pope's influence, while the CIA and Western intelligence used him as a leader against the Soviets. The ideological and political conflicts within the Vatican made it easier for intelligence agencies to manipulate the situation. These conflicts left the Pope isolated and more vulnerable. Foreign intelligence services exploited internal Church disputes to infiltrate the Vatican and manipulate certain groups. These complex dynamics became one of the main reasons Pope John Paul II was targeted.

The World in the Shadow of the Cold War
Towards the Assassination
What Was the World Like the Day Before the Assassination?

Picture 26. The Cold War is the name given to a period in which weapons remained in the shadows and wars were directed by unseen hands. The United States and the Soviet Union, donning the sword of their ideologies, challenged each other on the world stage. These were years when secrets were lost among whispers, spies hid behind shadows, and nuclear threats kept humanity on edge. From Berlin's divided streets to the dark rooms of deep states, a sense of tension could be felt everywhere. Although this cold yet burning war ended in 1991 with the collapse of the USSR, it left behind unresolved mysteries and echoes of whispers.

On the eve of the papal assassination that would shift the global balance, the political climate dominating the world stage was largely shaped by the ideological and geopolitical tensions brought about by the Cold War. The world resembled a stage breathing under the shadow of ideological contradictions and the Cold War, as if on the verge of a clue, surrounded by dark shadows. In those days, the silent whispers echoing behind the thick walls of intelligence agencies seemed to signal that a historical turning point was approaching.

On one side, the sharp divide between East and West symbolized a delicate balance trembling under the shadow of nuclear weapons. The streets of that era bore the scars of deep wounds left behind by ideological tensions and political intrigues, while also nurturing seeds of hope sprouting in the hearts of peoples suffering under both capitalist and communist oppression. People were living in a world where every corner whispered stories of both pain and resistance, both despair and belief. Almost everywhere in the world, terrorist acts carried out in the name of ideologies had become repetitive and even ordinary. At this point in the violence-filled century, as the world turned into a global village, the political arena became a stage where assassinations were committed for attention. However, society felt only temporary discomfort in the face of such violent acts. Assassination attempts, hijackings, prolonged hostage situations, and bombs detonated in the name of "freedom" had now become commonplace news.

The date May 13, 1981, stood right in the middle of this complex mosaic, on the threshold of an event that would change the course of history; humanity was breathing in the grip of conflicts, with an uncertain hope for the future.

A World Under Cold War Tension:

The world was caught in the middle of a sharp ideological, military, and political rivalry between the Western bloc led by the United States and the Eastern bloc led by the Soviet Union. The nuclear arms race, proxy wars, and international alliances were among the main elements shaping global politics. There were deep divisions between democratic liberalism and capitalism on one side, and communism on the other. This ideological conflict manifested itself not only in the political arena but also on cultural and societal levels. On the other hand, the leadership of Pope John Paul II, especially due to his emphasis on universal values such as faith, freedom, and human rights within the Catholic world, was seen as a symbolic form of resistance against communist ideologies.

SINIRDAKİ BÜYÜK OPERASYON

Suriye hududunda, bölücü bir örgüt için getirilen Rus yapısı silahlar ele geçirildi

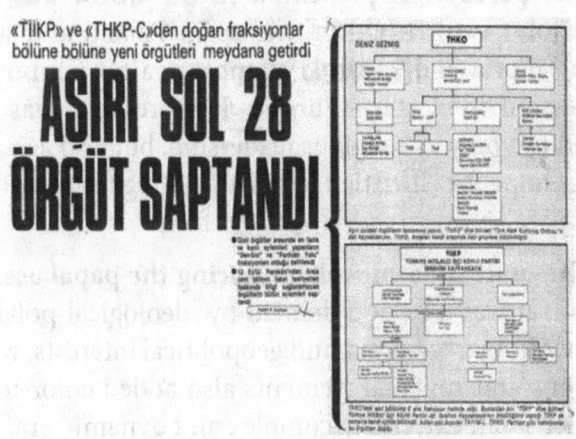

Picture 27 – 28 – 29. *The poles were clear, but the weapon of chaos was aimed in every direction. The Soviet mind tried to divide Turkey from within by burning both the right and the left in the same fire. Turkey became trapped between the poles; ideological chaos was inscribed into the destiny of its geography.*

The perception presented to the world was this: Pope John Paul II had grown up in Poland and was a strong moral and spiritual support against communist oppression in Eastern Europe. His presence was perceived not only as religious leadership, but also as a beacon of hope for Christian peoples fighting for freedom.

The political atmosphere during the papal assassination: It was a period defined by ideological polarization, Cold War tensions, and geopolitical interests, where religious and spiritual elements also added color to the conflict — an extremely complex and dynamic era. This environment left deep marks both internationally and locally, forming an unforgettable impression on the stage of history.

Turkey in the Shadow of the Cold War: The First Signs of the Papal Assassination in Turkey

During the Cold War, Turkey held a strategically significant position as NATO's forward outpost against the Soviet Union. With U.S. support, anti-communist policies were promoted while pro-Soviet groups were suppressed. The 1979 Iranian Revolution and the Soviet invasion of Afghanistan increased Turkey's geopolitical importance. Under the CIA-backed "Green Belt Project," the policy of supporting Islamic movements gained momentum. It was alleged that the Gladio network in Europe (NATO-backed secret anti-communist organizations) also operated in Turkey under the name "Counter-Guerrilla."

Picture 30 – 31. *In the shadow of the Cold War, the bullets echoing through the streets of Istanbul silenced Abdi İpekçi; years later, the same hand targeted a Pope in Rome. Mehmet Ali Ağca's bloody journey was etched into history like a shadow stretching from the assassination of Abdi İpekçi to the Vatican. His dark path, traced through intelligence games and deep connections, still stands as an unsolved riddle.*

Prior to the papal assassination, Turkey was experiencing significant political and social instability. Economic crisis, left-right conflicts, and foreign interventions had rendered the country unstable. During this period, Turkey—being one of the regions where the Cold War was most intensely felt—was engulfed in deep chaos and entered a new era under military rule following the September 12, 1980 coup.

Bullets Echoing Through the Streets of Istanbul: The Assassination of Abdi İpekçi

In the final quarter of the 20th century, Turkey writhed in the grip of seething political polarization, like a volcano on the verge of eruption. Streets, universities, factories—everywhere was consumed by a bloody struggle. Youth were divided into ideological camps; the right and the left were not just differing opinions, but opposing sides in a deadly war. In the second half of the 1970s, violent clashes between leftist and right-wing groups escalated. Revolutionary leftist organizations (such as THKP-C, Dev-Sol) and right-wing factions (primarily the Grey Wolves movement) increasingly clashed in universities, streets, and cities. As the influence of the MHP and its affiliated Grey Wolves grew on the streets, leftist groups also intensified their actions.

Every day brought another murder, every morning began with news of another assassination. The walls of the cities were riddled with bullet holes. University lecture halls had become battlegrounds echoing with slogans, no longer places of learning. Ideologies were no longer represented by ideas, but by the barrels of guns. This chaos, growing before the eyes of the state, was being fed by unseen hands, deepening the polarization. The 1978 Maraş

Massacre and the 1980 Çorum Incidents were among the starkest examples of societal conflict. One of the main justifications for the September 12, 1980 military coup was the surge of violence that could no longer be contained within a normal legal system.

It was in exactly such an atmosphere that the assassination of Abdi İpekçi took place.

Abdi İpekçi[16] was one of the most influential figures in Turkish journalism. As the editor-in-chief of *Milliyet* newspaper, he was known not only as a journalist reporting the news but also as a prominent voice advocating an end to political polarization in Turkey and someone with influence over the government. In his articles and editorials, he stressed his belief that dialogue between the right and the left was possible and that the violence could end. His writings had a powerful impact on both politics and society.

**The Evening of the Assassination
February 1, 1979**

That evening, Abdi İpekçi left the offices of *Milliyet* and was driving toward his home in the Nişantaşı district of Istanbul. Due to traffic congestion, he had to slow his vehicle, and a man approaching the car fired 4–5 shots through the open window. İpekçi died at the scene shortly after being shot.

---

16 Abdi İpekçi (1929-1979) was a Turkish journalist and writer. Born in Istanbul in 1929, his family was of Turkish origin, having migrated from Thessaloniki to Istanbul during the Ottoman period. He completed his education at Galatasaray High School and then attended Istanbul University Faculty of Law. İpekçi began his journalism career at a young age and became one of Türkiye's most prominent press figures. He served as editor-in-chief and editor-in-chief of Milliyet Newspaper. He wrote important articles on democracy, human rights, and freedoms.

The assassin was Mehmet Ali Ağca, a first-year economics student at Istanbul University and only 21 years old.

Following the murder, a major operation was launched across the country. Ağca managed to evade capture for months. While the police pursued him, one of the most striking pieces of evidence was a torn phone book page with İpekçi's address written on it. This small detail would become one of the critical elements of the investigation.

However, five months later, on June 25, 1979, Ağca was caught after an anonymous caller tipped off the police via the emergency radio system. He was arrested while playing cards in Marmara Coffeehouse—then a popular hangout for nationalist Grey Wolves and a center for heated political debate in Istanbul. Ağca appeared calm, composed, and self-assured. Even as he was taken into custody by police, there were no signs of worry on his face. But the murder would not be seen as merely an individual act; it would be alleged that a greater power and a deeper plan lay behind the assassination.

Ağca's arrest would, in fact, signal the beginning of a major scandal. Nationwide debates erupted, and all eyes turned to the judiciary and security forces. According to a statement by Ahmet Koç, the Martial Law Military Prosecutor at the time, the police had waited a full two weeks before searching Ağca's home. No action had been taken for a month and a half to investigate the addresses and phone numbers found on him. These revelations rocked the political landscape and shook the state apparatus to its core.

These revelations sparked claims that certain parties had deliberately delayed action in order to protect Ağca. When Ağca and his accomplices were finally caught days after the incident, he showed no sign of remorse. In his first statement to the police, he said calmly:

"I killed him because I rebelled. The only thing I will say is that I am neither right-wing nor left-wing; I am an independent terrorist acting alone."

Six months later, Ağca suddenly changed his testimony. At first, he denied the charges, then began making contradictory statements. Sometimes he claimed to have acted alone, other times he implied the involvement of greater forces behind him. Over the years, each statement he gave contradicted the last, blurring the line between truth and falsehood in the investigations.

Picture 32 – 33. The locks had been opened, the shadows had moved... Ağca did not escape; he was taken. This headline marked not just an escape, but the beginning of the bloody road leading to Rome.

The İpekçi assassination was not just the murder of a journalist—it also threw Turkey's political balance into chaos. The killing occurred during the bloodiest days of the right-left conflict in Turkey. But this conflict was not merely a grassroots movement—it was a game orchestrated by deep state structures, international interest groups, and players lurking in the shadows.

The İpekçi assassination was one of the most critical flashpoints in the right-left conflict. But it would also become one of the primary justifications for the September 12, 1980 military coup. While youth were being pitted against each other in the streets, others were simply waiting for the right moment to push the button. And those who ultimately won were the ones who remained in the shadows. Amid all these debates, Ağca was arrested and sent to Maltepe Military Prison.

The Great Escape Plan That Shook Turkey

While political assassinations continued unabated, on the morning of November 25, 1979, Turkey would wake up to an event that would leave a lasting mark in its history. News agencies were reporting an incident that rocked the country. Mehmet Ali Ağca, who had unexpectedly escaped from Maltepe Military Prison due to the Abdi İpekçi assassination, would stun the nation.

Within the walls of the Maltepe Military Prison, protected with high-level security measures, Mehmet Ali Ağca slipped through like a shadow and vanished into thin air. After being arrested for the İpekçi assassination and placed in this prison, Ağca, while awaiting trial, disappeared that day through the iron gates of the prison with the alleged complicity and active assistance of security personnel.

The prison walls, said to be of high security, could not stop Mehmet Ali Ağca. On the night of November 25, only 128 days after entering the prison, Ağca carried out one of the most mysterious escapes in history. Rightwing soldiers were helping Ağca in his escape.

A soldier at the prison who assisted in the escape, Bünyamin Yılmaz, would say years later:

"I was ordered to help Ağca escape. I gave my word, and I didn't go back on it. I helped him escape all by myself... If I were a civilian, I'd do it again, but I regret doing it while I was in the military."

Yılmaz took a note sent to him by Ağca to Oral Çelik, one of the figures connected to the assassination. Çelik provided the money and weapons needed for the escape. Yılmaz gave his military uniform to Ağca to help him flee. Even the guards on duty didn't notice during the escape. Yılmaz paid a heavy price for this escape; he was caught and served eight years in prison.

Later, in a letter sent to Milliyet newspaper, Ağca said of the escape: "Please don't exaggerate it—it was a simple event."

This escape triggered a major scandal that shook Turkey internally; security vulnerabilities became a topic of national debate, and the effectiveness of the judiciary system came under scrutiny. The impact of the incident spread to every corner of the country; large-scale investigations were launched, but Ağca soon disappeared abroad. After leaving Turkey, he went to Iran under the Khomeini regime. After staying there for a while, he vanished in the Middle East.

Ağca's escape from Maltepe Military Prison was not merely a prisoner's release—it became a symbol of Turkey's fragile security and judicial systems, of the ongoing ideological conflicts in the international arena, and of the games of intelligence agencies. This event took its place in the country's modern history and in the eyes of international public opinion as an unforgettable turning point echoing the silent yet powerful reverberations of dark intrigues and ambiguous power balances.

Later, during his imprisonment in Italy for the attempted assassination of Pope John Paul II, Ağca summarized the Maltepe escape with the following statement:

"I met a young soldier named Bünyamin Yılmaz. I told him I was innocent. He believed I hadn't committed murder. I asked for his help. He was somewhat sympathetic to the nationalist cause. He helped me on his own. Many non-commissioned officers, soldiers, and privates were under suspicion. I was really upset. No one else was responsible—only Bünyamin Yılmaz... He brought me a military uniform. For the first time, I wore a Mehmetçik's [Turkish soldier's] uniform... We went out in military attire. As we were leaving, there was something I'll never forget... One foot was outside, one foot still inside. Just as I was about to leave, the guard asked, 'What time is it?' I was like, God... I stayed calm, checked the time—it was quarter to three, I'll never forget that."

The Dark Secret Behind the Escape

The Turkish press alleged that Ağca's escape was not just a simple breakout, but part of a larger organization. The question was: Was the team that helped him escape abroad part of a greater scheme?

Before leaving, he wanted to leave a message behind.

Once again, he chose the Milliyet newspaper. He made a phone call, asking them to check the mailbox. The first check came up empty. Then another call came—this time, they were told to look in the trash. And from the trash came a note, heralding a new assassination plot.

The target was the Pope…

Mehmet Ali Ağca's Journey to Rome
Footsteps of the Man in the Shadows

Some journeys are such that they change not just one person, but the entire world. The road Mehmet Ali Ağca took to Rome was a journey full of unsolved mysteries to this day. This was not a simple escape; it was a path hidden in the mists, leading to one of the greatest assassination attempts in history.

When he walked that path, was he merely a lone man shaping his own fate? Or was he a figure moving in the shadows of secret services, intelligence agencies, ideologies, and prophecies?

Ağca's prison escape was never just the flight of an ordinary criminal. He was wanted—internationally. Just months earlier, he had become the most talked-about figure in Turkey due to the Abdi İpekçi assassination. But Ağca's escape plan was not just about evading Turkish law enforcement. This journey that began after his escape was the first move in a grand game that would take him to one of the most significant assassination attempts in history.

Picture 34. Secrets lost in the trail of an assassin: Mehmet Ali Ağca's shadowy journey through Europe bears the marks of intelligence wars, deep connections, and an assassination that turned into an unsolved riddle. Ağca's journey in the shadows is like a secret echoing through the foggy corridors of the Cold War... The escape route stretching from Istanbul to Tehran, from Sofia to Zurich— did it carry the traces of intelligence agencies, dirty dealings, and dark connections? In Rome, the bullet fired targeted not only a Pope but also the unanswered questions buried deep in history. The courts have closed, yet the map of this dark journey remains incomplete.

FROM ISTANBUL TO SOFIA: IN THE SHADOWS OF DEPTH

Shortly after his escape, Ağca's trail was lost. Some believed he had gone to Iran; others thought he was hiding in the Middle East. He was leaving deep traces along this route that awaited unraveling. But his real destination was clear: Europe. This journey, which began in Turkey, took him to Bulgaria.

In the early 1980s, Bulgaria was one of the darkest corners of the Eastern Bloc. Under the shadow of Soviet intelligence agency KGB, Bulgaria's secret service Darzhavna Sigurnost (DS) was the center of many covert operations against the West. Whom did Ağca meet here? Which doors were opened to him? These questions were keys to secrets that had remained unanswered for years. Ağca's entry into Bulgaria and his stay there marked the beginning of many entangled threads.

According to one theory, Ağca met with KGB-affiliated agents in Sofia. Did Bulgarian intelligence have a role in the assassination attempt on the Pope? Was this pure speculation or evidence of deep state mechanisms? The only certainty was that Ağca wouldn't stay long in Sofia. He was provided with a fake passport and began a long journey toward Europe.

FINAL STOP BEFORE ROME: AUSTRIA AND SWITZERLAND

By 1981, Ağca was already in Europe. It was alleged that he traveled through Austria and into Switzerland using false documents. During the Cold War, Switzerland was a hub for intelligence agencies. Western intelligence, Eastern Bloc agents, and even those close to the Vatican held secret meetings there. Who helped him at this stage? Where did he obtain the logistical support for the assassination? How long did he stay there? At which table was the decision made that would lead him to Rome? These questions would be asked for years.

According to some documents, Ağca spent a brief time in Milan before reaching Rome. Who were his contacts in Milan? By what means did he travel to Rome? No one knew for sure. But what we do know is this: In the spring of 1981, Mehmet Ali Ağca took his first step into the heart of the Vatican.

ARRIVAL IN ROME: THE SHADOW OF ASSASSINATION

Throughout history, Rome has been a city of conspiracies and assassinations. In this city, where Caesar was murdered and intrigues stretched sky-high, preparations for a new assassination were underway. Ağca's target was clear: Pope John Paul II.

And on May 13, 1981, one of fate's darkest moments would unfold in St. Peter's Square.

Mehmet Ali Ağca's journey to Rome remains a mystery still not fully unraveled. Was this the work of a single man, or part of an operation carried out under the shadow of greater powers?

Picture 35. Pope John Paul II's visit to Turkey was an event that spiritually and diplomatically reinforced Turkey's place on the Western front during the Cold War. This visit skillfully combined both political and religious messages, making Turkey an indispensable ally for the Western world.

What we know is that Ağca didn't just go to Rome. He left a trace in the deep corridors of history—a trace that continues to draw pursuers into a veil of mystery even years later. This journey was not just one man's story, but the beginning of one of the greatest mysteries in world history.

VATICAN-TURKEY RELATIONS AND THE POPE'S VISIT TO TURKEY

Historical Background of Vatican-Turkey Relations

Relations between Turkey and the Vatican have historically been shaped by religious and diplomatic contacts dating back to the Ottoman era. During the Ottoman period, discussions occasionally took place with the Vatican to protect Catholic communities and manage relations with Europe. In the modern Republic of Turkey, official diplomatic relations with the Vatican remained limited until the 1960s, after which contacts between the two states began to increase.

Adnan Menderes was the first Turkish statesman to visit the Vatican as a head of government. Alongside Foreign Minister Fuad Köprülü, he visited Pope Pius XII and received special attention from the Vatican, including golden medals awarded to both men. According to Turkish press reports, during the meeting, officials discussed anti-communist efforts and how to initiate official diplomatic relations and assign representatives to each other. Though clerics like Pope John XXIII[17] played a role in the warming of relations following WWII and Turkey's

---

17 Recent Türkiye Research Issue/Issue: Ramazan Erhan Güllü, Research Article 36, 2019

transition to multiparty politics, the primary factor was the strategic idea of forming an anti-communist alliance.

In the 1960s, Turkey officially established diplomatic relations with the Vatican, marking a new era. In 1984, the Vatican opened a permanent representative office in Turkey. This development contributed to the strengthening of diplomatic and cultural ties between the two states.

The relationship between the Vatican and Turkey has been shaped around themes like religious tolerance, cultural exchange, and support for peace, with papal visits to Turkey being a crucial part of this dynamic.

POPE JOHN PAUL II'S VISIT TO TURKEY (1979)

Pope John Paul II's visit to Turkey from November 28–30, 1979, marked a significant turning point in Turkey–Vatican relations. During the visit, the Pope held meetings in Ankara and Istanbul, visited religious and historical sites like Hagia Sophia and the Blue Mosque, and met with the then-President of Turkey, Fahri Korutürk.

The Pope emphasized the importance of dialogue between Christians and Muslims and conveyed messages of religious tolerance. Though viewed as a critical step in Vatican-Turkey relations, this visit was met with backlash from Mehmet Ali Ağca and certain circles, overshadowed by threats of assassination.

The Pope's Visit to Turkey and Ağca's Threat Letter

"I Will Definitely Shoot the Pope. I Escaped to Kill."

One of the most significant threats to Pope John Paul II's Turkey visit came from Mehmet Ali Ağca, who would later become known for his assassination attempt. Ağca described the Pope's visit as a "provocation against Islam" and issued a letter publicly announcing his intention to assassinate the Pope.

In the threat letter sent to Milliyet newspaper, Ağca wrote:

"Western imperialists, afraid of the emergence of a new political, military, and economic power in the Middle East with Turkey and its Islamic brother countries, are hastily sending a Crusader commander disguised as a religious leader, John Paul, to Turkey during a sensitive time. If this untimely and meaningless visit is not canceled, I will definitely shoot the Pope. The only reason I escaped from prison was to do this."

This letter heightened security concerns regarding the Pope's visit and was taken seriously by Turkish authorities. Nonetheless, the visit proceeded under tight security as planned.

Picture 36. Pope John Paul II's Visit to Turkey. November 28-30, 1979. Silence reigns as a storm approaches...Pope John Paul II was delivering messages of peace in Turkey, but a threat was growing in the shadows. Ağca's warning hung in the air. Was it a harbinger of a prophecy that would resonate in Rome?

Although the Pope's 1979 visit aimed to foster interfaith dialogue, it was marred by threats. Right-wing newspapers reacted harshly to the visit. This episode highlighted the fragile balance between diplomatic efforts and security risks in Turkey–Vatican relations.

Reactions to the Visit in the Turkish Press

The Turkish press gave significant coverage to the Pope's visit, with both support and criticism emerging from different segments.

Secular and Mainstream Media: Newspapers like Cumhuriyet, Milliyet, and Hürriyet treated the visit as a diplomatic engagement. They emphasized its importance for the development of Vatican–Turkey relations and viewed it as a positive step toward promoting interfaith dialogue.

Conservative and Nationalist Publications: Right-wing and conservative outlets took a more skeptical stance. They portrayed the visit as religiously motivated and part of a broader Vatican strategy toward the Islamic world. Some newspapers viewed the Pope's visit to Hagia Sophia as symbolic and contradictory to Turkey's secularism.

Radical and Extreme Reactions: Ağca's threat targeting the Pope received widespread coverage. He saw the visit as a political maneuver by Western powers and insisted it should be canceled. Some newspapers ran headlines about Ağca's prison escape and threat letter, highlighting the visit's security aspects.

Ağca ultimately failed to carry out his threat during the visit. However, about a year and a half later, in his statements following the assassination attempt, he implied that the Pope's 1979 visit to Turkey was a trigger for his later actions.

Picture 37. This headline was the first whisper of an ancient plan that led to Rome. It was the beginning of the shadowy road to Rome. Prophecy or a pre-written game? Ağca was walking, but who had drawn the path?

Ağca's Trial in Martial Law Court and Death Sentence

Ağca was taken into custody on June 25, 1979, for the murder of journalist Abdi İpekçi. He was arrested on July 11, 1979, and escaped prison on November 25, 1979, after 158 days in custody. He was tried by the martial law military court. The nature of the murder, Ağca's escape, and the mysterious connections behind the assassination transformed the case from an ordinary criminal matter into one with political implications. Ağca confessed during police and court proceedings, but his later statements were full of contradictions, raising questions about a possible larger force behind the assassination.

Death Penalty Sentence

On April 28, 1980, the Istanbul Martial Law Military Court sentenced Ağca to death. His lawyers appealed, insisting that he was not the assassin. But on August 20, 1980, the Military Supreme Court of Appeals unanimously upheld the verdict under file no. 1980/279, decision no. 290. The decision became final, and the implementation of the death sentence was approved by Law No. 2630 published in the Official Gazette on March 12, 1982. At the time, the death penalty was frequently used for politically motivated murders and public order crimes in Turkey.

Reasons for Ağca's Death Sentence:

- The murder of Abdi İpekçi was seen as more than just a personal crime—it was a national trauma.
- The killing was meticulously planned and professionally executed.
- Ağca's calm demeanor in court mirrored how he acted while committing the crime.

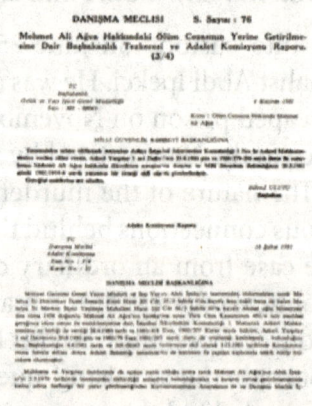

Picture 38. The Advisory Council's critical decision: The bill regarding Mehmet Ali Ağca's execution marked the beginning of a process that changed the course of history. This decision, made in Turkey's political and legal arena amidst the tense atmosphere of the Cold War, marked the beginning of a process that would profoundly impact not only a court process but also the international balance of power. This proposal, following Mehmet Ali Ağca's execution, was a reflection of an era shaped not only by the legal world, but also by the worlds of diplomacy and intelligence.

The verdict was sent to the Turkish Parliament, and on March 3, 1982, discussions on approving the execution began in the Consultative Assembly.

Execution Vote in the Consultative Assembly

The bill regarding the execution of the death penalty against Mehmet Ali Ağca was brought to the Consultative Assembly and as a result of the vote, the execution of the death sentence given to Ağca for the murder of İpekçi was approved.

Voting results:
- Members: 160
- Voters: 137
- Yes: 131
- No: 1
- Abstentions: 23

Kamer Genç's Opposition to the Death Penalty

The only member who opposed the execution was Tunceli representative Kamer Genç. As the lone dissenter in the assembly formed by the coup regime, Genç faced immense pressure but did not back down. He shouted "No!" three times during the vote. This stance cost him dearly—he was soon ostracized and his 1983 independent parliamentary candidacy was vetoed by the National Security Council (MGK). He resigned from the assembly in protest and later joined left-wing movements, serving many years as Tunceli's MP. Genç's opposition, despite holding opposing views from Ağca, is remembered as a notable moment in Turkish political history.

Ağca's Escape and Non-Implementation of the Death Sentence

Despite the death sentence, Ağca's escape made execution impossible. After breaking out of prison in Turkey, he initiated an international escape plan, traveling through Iran and Europe to reach the Vatican.

News That Shook the World and the Road to Rome

Ağca's escape made global headlines, but he remained elusive. A red notice was issued, placing him on the international wanted list. Reports from the U.S. suggested the case might involve broader connections than previously thought. Ağca's route, seemingly carefully planned, caught the attention of global intelligence agencies. According to leaked CIA reports, Ağca's escape was no ordinary prison break—it was directed by powerful forces intending to bring him to the Vatican. Even more striking were U.S. claims suggesting Ağca was part of a plot far bigger than the murder of İpekçi—possibly targeting the Vatican.

Final Days Toward Rome and Another Assassination Attempt That Shook the World

Ağca's escape had gone beyond being a mere tale of prison break, transforming into an adventure filled with international intrigue. As he advanced step by step toward Rome, forces that wished to stop him also began to mobilize. However, despite all obstacles, only 44 days remained until Ağca would reach the Vatican. This process was not just an escape, but also the beginning of a series of events that shook global politics.

Just as Ağca was moving toward Europe, another shocking event occurred in the United States. On March 30, 1981, there was an assassination attempt on U.S. President Ronald Reagan.

While this incident was being thoroughly investigated by international security agencies, potential connections with Ağca's escape came under discussion. The time proximity between the two assassination attempts, the profiles of the attackers, and the questions surrounding the forces behind them suggested that these events were not merely coincidental. Information leaked from American intelligence sources indicated that Mehmet Ali Ağca's escape was no ordinary breakout. According to a special report published by the Washington Post, Ağca's escape was allegedly supported by an international organization, which was claimed to be linked with certain European intelligence services. CIA reports stated that Ağca's breakout was not a coincidence; rather, it was orchestrated by specific forces that would ensure his arrival at the Vatican.

Even more striking were the claims from U.S. sources that Ağca might not only have been involved in the assassination of Abdi İpekçi but could also be part of a much larger attack targeting the Vatican. This news created a major stir in the global media and further darkened the truths behind Ağca's escape. The escape and subsequent developments continued to be debated for many years both in Turkey and on the international stage. The powers behind the scenes and the true reasons behind this escape have still not been fully revealed.

Picture 39. A leader, a hitman, and a moment of chaos... Bullets were fired, bodyguards shielded the situation, and the world held its breath. Another assassination attempt took place on the stage of history, but who was behind the scenes?

Intrigues in the Shadows of the Cold War

The Cold War era was not limited to military and economic competition; it was also shaken by mysterious assassination attempts on world leaders. In 1981, U.S. President Ronald Reagan and the leader of the Catholic Church, Pope John Paul II, were subjected to assassination attempts within very close dates. The two attempts, occurring 44 days apart, were interpreted not merely as individual attacks, but as consequences of international power balances and intelligence wars.

Assassination Attempt on Ronald Reagan

March 30, 1981... Washington, D.C.

Having been elected President of the United States in the 1980 elections, Ronald Reagan had become the leader of the Western world during one of the most critical periods of the Cold War. When Reagan assumed office in the White House after a sweeping victory in the 1980 presidential election, he was seen as a leader who would intensify the U.S. rivalry with the Soviet Union. His economic and military strategies were planned to strengthen the U.S., and this caught the attention of certain circles both domestically and internationally.

There are moments in history that can change the fate of a nation and the course of world politics in just a few seconds. One such moment occurred on March 30, 1981. On a cold but sunny day in Washington D.C., America's fresh new president Ronald Reagan came face to face with death.

2:27 PM...

A crowd had gathered in front of the Washington Hilton Hotel, excited for a chance to see their new president up close. Hidden in that moment was an invisible shadow preparing to write his own fate and that of the nation.

The assassin, John Hinckley Jr., armed with a small and seemingly harmless handgun, was determined to shoot a bullet that would alter the flow of history. As he fearlessly fired his weapon at his target, six bullets rang out in succession. One bullet struck a Secret Service agent in the chest, another brought a police officer to the ground. One bullet hit White House Press Secretary James Brady in the head, and he collapsed to the ground with a painful scream; each person struck became a line in history.

The final bullet struck President Reagan himself, piercing his lung.

In that moment, time stood still. The President's body bent forward, and he gasped for breath. But that was not the final line history had written for him. In the thin space between life and death, Reagan resisted like a warrior in pain. Despite the bullet piercing his left lung, he was saved by emergency medical intervention.

Reagan's survival turned global balances upside down; it strengthened his leadership and helped him gain more support from the American people. The March 30, 1981 assassination attempt on Ronald Reagan would be interpreted not just as an individual attack, but as a consequence of the complex political and psychological factors brewing in the shadow of the Cold War.

This event marked a turning point that affected U.S. domestic security policies, political balances, and global stability. After the attack, Reagan pursued a more aggressive foreign policy and toughened his strategies against the Soviet Union, which he called the "Evil Empire."

Shortly after this incident, the leader of the Vatican, the Pope, would also be the target of an assassination attempt. The survival of both Reagan and Pope John Paul II would become a unifying factor for the Western world against the Soviets. Following these two events, the U.S. and the Vatican intensified their intelligence and diplomatic efforts to diminish Soviet influence. The secret collaboration between Reagan and the Pope accelerated the fall of the Soviet Union, securing both leaders a prominent place in history.

These events would go down in the history books as one of the deepest intelligence wars ever seen.

Protests for the Revelation of the Third Secret

While the world was shaken daily by new sensational news during the Cold War, various groups held protests demanding that the Vatican reveal the "Third Secret" of Fatima. These protests included hunger strikes and even a plane hijacking. Especially before Mehmet Ali Ağca's 1981 assassination attempt on Pope John Paul II, speculations about the Third Secret of Fatima increased, and pressure on the Vatican to disclose it intensified.

During this period, some fanatic Christians organized hunger strikes to force the Vatican to reveal the secret, and one person even hijacked a plane.

The Holy Hijacker

The Hijacking Incident in Pursuit of Fatima's Third Secret

May 2, 1981… Dublin Airport…

In May 1981, the skies over Dublin were covered with the shadows of an approaching storm. As Aer Lingus Flight EI 164 prepared to depart from the Dublin runway for France, passengers thought they were beginning a routine journey. However, this flight would mark the beginning of an incident that would be written in the darkest pages of history. A former priest from Western Australia was determined to expose a tightly held secret of the Catholic Church. The hijacker on board involved Ireland, France, and Iran in one of the strangest airplane hijackings in history.

At the time, hijackers usually acted with political or ideological motives. But this hijacker would make no demands for the release of terrorists, nor issue any political statement.

One of the flight attendants would later describe him: "Very well-dressed, gray-haired, and tanned. At first glance, he looked like a wealthy businessman." But this mysterious passenger was no ordinary person.

This mysterious passenger was Lawrence James Downey.

Downey had a rather strange and dark past: he had been a mercenary, a merchant ship captain, and a professional boxer—and now he was about to hijack a plane with a bottle he claimed contained cyanide and with his religious beliefs.

And he was no ordinary terrorist. In the 1950s, Downey had been a Trappist monk in Rome but was expelled from the order after punching the superior in the face.

Born in 1930 in Scotland, Downey was a former monk. After living a religious life as part of the Trappist order, he was expelled from the monastery for reasons related to mental instability. After leaving the monastery, he traveled widely and over time became obsessed with mystical and religious subjects.

A Demand for a New Constitution

One flight attendant said, "When I stood up and turned around, he was there, covered in gasoline." She added, "He had two small bottles which he claimed contained cyanide gas. That's how it all started."

Downey quickly moved to the cockpit and demanded that the plane not land in London but instead continue to Tehran. According to him, he had prepared "a new constitution for the people of Iran."

Captain Edward Foyle stated that they needed to refuel, and diverted the flight to Le Touquet Airport in the Normandy region of northern France. As French authorities prepared for the plane's arrival, there was a tense eight-hour standoff.

The Irish government in Dublin was also informed of the incident. Then Minister of Transport (and future Prime Minister) Albert Reynolds was mobilized from Dublin Airport.

Journalist Sam Smyth noted that Reynolds was deeply concerned during the crisis: "He was worried for both the crew and passengers, and for the Aer Lingus plane."

What Was the Real Purpose?

When the Holy Hijacker was stranded on the runway in Le Touquet, he revealed his true purpose: Fatima's Third Secret was of special importance to him, and he had hijacked the plane to force the Vatican to reveal it.

He wanted Pope John Paul II to disclose the Third Secret of Fatima.

Two of Fatima's Three Secrets had been revealed in 1941, supposedly relating to the World Wars. However, the third secret was kept sealed until 1960 and, when read by Pope John XXIII, it was rumored to have horrified him.

Though Downey's demand was viewed as "bizarre," the situation had to be taken seriously. There were 112 people on board, and Downey claimed he was armed with cyanide. Some hijackers in history had not hesitated to kill hostages.

Downey demanded that The Irish Independent, Ireland's best-selling newspaper, publish efforts to reveal the Third Secret of Fatima. Contact was made with the paper's editor, Vincent Doyle, to fulfill this demand.

Downey penned a 3,500-word manifesto, which was sent via telex to the newspaper. However, before the content was published, French paratroopers stormed the plane. Without a single shot fired, Downey was subdued and the operation was successfully concluded.

Picture 40. On May 2, 1981, Laurence Downey, wanting to track down the Third Secret of Fatima, hijacked a plane and sent a message to the Vatican. Was it a twist of fate or part of a grand plan?

The curious part of this event is that it happened just 11 days before Mehmet Ali Ağca's assassination attempt.

In February 1983, Downey was sentenced to five years in prison in France for air piracy but was released 16 months later and deported to Australia.

In an interview years later, Downey stated that "knowing the contents of the secret did not bring him happiness."

"I have felt lonely all my life, as if I were the only person on Earth," he said.

Picture 41. City of secrets... Silent walls for centuries, whispered prophecies, and a truth hidden in the shadows... Vatican City is not just a city, but a labyrinth where time and fate are sealed.

One of the most bizarre hijacking events the world has ever seen became the subject of documentaries, comedy plays, and radio dramas in Ireland.

This incident, which deeply shocked global public opinion, opened a door to a period where mystical and political reckonings became intertwined. Was Downey's act simply a madman's frenzy, or the echo of a sacred message?

Mehmet Ali Ağca's Days in Rome and the Assassination Preparations
Journey to Rome: A Fugitive in Hiding

While the world's attention was focused on the attempted assassination of U.S. President Reagan, Mehmet

Ali Ağca had meticulously planned a cautious journey to reach Rome. To conceal his identity, Ağca used various methods and entered the city traveling on a bus carrying 100 Italian tourists. By blending in with a large group, he successfully evaded the attention of the security forces. Upon arrival in Rome, he acted like an ordinary traveler, but his intentions were far from those of a typical tourist.

The Hitman Hidden in a Luxury Hotel

When Mehmet Ali Ağca arrived in Rome, he was not just a fugitive, but one of the most wanted men in the world, with a red notice issued for his arrest. Yet he skillfully diverted all attention and checked into one of Rome's hotels. Highly skilled in using false identities, Ağca made a reservation with fake documents and behaved like an ordinary tourist to deflect suspicion.

During this time, he was preparing for the significant task awaiting him in his hotel room. His plans for acquiring a weapon, establishing escape routes, and timing the assassination revealed a level of professionalism beyond that of a typical hitman—this was part of a well-orchestrated operation.

A Man in the Shadow of an Assassination

While wandering the streets of Rome, Ağca was not simply sightseeing; he was carefully studying the Vatican and the Pope's movements. He acted like a shadow, trying to identify the most opportune moment for the assassination. For days, he observed St. Peter's Square, learned Pope John Paul II's routines, and tested the security measures.

Rome's intelligence units were trying to trace Ağca's whereabouts in Europe, but they had no clue about the specifics of the assassination plot. While intelligence agencies still believed Ağca was on the run, they were completely unaware of the looming catastrophe within the Vatican.

The Final Stages of a Deadly Plan

By the time Ağca selected the day for the assassination, every detail had been meticulously calculated. The weapon had been secured, the escape plan prepared, and communication with his supporters established. The most critical element, however, was waiting for the right moment.

On May 13, 1981, as Pope John Paul II prepared to meet the public in St. Peter's Square, Ağca was ready to execute his plan. The world had no inkling of the horror that was about to unfold. This assassination attempt was not just an attack on an individual; it marked the beginning of a chain of events that would deeply impact global politics.

Picture 42. The Bullet That Broke the Silence in the Vatican: The gunshot that echoed through St. Peter's Square on May 13, 1981, was not just an assassination attempt, but also a sign of one of the Vatican's greatest mysteries. Was Pope John Paul II trying to prevent the Third Prophecy of Fatima from coming true, or was he in the midst of it? The moment Mehmet Ali Ağca pulled the trigger became not just a crux of an attack, but the crux of the secrets hidden by the deep state, intelligence agencies, and the Vatican. This assassination remains one of history's greatest mysteries, unsolved to this day.

Mehmet Ali Ağca's time in Rome and his preparations for the assassination remain filled with unanswered questions. Who helped him? Which powers were behind this plot? And most importantly, what would be the global consequences of this act? These questions would continue to be debated for years.

The Bloody Day in Vatican Square and the Third Secret
May 13, 1981, Rome...

The May sun bathed the stone walls of the Vatican in gold. As on every Wednesday afternoon, thousands had gathered in St. Peter's Square. Catholics and non-believers, priests and ordinary tourists—all had come to see the Pope.

In the past, the Pope's public meetings were held indoors at St. Peter's Basilica. He would be carried on a portable throne called the Sedia Gestatoria, visible from a high point and far from the crowd.

But Pope John Paul II was very different from previous Popes. He believed it was his duty to personally deliver God's word to everyone. Therefore, he wanted to be among the people, to physically touch them and convey his message directly. Now, under his leadership, every Wednesday, papal general audiences were held outdoors in St. Peter's Square. The Vatican distributed free tickets, and visitors gathered freely in the vast square.

But everything was different on May 13. Beneath the magnificent stones of St. Peter's Square—where prayers and hopes intertwined—the square would soon host a pivotal moment in history.

At around 19°C, about 15,000 people had flocked to the square. The multinational and multicultural crowd was there to listen to the Pope: people from Poland, the Pope's homeland; cyclists from Northern Italy; visitors from the U.S.; and ever-present Japanese tourists.

At precisely 5:00 PM, Pope John Paul II passed under the famous "Arch of Bells" in the open-top vehicle known as the Popemobile, greeting the people. The Pope appeared joyful and serene. The Popemobile was nearing the end of its route. The Pope touched the hands of the crowd, blessed babies, and reached out to those around him.

Meanwhile, 2.5 kilometers away in Piazza del Popolo, a rally organized by Italian political parties was taking place. Both left- and right-wing parties were protesting a referendum proposal supported by Pope John Paul II.

"Like Shooting God"

Pope John Paul II, dressed in his white cassock, smiled as he moved among the people. For Catholics, he was as always—humble, a figure radiating the light of God. The crowd gathered in St. Peter's Square moments before history was made, basked in a sacred sense of peace.

The Pope smiled, lifted his hands in blessing, and touched a small blonde girl standing beside him, gently stroking her head.

But no one noticed the shadow in the depths of the crowd. Amid the cheers and prayers, a figure from the dusty pages of history emerged—like a legend: the mysterious assassin!

This enigmatic figure appeared like a dark shadow in the midst of this divine scene—perhaps aiming to alter history's course, ignite ideological conflicts, or reveal the deepest contradictions of existence. No one but this figure in the excited crowd knew that within minutes, a tragedy would be etched into the history books.

His presence embodied the cold sorrow of invisibility and silence. Slowly lifting his gun, he felt the weight of the cold metal in his hands. His eyes were blank. "Today, history will be made," he whispered. As the Pope waved to the crowd in his white Fiat Campagnola with the open top, the target drew closer. Then came the sound that shattered everything...

At exactly 5:17 PM, gunfire rang out. Time seemed to freeze in the square. Three or four shots were fired—no one knew exactly how many. But the crowd instantly realized what had happened.

Two bullets... One struck his abdomen, the other his hand. Realizing he had been hit, he first looked at his hands. When he saw they were covered in blood, he went into shock. For a few seconds, he stood still, then slowly collapsed backward into the arms of his private secretary, Stanislaw Dziwisz. Both men's hands were soaked in blood. The white cassock was drenched.

As the crowd's screams rose, the expression on the Pope's face froze—a mix of shock, pain, and something else: mystery.

Who was this man? Where had he come from? The silhouette appearing in that moment, in the most sacred of Christian sites, filled hearts with fear and confusion.

As the white robe became stained with blood, the aura of sanctity gave way to the cold shadow of death. The Pope's eyes stared into the void; his body slowly crumpled inward. A holy figure had come face to face with death. In that moment, ancient whispers echoed through the Vatican's shadowy corridors, bringing to light a long-hidden truth. Was the Third Secret of Fatima being fulfilled?

That moment, the sacred square became a site of sacrifice. The cries of thousands were so powerful they could frighten death itself. The blood that stained the white robe seemed like a death sentence for sanctity. But once blood was spilled, there was no turning back.

A child cried. A woman collapsed to her knees, hands raised to the heavens. A man screamed, but his voice was lost among the others. The world was witnessing the fall of the sacred.

A woman's voice rose, torn and raw: "My God!"

The Pope had been shot. Blood seeped between the stones, sanctifying the ground like an immortal seal. The crimson on the Pope's white robe became a symbol of fear. The crowd scattered like a massive wave. Some dropped to their knees to pray, others fled screaming. To prevent a second attack, the Popemobile sped away, exiting under the "Arch of Bells." It headed toward a standby ambulance waiting at the square's edge.

The Pope's ancient Swiss Guards were now in a desperate race against time. As they carried his limp body, the crowd was mired in fear. Sirens echoed across the square, blending with the screams as the Vatican descended into the greatest chaos in its history. The bloodstained white robe was no longer a sign of safety—it was perhaps a symbol of betrayal, perhaps a dark conspiracy.

The ambulance rushed the Pope to a hospital. Because the Vatican clinic was too small, he was taken directly to Rome's premier hospital, Gemelli. On the way, the only words he spoke were:

"Madonna, Madonna…" (He was praying to the Virgin Mary.)

He was losing a lot of blood. When the ambulance reached the emergency entrance, hospital staff rushed out to bring him inside. As initial treatment began, nurses and doctors in the hospital corridors were in shock: "It's the Pope! The Pope has been brought here!"

He was immediately taken into intensive care and given a blood transfusion. The first bullet had grazed his left hand, striking his right arm. The second hit his abdomen, damaging his intestines but not his pancreas, kidneys, or major arteries. Doctors removed parts of his intestines and performed a colostomy.

Upon arrival, doctors warned he was at risk of death due to blood loss. The surgery lasted 5 hours and 25 minutes.

During the operation, while still semi-conscious, the Pope asked:

"Perché l'hanno fatto?" ("Why did they do it?")

Who? Why?

The answers to those questions lay hidden in the shadows. And those shadows would change the balance of the world forever…

Panic and Chaos in St. Peter's Square

While the Pope was being rushed to the hospital, the square that had been filled with joy and peace moments earlier was thrown into total chaos. Two women were also accidentally shot during the attack. One was Rose Hall, an American-born nun working as a missionary in Germany; the bullet passed through her left arm. The other was 58-year-old Ann Odor, a Catholic from the U.S., who suffered life-threatening injuries from a bullet to the abdomen and underwent emergency surgery.

Many in the crowd dropped to their knees in tears, praying for the Pope. A 450-person Polish group sang hymns in their native language in honor of their homeland's most revered son.

Everyone was asking the same question: Who was the assassin?

Some witnesses claimed the attacker was "Arab," others thought he was "South American or a Soviet agent." Amid the chaos, the true facts would only emerge hours later.

The Mysterious Assassin

The echoes of gunshots continued, and a man was trying to escape from the scene. The attacker ran toward the area with postal trailers, in the shadow of the Bernini Columns.

He threw his gun to the ground and tried to blend into the crowd. But he was too late—the security guards had already caught this mysterious assassin with smoke still rising from his hands, and initially took him to the Vatican police station. Since the Vatican only has jurisdiction over religious crimes, he was later handed over to the Italian police at the central station Kommissariato Borgo. The crime began to be investigated by the Italian state.

Who was this man? Why had he committed this attack? The world would be shaken by the shooting of the Pope. But the assassin's identity would further obscure the darkness behind the assassination, and he would not speak immediately after being caught. Yet when he finally spoke, the background of the event would deepen like a labyrinth.

His first words were: "The real plan was inside the Vatican."

Ağca's Identity and Past Revealed

After approximately 12 hours of interrogation, the assassin's identity was confirmed: Mehmet Ali Ağca, 23 years old, Turkish citizen.

A fugitive previously convicted of murder and wanted on a red notice. In his interrogation by Rome's anti-terror unit, Ağca described Rome as a "terrorist capital." It was believed that he was affiliated with an Islamist neo-fascist organization. Police found a note in Ağca's pocket that read: "I'm killing the Pope because I am against the imperialism of the Soviet Union and the USA, and I protest the genocides carried out in El Salvador and Afghanistan." However, the clearest thing about Ağca's mental state, according to the police, was the intensity of hatred within him.

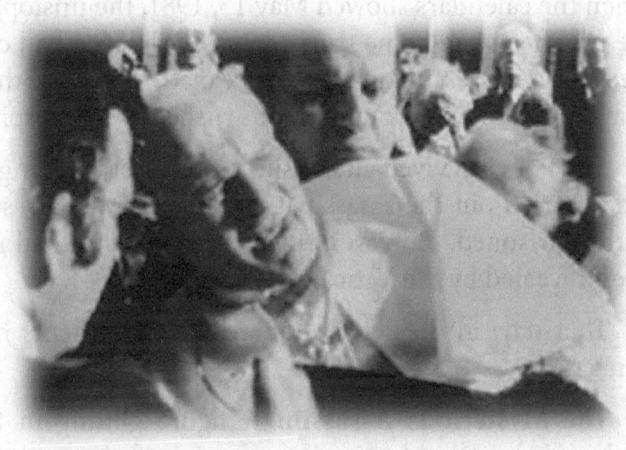

Picture 43. The sky trembled, time stood still…Fatima's secret echoed, but no ears heard. And then, the man in white was shot. Blood fell to the ground, time was sealed in blood.

The first questions, comments, and conspiracy theories regarding the background of the incident began to pour in. Was it the Soviet Union? The CIA? The Freemasons? An internal reckoning within the Vatican?

In fact, the third secret that the Vatican had kept hidden for years had come true. Just like the Virgin Mary's appearance to the children, an assassination attempt had taken place on the 13th day of a month, targeting a reigning Pope. Even though the Vatican, which knew the secret, took special security measures on the 13th day of each month, security was at its highest on the day of the incident. The Swiss Guards, who had been tasked with protecting the Pope for 500 years at the cost of their lives, were extremely cautious. Despite all these measures, when the calendars showed May 13, 1981, the unstoppable prophecy had come true. Mehmet Ali Ağca had carried out an assassination attempt exactly on the 13th of May, and the Pope, wounded, was rushed to the hospital.

The Pope survived after a successful operation. Ağca, who carried out the assassination attempt, was arrested and imprisoned. However, the third secret still had not been revealed by the Vatican.

That day, in St. Peter's Square, three elements had converged:

The Mysterious Assassin: A figure gliding in the dark, unknown in identity, intent on interfering with the fragile balances of history;

The Pope: The voice of the Catholic faith, a divine bell ringing in the hearts of people for resistance and salvation;

The Third Secret of Fatima: A sacred message symbolizing a warning from the past and a hope-filled promise for the future, hidden deep within the human soul.

Picture 44. May 13, 1981: The bullet fired in St. Peter's Square targeted not only the body of Pope John Paul II but also the fragile balance of power in the Cold War. While a Polish Pope's call for freedom terrified the Eastern Bloc, the bullet fired from Mehmet Ali Ağca's gun echoed across the invisible frontier between West and East. This moment changed the course of history.

These three elements were the main factors of a sharp turning point in history and an unforgettable story. Each one harbored within it both a mystery and a tragedy; and soon, humanity, which would receive the news, would become witnesses to that singular moment.

Vatican Radio: The Voice That Announced the Papal Assassination to the World

At exactly 17:17, the sudden sound of gunfire shattered the silence of the sacred square. For a moment, time faltered, and the air, once echoing with the sound of bells, turned into a scene of deadly terror. And at that moment, behind the ancient stone walls of the Vatican, a voice filled with sorrow and pain was preparing to be heard.

Doomsday at Vatican Radio

Vatican Radio, long a cathedral-like medium that had carried the voice of the Church to the world, had always been the bearer of sacred news. But that evening, the only thing echoing in this holy place was chaos. In St. Peter's Square, where thousands had gathered in the hope of a blessing, blood and silence now reigned. Vatican Radio had fallen silent… because the world had come to a standstill. At that moment, the four gunshots that rang out in the heart of Rome struck not only Pope John Paul

II, but also the souls of millions. Footsteps echoed down the corridors, screams rang out, and papers spilled across the newsroom desks…

Yet just minutes earlier, Sean-Patrick Lovett, director of the English program, had been preparing an ordinary broadcast schedule. Now, the fingers on his typewriter trembled, and the words forming in his mind turned into a chaotic vortex. And one question echoed: "Is the Pope alive?"

To deliver false news would be a disaster. But telling the truth was impossible; because no one yet knew whether the Pope was alive or dead.

A Voice Echoing Through Uncertainty

Sean-Patrick Lovett, then 24 years old and director of Vatican Radio's English Program, thought it would be just another ordinary day in journalism. Yet that day, he would witness and become the first voice of a dark page in world history.

17:17… Lovett says he can never forget this time. Later, he would describe those moments: "In Italy, the number 17 is considered unlucky. What 13 is in the Anglo-Saxon world, 17 is in Italy. Maybe it was a sign of fate…"

At Vatican Radio, doors flew open, people began to run. Some shouted, "The Pope is dead!" Others yelled, "A bomb exploded!" Fear knew no language.

Some in the crowd were fleeing in the opposite direction in panic. The truth had been lost amid the rumors. Some claimed there were four assassins. Others spoke of bombs. No one knew what had really happened.

An emergency meeting was held at the radio. But what was there to say? In an age without modern technology, Vatican Radio was the only news source, and what it said was absolute truth for millions. But even the truth itself was unknown. All they knew was that the Pope had been shot and was fighting for his life.

They immediately went on air—but what could they say? The phones rang nonstop. People were waiting for news from Vatican Radio. But Vatican Radio was engulfed in immense uncertainty. They didn't know whether the Pope was alive or not. Inside the newsroom, there was a deathly silence. The only announcement they made was that he had been taken into surgery and one person had been arrested. But this was only a small piece of the truth.

As the darkness of the evening seeped into the thick walls, Lovett, sitting at his desk, took a deep breath. And at that moment, his voice spread across the world:

"Pope John Paul II has been shot and taken to the hospital. There is no confirmed information yet about his condition. Please, keep him in your prayers…"

These words filtered through the stone walls of the Vatican, into the streets of Rome, and from there to the whole world. Millions waiting by their radios were stunned by these words. News agencies, televisions, state officials… The world had learned that the Holy Father was walking a fine line between life and death.

The World Was in Shock!

Is the Holy Father Alive?

After hours of anguished waiting, word finally reached the Vatican. A message from the hospital confirmed that, miraculously, the Pope was alive. But at that moment, they didn't even know how to announce this news. Lovett closed his eyes, gathered his breath, and whispered these words to the world:

"The Holy Father is alive. Keep your prayers with him."

This sentence drifted into the air like a prayer. The stone walls of the Vatican, which had witnessed thousands of moments in history, now recorded perhaps the holiest of all. These words were not just a news report—they were a message of hope to the people.

After the Silent Screams

The Pope had been brought back to life by doctors, and the world had narrowly escaped a tragedy. But the voices echoing through Vatican Radio that night were etched into the pages of history. Everyone in the studio knew they were not just delivering news—they were witnessing the turning point of an era.

Even today, the recordings from the night of May 13, 1981, remain in the archives. The sorrowful words whispered by Vatican Radio are remembered as one of the darkest moments in human history.

The Pope's Forgiveness

Rome had been buried in silence for days. The streets were empty; people waited for news about the Pope's condition. Then the miracle happened—the Pope survived.

Only a few days after the event, the world was stunned by the Pope's words from his hospital bed at Gemelli Hospital:

"I forgive the brother who shot me."

Picture 45. The trigger was pulled, and the world held its breath... After the bullets echoed through Vatican Square, Ağca was no longer just a man, but the protagonist in a global enigma. He was in handcuffs, but where were the real culprits?

Who forgives an assassin? But the Pope did. And he didn't just say it—he showed it in action. Later, in 1983, he would go to the prison and meet with his would-be assassin, Ağca. The 21-minute conversation between the two would remain one of history's greatest mysteries.

World Press in Shock

The assassination attempt on Pope John Paul II had a shocking impact on the world press. On May 14, 1981, the entire press featured the assassination attempt on their front pages:

"On May 13, 1981, in St. Peter's Square at the Vatican, Ağca fired four shots with a 9 mm Browning pistol..."

As the identity of the mysterious assassin finally came to light, the world press trembled in astonishment and curiosity. Photos of the Turkish-born assassin Mehmet Ali Ağca adorned newspaper headlines and would be remembered as symbols of both tension and tragedy.

The whispers echoing through press rooms, rapid-fire phone calls from news agencies, and the constant live coverage from cameras conveyed the gravity of this historic moment. The mystery of the event went beyond just an assassination attempt—it raised questions about ideological conflicts, international intrigues, and dark balances of power.

This assassin, whose identity had been revealed, seemed to have emerged from the shadows of the past and left an unforgettable mark on the stage of history. The world held its breath, wondering: Was this dark silhouette of an assassin an intelligence agent? Had he emerged as a product of radical ideologies? Or were there more complex relationships behind the incident? What message was being sent to the world through the assassination attempt on the Pope? His emergence whispered harsh truths lying behind hidden secrets and mysterious plans to an observing world.

While the world press analyzed this shocking development with intense interest, headlines began to feature dramatic phrases such as "The Mysterious Assassin Unveiled!" and "The Truth Hidden Under Dark Shadows." The news, which resonated through international media, reflected not only the actions of an individual but also the complex nature of that era, at the intersection of global politics, ideology, and religious conflict.

In an arena dominated by ideological chasms, international intrigues, and individual dramas, the name

Mehmet Ali Ağca was etched in memory as a symbol of both fear and curiosity, of horror and secrecy.

Thus, the mysterious assassin Mehmet Ali Ağca did not only act in a single incident in the course of history—he took his place on the world stage as a controversial and multi-dimensional character who embodied some of the most striking paradoxes in human history.

The World's Reaction to the Assassination Attempt on the Pope

The assassination attempt on Pope John Paul II caused shock and outrage across the globe. Many statements referenced the Pope's international diplomatic identity and influence. "The shooting of a Pope, who is also a symbol of peace and hope for millions, was seen not only as an attack on a religious leader, but on humanity itself."

Israeli businessman Amos Barak summarized the gravity of the attack with these words:

"Assassinations have now become part of politics. But attacking the Pope... That's like shooting God!"

This statement revealed that the papal assassination attempt was being viewed not merely as an attack, but as a global message. World leaders, however, interpreted the event from various perspectives.

USA: "An Attack on Freedom"

Just 44 days before the papal assassination attempt, U.S. President Ronald Reagan had survived an assassination attempt himself. In his statement after the attack, Reagan said: *"The Pope is a figure who represents peace and love for humanity. This vile attack on him is not only an attack on the Vatican, but on the values of freedom and faith."*

Reagan considered the event not merely an assassination attempt, but a threat directed at the Western world within the context of the Cold War. The U.S. began investigating possible intelligence links behind the attack, suspecting a Soviet-backed conspiracy. The CIA started probing whether Bulgaria and the Soviet KGB were involved. At the beginning of the 1980s, the Pope's words encouraging people in Eastern Europe to oppose communist regimes posed a serious threat to the Soviets. Despite Ağca's statement, Americans considered it unlikely that he had planned the attack alone.

Soviet Union: "We Have Nothing to Do with It"

Soviet leader Leonid Brezhnev made no official statement about the attack. However, Kremlin officials quickly labeled the Western media's attempts to associate the attack with the Soviets as "baseless propaganda."

The official Soviet newspaper Pravda described the assassination attempt as "the act of a madman," insisting that there was no state support behind the incident.

Nevertheless, in the Western world, claims that the KGB and Bulgarian intelligence may have assisted in the assassination attempt on the Pope were already spreading rapidly.

Europe: "A Knife Stabbed Into the Heart of the Vatican"

Italian Prime Minister Arnaldo Forlani stated after the attack:

"This is an assault not just on one man, but on the conscience of humanity."

British Prime Minister Margaret Thatcher described

the attack as "a horrific act of terror against all faiths." French President Valéry Giscard d'Estaing, who had narrowly escaped a similar attack in Corsica just weeks before, sent a message of "deep sorrow" to the Vatican. A consultant present when he heard the news said:

"The President froze—he experienced the news as a profound shock."

François Mitterrand, who was elected a few months later to succeed Giscard d'Estaing, emphasized that the assassination attempt was not only an attack on the Vatican, but also on Europe's spiritual identity:

"One of Europe's most important moral leaders was targeted. This is a direct attack on the values of our continent."

West German Chancellor Helmut Schmidt, upon hearing the news, made the following statement:

"I feel as if I've been shot in the stomach."

Poland: A Day of National Mourning

For Poles, Pope John Paul II was a hero—he symbolized both the Catholic Church and the struggle for independence. Following the attack, an atmosphere of mourning spread across Poland. Thousands gathered in Warsaw's St. John's Cathedral to pray for the Pope, while Deputy Prime Minister Stefan Grzybczynski's message was broadcast over loudspeakers. *"I too struggle with many illnesses. But what I am experiencing is nothing compared to these attacks on the Church."*

Meksika'da suikasti protesto eden 7 kişi intihar etti

MEXICO CITY, AFP (AA)

BAŞKENT Mexico City'de yaşayan hepsi de koyu Katolik 7 kişi, Papa'ya yapılan suikasti protesto amacıyla intihar etmiştir. Canlarına kıyanlardan altısı erkek, biri de kadındır. İntihar edenlerden dördünün işçi, birinin öğretmen, birinin öğrenci, birinin de ev kadını olduğu bildirilmiştir.

Picture 46. An assassination not only shattered a leader, but also the fragile intersection of faith and politics. Its shockwaves spread across the world without borders.

Mexico and Latin America: Rebellion and Rage

Countries in Latin America, such as Brazil and Argentina, associated the attack with the increasing violence on their continent. According to them, the Pope was delivering bold messages on human rights and poverty in Latin America. They interpreted the attack not merely as an assassination attempt but also as a message directed at all who were fighting for justice and peace.

During one of his first international trips in 1979, the Pope had visited Mexico. Mexicans said, *"The Pope is a very special person for all Mexicans. How could someone target a heart like his?"* After hearing of the attack, Brazilians recalled the Pope's speech in Rio de Janeiro the previous year and prayed:

"Pray for the Son of God."

Asian Countries

Indian Prime Minister Indira Gandhi described the assassination attempt as "a blow to the conscience of humanity" and told journalists: *"I was so shocked by this news that I am at a loss for words. What can I say?"*

Japanese Prime Minister Zenko Suzuki stated that the Pope was an important figure for universal peace and said, *"This attack is a sign of rising extremism around the world."*

Many other leaders made statements viewing the attack on Pope John Paul II not as an assault on an individual but as one targeting the spiritual values of humanity.

Communist Governments

Communist governments issued brief and formal messages wishing the Pope a recovery. For example, the Soviet government sent a telegram out of courtesy but avoided giving an impression of solidarity.

> **Roma Savcısı:**
> **«Bu olay uluslararası terör örgütlerinin işidir»**
>
> ● Savcı Galluci, "Bir insan böylesine kusursuz bir suikast girişimini tek başına başaramaz" dedi
> ● İtalyan basını: "Suikast uluslararası bir komplodur"
>
> Haberleri 6. Sayfada

Picture 47 – 48 – 49. *An assassination targets not just a life, but a balance. Mehmet Ali Ağca's trigger was read like the unpredictable move of a pawn in Cold War chess. The bullet ricocheted off the Pope's body, echoing through NATO's southern flank, the heart of the Warsaw Pact, and the diplomatic corridors of the Vatican. It was a warning, not driven by individual hatred, but by global calculations.*

The Pope's global identity as a defender of peace and human rights led to interpretations that the attack carried an "ideological message." History would record this assassination attempt not just as an attack, but as one of the greatest spiritual and political mysteries of the modern era.

Initial Investigation and Debates

When Mehmet Ali Ağca was captured and interrogated in Rome following the incident, intelligence agencies and governments worldwide were on high alert. The details that emerged during this process led to various international speculations. Ağca's past and the potential organizations behind the assassination became the subject of the initial investigation.

Picture 50. The headline of a New York Times article read: "...Fugitive Killer Turk Captured." The article addressed allegations that Mehmet Ali Ağca, accused of shooting Pope John Paul II, had ties to Turkey's Nationalist Movement Party and far-right groups in Europe. While Rome police and international journalists found clues linking Ağca to right-wing Turkish extremists, intensive investigations in Western Europe have yielded no definitive evidence that the attempted assassination of the Pope was an international conspiracy. The article also emphasized that no concrete information had been found to suggest that Ağca had contact with any non-Turkish terrorists in the past year or that he had acted as an agent of any specific organization.

Initial Findings About Ağca Before the Assassination

According to Italian police, Mehmet Ali Ağca left Turkey using a passport belonging to a person of Indian nationality, joined a group tour in Majorca, and traveled with about 100 Italian tourists. After his arrest following the assassination attempt, a search of Ağca's last hotel room revealed an escape plan drawn on a piece of paper and hair dye. Police officials described Ağca as someone "determined to carry out what he set his mind to, even at the cost of his life," adding that he would not easily give up those who helped him.

The New York Times reported that Italian police found no concrete evidence that Ağca was supported by an international organization. The British Guardian claimed that Ağca was one of Turkey's notorious right-wing professional assassins and was trying to hide his connection to the far right during the investigation. In the European press, particularly Dutch television and several media outlets ran stories with headlines like "MHP member Ağca shot the Pope."

Ağca's Initial Interrogation

During his police interrogation in Rome, Ağca answered only the questions he wanted to and ignored the rest. Occasionally, he asked questions to his interrogators and frequently inquired about the Pope's health. He claimed that the assassination attempt was meant as a "protest against the Soviet Union and American imperialism," citing massacres in El Salvador and Afghanistan as examples.

A handwritten note found in Ağca's pocket contained the following statement:

"I am killing the Pope to remind the world of the thousands of people victimized by imperialism and the Soviet Union in Palestine, El Salvador, and the Third World."

The head of Rome's Anti-Terrorism Unit, who interrogated Ağca, stated that he "had all the characteristics of a professional assassin—extremely calm, arrogant, confident, and in very good physical and psychological condition."

In an interview from prison with the Italian magazine Poesa Sera, Ağca said, "Contrary to what all newspapers write, I am neither a fascist nor a communist... I am someone who acts independently. I do not like the way the world is going." These statements were interpreted as attempts to deliberately obscure his identity or mislead interrogators.

Police Traced Ağca From Turkey to St. Peter's Square

Mehmet Ali Ağca's assassination attempt on Pope John Paul II led to a major international investigation, and his movements from Turkey to Rome were meticulously tracked by security forces. While Rome's Anti-Terrorism Department tried to determine who had guided or supported Ağca, his efforts to portray the assassination as a purely "individual act" drew attention.

Rome police official Alfredo Lazzarini stated after Ağca's interrogation, "He is a cool-headed, sane, and definitely well-trained terrorist with a capital 'T'." This comment raised suspicions that Ağca may have received military or intelligence training.

Italian authorities tried to uncover who helped Ağca escape from prison in Turkey, who funded his travels in Europe, and how he managed to use fake identities. Initially, it was determined that he carried Swiss and Italian banknotes and had traveled through France, West Germany, Bulgaria, Yugoslavia, and Spain. He used fake passports under various names.

However, Italian government sources initially seemed convinced that Ağca acted alone in the assassination attempt. There was a belief that he had no accomplices at the scene in St. Peter's Square and no one aiding him in Italy. This confirmed the New York Times' initial report.

In Ağca's pocket was a brochure draft written not by any organization but by himself. It read: "I, Ağca, killed the Pope so that the world may know the thousands of victims of global imperialism." This statement strengthened the claims that he acted with personal rather than ideological motivations.

AĞCA'NIN SORGUSUNA KATILMAK ÜZERE 3 KİŞİLİK BİR HEYET BUGÜN ROMA'YA GİDİYOR

- Adalet Bakanı, "Türkiye'den bir heyet gitmesi iki hükümet arasındaki anlaşma ile oldu" dedi

- Sorgu için daha önce 2 kişilik bir heyet Roma'ya gitmiş, ancak sorguya katılamadan geri dönmüştü

AĞCA'YI TÜRK GÖREVLİLER SORGUYA ÇEKİYOR

ROMA, AA

Papa 2. Jean Paul ve 2 Amerikalı turisti öldürmeye teşebbüsten sanık terörist Mehmet Ali Ağca, 3 Türk görevli tarafından sorguya çekilmiştir.

Roma'daki Rebibbia Cezaevi'nde sorguya çekilen Ağca'nın saldırı sırasında tek başına hareket edip etmediğini açığa çıkarmaya uğraşmaktadırlar.

Hafta sonu Roma'ya gelen 3 Türk görevli, Mehmet Ali Ağca'nın Türkiye'de cezaevinden kaçtıktan sonra gittiği ülkeleri ve yaptıklarını tek tek ortaya çıkarmaya çalışmaktadırlar.

Roma sulh yargıçlarından Claudio D'Angelo ve Nicolo Anata da, sorgu sırasında Ağca'nın hücresinde hazır bulunmuşlardır.

"Teröristlere dışarda kucak açılırsa bu olur"

Picture 51 – 52 – 53. Ağca's bullet struck not only the Pope's body, but also NATO's defense lines, Soviet intelligence networks, and global political maneuvering. The real battle was being played not on the field, but on the chessboard.

Yet investigators could not definitively determine whether Ağca was left- or right-wing. His ability to travel freely in Europe and obtain fake documents raised suspicions of a support network. But police found no evidence that Ağca had committed any theft or robbery to obtain money or forged papers, which increased the likelihood that he was supported by an official or unofficial group in Turkey or another country.

Kenan Evren's Reaction to the West and the Vatican's Request for Assistance

General Kenan Evren, who seized power in Turkey following the September 12, 1980 military coup, made a sharp criticism of Europe in his statement on the assassination attempt:

"I think our European friends who are usually lost in the clouds may have come to their senses a little with this event. If many of our European friends keep embracing these people as 'political refugees,' this is the result."

The Vatican requested assistance from the Turkish government to clarify the assassination, and Kenan Evren agreed to cooperate by sending two officers from Istanbul's Political Police to Rome. Ağca's investigation was conducted by four prosecutors, including the Chief Prosecutor of Rome, with input from Istanbul police.

Picture 54. (TIME, May 25, 1981): The moment of an assassination, a question echoing in the headlines of the world press: "Why did they do it?" Pope John Paul II was shot in the middle of a crowd but survived. Was it a coincidence, or had the prophecy already been written?

Thus, the assassination and subsequent investigations stirred great debate in international political balances and led to various conspiracy theories.

Did Ağca Want to Trigger Global Collapse?

"Targeting Peace"[18]

On May 25, 1981, the world-renowned Time magazine featured the moment of the assassination attempt on its cover. Every detail of the incident was covered in

---

18 May 25, 1981, Volume 117, No. 21

the issue. The analysis by Lance Morrow drew particular attention. The article suggested that Ağca aimed to start a world war. The analysis stated:

"This, of course, is not the first time such an event has occurred. When a Hindu nationalist shot Mahatma Gandhi in 1948, George Bernard Shaw said: 'It is dangerous to be too good.'

The assassin's main goal is always to attract attention and create a dramatic scene. The most important element of his craft is choosing the symbolically correct victim. Mehmet Ali Ağca's choice of the Pope was not just a political murder—it was a grand moral assault.

• Pope John Paul II was one of the few spiritual leaders of the world.

• His assassination would have been one of the greatest blows to the spiritual and moral balance of humanity.

This was one of the harshest examples of terrorist logic, because:

• The target chosen had to shake not only the legal system but also the spirituality of people.

• The terrorist aims to create fear and despair by attacking what people value most.

• Every terrorist dreams of clutching the main artery of civilization and paralyzing it."

The Assassin's Calculations

Mehmet Ali Ağca aimed to create an impact like that of history's great assassins.

• Just as Gavrilo Princip, a Bosnian student, triggered World War I by assassinating Archduke Franz Ferdinand in 1914, did Ağca want to spark a global collapse?

But Ağca could not fully achieve this goal.

- At first glance, he appeared to be a complex and incomprehensible political figure.

- His mind seemed to host both extreme right- and left-wing ideas at the same time, as if these two extremes complemented each other.

Ağca resembled the "dark little men sowing seeds of trouble" described in Joseph Conrad's novels.

- Ideologically shallow but capable of creating political chaos.

- Lacked the depth of characters portrayed by Dostoyevsky.

- Was one of those well-dressed young men traveling Europe with fake passports, studying weapons catalogs.

- These types of individuals were becoming more common and dangerous.

- Or at least, Ağca wanted the world to think so.

Assassination and the Ideological War in the Media

During the Cold War, the bipolar global political structure was reflected in how news was presented. Media outlets interpreted events according to their ideological perspectives. The assassination attempt on Pope John Paul II on May 13, 1981, became part of this media war. Ağca's attempt sparked a multilayered investigation and international debate. Although Italian authorities initially claimed he acted alone, suspicions later emerged that he had a support network during his European travels.

Western Media: Democracy and the Shock Factor

Western press presented the incident with shocking and dramatic headlines, interpreting the assassination as an attack on democracy and human rights:

- **New York Times (USA):** "A Bullet for God's Representative! Pope John Paul II Shot in Vatican Square"

- **The Times (UK):** "Bloody Day in the Vatican! Pope Faces Death"

- **Le Monde (France):** "Attack on the Pope: Vatican in Shock!"

- **Corriere della Sera (Italy):** "Assassination in Rome! Pope Shot"

- **L'Osservatore Romano (Vatican):** "Miracle of the Virgin Mary: Pope Survives Bullets!"

- **El País (Spain):** "Assassination Attempt on Pope! World in Shock"

- **The Guardian (UK):** "The Most Terrible Day in Vatican History!"

- **Hürriyet (Turkey):** "Mehmet Ali Ağca Fires at the Pope in the Vatican!"

After these initial reports, Western media speculated on which powers might be behind the assassination, linking it to the Soviets or broader conspiracy theories.

Eastern Bloc Media: Capitalism's Crisis and the West's Guilt

Eastern Bloc media ignored the ideological context of the attack, presenting it as merely a "crime story" and blaming Western moral decay. When Western media suggested Soviet or Bulgarian involvement in the attack, Soviet media called this a "fabricated conspiracy to defame socialist states." A 1982 commentary in Pravda stated: "The Vatican and CIA are inventing fake scenarios to smear socialist countries."

While the Eastern Bloc avoided using the assassination for ideological propaganda, the Western Bloc amplified its political dimensions and speculated about Soviet involvement.

- **Pravda (USSR):** "The West's Hypocrisy: Is the Assassination a New Anti-Communist Scenario?"

- **Izvestia (USSR):** "Terror Attack in Italy"

- **Neues Deutschland** (East Germany): "The West's Culture of Violence and Chaos"

- **Trybuna Ludu (Poland):** "Incident in the Vatican: Who Is Using Whom?"

- **Rabotničesko Delo (Bulgaria):** "CIA Behind the Terrorist" – featured Bulgaria's denials of the accusations.

Eastern Bloc newspapers attempted to minimize the political and religious dimensions of the assassination and ignored the Pope's potential to inspire anti-regime movements in Poland.

Key Messages in Soviet Media

"The West is a system that breeds terrorism."

"The Pope is the religious mask of capitalism."

"Socialist countries never engage in such dirty deeds."

This situation in the media was a striking example showing that the Cold War was not just a military and political rivalry but also a perception war waged through the press.

The Pope's Homeland Poland's Approach

In Poland, where the Pope was a national hero, the news received broad coverage but remained under state control. The official media reported the attack but did not praise the Pope's role in inspiring anti-regime movements. The Catholic Church in Poland held masses for the Pope's recovery; the state did not block this, but also did not highlight it in the media.

Trybuna Ludu (Poland): The event was reported with the headline "The West's Hypocrisy on Human Rights." The connection between the Solidarity movement and the Pope was censored.

Picture 55 – 56. A hitman, two assassinations, and the headlines echoing in the world press... Ağca first targeted a journalist, then a Pope. So, did the bullets only hit bodies, or did they carry a message that echoed through the dark corridors of history?

How the Italian Press Approached the Incident

In the early days of the incident, the Italian press evaluated the assassination attempt with great shock and horror. While Mehmet Ali Ağca's personal motivations were being questioned, over time, the idea that this attack might be part of an international conspiracy began to gain traction.

Right- and center-leaning newspapers (Corriere della Sera, Il Giornale, La Stampa) claimed that the assassination was organized by the Soviet Union and Bulgaria. On the other hand, leftist and independent newspapers (La Repubblica, Il Manifesto, L'Unità) suggested the incident might have been a NATO-CIA-linked operation.

The Pope's act of forgiving Ağca also resonated widely in the Italian media and fueled political debates. Overall, media organizations rapidly framed the incident within a Cold War scenario, and the topic remained on the public agenda for a long time.

The Ideological Divide in the Turkish Press's Coverage of the Incident

During the Pope assassination process, the Turkish press developed differing interpretations based on ideological lines. Left- and center-aligned newspapers (Cumhuriyet, Milliyet, Nokta) claimed that Ağca was a "pawn" and used by the West as a propaganda tool against the Soviets. In contrast, right-leaning newspapers (Tercüman, Güneş, Türkiye) argued that the assassination might have been supported by the Soviet Union and Bulgaria, backing the "Bulgarian Thesis" which had become widespread in Western media.

Some Islamist publications suggested that the attack on the Pope could be seen as retaliation from the Islamic world against the West's religious leader. However, the Turkish state and official media outlets strongly condemned the assassination, emphasizing that the incident placed Turkey in a difficult position on the international stage.

In the early days, the assassination was evaluated as an individual attack, and Ağca's past was closely scrutinized. However, as Western media increasingly focused on the "Bulgarian Thesis," the Turkish press also took interest in the subject, though no consensus was reached.

Different opinions emerged based on ideological differences:

Left-wing media (Cumhuriyet, Milliyet) argued that the event was orchestrated by the CIA and the West.

Right-wing media (Tercüman, Güneş) suggested it was connected to the Soviet Union and Bulgaria.

The Pope's forgiveness of Ağca was interpreted in the press both as a "religious act of mercy" and a "political strategy." Overall, the Turkish press handled the assassination attempt in parallel with international developments but adopted a cautious approach so as not to harm Turkey's foreign policy standing.

Picture 57. A courtroom, iron bars, and a moment where history is put on trial... Ağca was questioning not only himself but the world order. Was justice served, or did the secrets behind the scenes deepen?

The Question the Rome Police Sought to Answer
Did he act alone, or was he an agent of unknown powers?

Before the assassination, a note found in the hotel room rented by Mehmet Ali Ağca read "I killed the Pope." However, the case was much more complex. The Italian police were investigating the truth behind the assassination attempt on Pope John Paul II.

Was Ağca merely a lone fanatic?

Or was he a hitman backed by a large organization?

The Italian police announced that during interrogation, Ağca claimed, "I acted alone, completely on my own." However, the investigation included suspicions of "collaboration with unknown individuals."

Ağca's Own Statements: Changing Stories and Contradictions

In his initial interrogation, Ağca claimed he had been trained by the PFLP (Popular Front for the Liberation of Palestine), a Marxist-oriented organization. However, a spokesperson for the PFLP's leader George Habash told TIME: "We don't know this man. We've never heard of him. He has no connection to us."

At the end of the first week of the investigation, Ağca changed his story and claimed he received training in Syria in 1980. However, the Marxist connection seemed strange because Ağca was listed by Interpol as a far-right terrorist.

Based on information received from Turkish officials, the police quickly obtained details of Ağca's past in Turkey. According to police records, his identity was quickly confirmed after his capture.

Rome Police Department: Initial Findings and Investigation Report

Date: May 13, 1981

Location: St. Peter's Square, Vatican

Crime: Armed assassination attempt on Pope John Paul II

Suspect Name: Mehmet Ali Ağca

Place of Birth: Malatya, Turkey

Date of Birth: January 9, 1958

Education: Attended but did not complete studies at Ankara University (Faculty of Literature) and Istanbul University (Faculty of Economics)

Criminal Record: Convicted in Turkey for the assassination of journalist Abdi İpekçi; escaped prison in 1979

Interpol Status: Listed on Interpol's red notice for international terrorism charges

Incident Description:

On May 13, 1981, at 17:19, Pope John Paul II was shot during a public address at St. Peter's Square in the Vatican.

The assailant blended into the crowd and fired two shots at the Pope, wounding him in the chest and abdomen. The Pope collapsed into his vehicle. Two American tourists were also injured and taken to hospital.

Initial Findings from the Crime Scene:

The assassination was likely professionally planned.

The attacker did not attempt to flee.

Weapon used: Browning 9mm semi-automatic pistol.

The assailant was quickly apprehended by police and taken to the Rome Police Department.

Suspect's Previous Criminal Connections:

Linked to the ultra-right Nationalist Movement Party (MHP) in Turkey.

Convicted of the 1979 assassination of journalist Abdi İpekçi but escaped from prison.

Cooperated with far-right groups in Turkey, and allegedly had ties to Palestinian militants.

Ağca's Initial Statements: Contradictions and a Chaotic Interrogation Process

In his first interrogation at the Rome Police Department, the suspect stated:

"I acted alone, no one helped me."

"It was my mission to kill the Pope."

"I had been preparing for this for a long time."

But as the interrogation continued, Ağca's statements began to change constantly:

Contradictory points in his statements:

Initially claimed he was trained by the PFLP.

Then said he received training in Syria.

Finally, claimed he acted independently after escaping from prison.

Due to these contradictory statements, the police are investigating the possibility that Ağca did not act alone.

Ağca's Movements in Europe According to the Police Report

Ağca's known movements in Europe before the assassination were as follows:

- Escaped from prison in Turkey in November 1979 and fled to Iran, then entered West Germany.
- Traveled to various countries in Europe using a fake passport.
- Enrolled at the University of Perugia in Italy in April 1981 with a false identity.
- Later traveled to Palma de Mallorca in Spain, then returned to Rome.

In the report, Ağca's movements before the assassination are detailed.

On May 10, 1981, Ağca returned to Rome and stayed at a hotel called Pensione Isa.

The Rome police found the following items in his hotel room:

A fake passport.

Written notes outlining the assassination plan.

Spare magazines for the Browning 9mm pistol.

Ağca exhibited suspicious behavior prior to the assassination:

Conducted repeated surveillance of St. Peter's Square.

Identified the best shooting positions during the Pope's speeches.

Made plans to smuggle the weapon in.

Rome Police's Initial Assessment

According to initial police reports:

"There is no definitive evidence that Ağca acted alone. His statements are contradictory and constantly changing. The detailed planning of the assassination raises the suspicion that he received professional support. Ağca's past connections and movements in Europe suggest he may have been directed by an international organization. The true masterminds behind the attempted assassination of the Pope have yet to be identified."

Ongoing Phases of the Police Investigation

The Rome Police Department initiated international cooperation to determine whether Mehmet Ali Ağca's attempt on the Pope was the act of a lone fanatic or part of a larger conspiracy.

Key questions being investigated:

Who were the powers behind Ağca?

Was there an organization that financed him?

Which intelligence agencies align with his connections in Europe?

As the investigations continued, Ağca's true motives and affiliations remained a mystery.

The P2 Dossier[19] and the Great Test of the Italian Judiciary

While the investigation into the Pope's assassination continued, in 1981 the Italian judiciary was rocked by one of the biggest scandals in modern history. Shortly before the Pope's assassination, the Italian legal system was shaken by the P2 (Propaganda Due) dossier. Now, with the "assassination case," the Italian judiciary was preparing for a major trial under global scrutiny.

---

19 The P2 Case: The Secret Power in Italy's Shadow. The clandestine Masonic lodge known as Propaganda Due (P2) had infiltrated the most critical positions in the state and become a power center that ruled the country from behind the scenes. A police raid revealed a list of 962 members, revealing how deeply rooted the lodge was in the Italian government, intelligence agencies, military, media, and business world. This clandestine structure operated as a state within the state. Led by Licio Gelli, the lodge manipulated government policies, controlled economic balances, and was even alleged to have been involved in political assassinations. By exploiting the media for its own ends, it manipulated public opinion and aimed to undermine the democratic system from within. In 1981, a police raid on Gelli's home uncovered the secret membership list, revealing the P2's shadowy presence over the state. Following the scandal, Prime Minister Arnaldo Forlani resigned, numerous government officials were dismissed, and the lodge was officially banned. However, this process became one of the greatest tests of the Italian judiciary. The trials dragged on for years, many people were tried, but many crimes remained unproven. The P2 and Ağca Trial: While the repercussions of this major scandal continued, Mehmet Ali Ağca's trial for the assassination of the Pope was also testing the Italian judiciary at the same time. Ağca's trial had become a stage where not only a crime but also deep state connections, international intelligence agencies, and shady interests were tried. The Italian judiciary, shaped by the P2's shadow, was now pursuing justice and truth before the eyes of the world. This trial went down in history as a time when Italy tried not just a criminal but also the dark corners of its own system.

Taking place in the shadow of political scandals in Italy, this trial had the potential to expose deep state structures embedded within the government. The Italian judicial system was about to face one of its greatest challenges.

Many journalists wrote that this historic trial would eclipse all others and leave a mark on Italy's legal history. However, how the court proceedings would unfold under the influence of hidden powers remained a mystery.

The Ağca Trial: An Individual Terrorist?

Amidst the ancient stones of Rome, the footsteps of a trial that would change the course of history echoed as a drama filled with international intrigue, ideological reckonings, and the depths of the human psyche.

Mehmet Ali Ağca, handcuffed and cold-eyed, stood before justice. He was not just an assassination suspect; he was a figure at the center of a complex web woven by time — the protagonist of a riddle shaped by fate's fine threads.

The headlines declared: "Ağca to be tried as an individual terrorist." Yet, if not in this trial, the Rome courtroom would eventually become a stage for international reckoning.

The Symbolic Trial of the Cold War: Mehmet Ali Ağca's Two Trials in Rome – Proceedings and Verdicts

Mehmet Ali Ağca was tried twice in Rome for his May 13, 1981, assassination attempt on Pope John Paul II at St. Peter's Square. The first trial began shortly after the incident in 1981 and concluded with a verdict. The second trial began in 1985.

Both trials resonated deeply within the Vatican and

the international public, fueling speculation and conspiracy theories in the tense climate of the Cold War.

First Trial: The Assassination of the Pope (1981)

Following the assassination attempt, Ağca was arrested by Italian authorities and subjected to a legal process. The trial, held in a high-security court in Rome, attracted intense international media attention.

The hearings, which began on July 20, 1981, focused on why Ağca committed the assassination, whether he acted alone or was directed by an organization.

Prosecutors emphasized Ağca's background, his crimes in Turkey, and his plan to attack the Vatican. It was documented that he had been involved in the 1979 assassination of journalist Abdi İpekçi, escaped from prison, and traveled through Europe with a fake passport.

Italian prosecutors suggested that Ağca might have been just a hitman and that a larger organization could be behind the attempt. However, Ağca avoided providing clear answers.

Pope John Paul II's survival from the attack prevented Ağca from receiving the death penalty. Under Italian law, on July 22, 1981, the court sentenced Ağca to life imprisonment for the "attempted assassination of the Pope."

Following the verdict, Ağca remained calm in court and did not appeal the decision. However, in his statements to the press, he made mysterious remarks such as "I fulfilled a mission," avoiding revelations about the plot's background.

His life sentence in 1981 sparked major international debate. Western countries in particular questioned whether the Soviet Union and the Eastern Bloc were involved in the attack. But the Italian court never reached a definitive conclusion about whether Ağca acted alone or was guided by an intelligence agency.

SECOND TRIAL: THE TRIAL OF THE CENTURY
1985 Hearing

In 1985, a second trial was opened to investigate the possible international connections behind Ağca's assassination attempt. During this process, allegations that Bulgaria and the Soviet Union were involved in the assassination were particularly prominent. The second trial in Rome was closely followed by international intelligence services and diplomatic circles.

In the second trial, three Bulgarian officials alleged to be connected to Bulgarian intelligence and members of the Italian mafia were tried. However, the court found the defendants not guilty due to lack of sufficient evidence, and Ağca's claims could not be proven. This case went down in history as one of the most controversial incidents of the Cold War era.

The two trials in which Mehmet Ali Ağca was tried in Rome raised the question of whether the assassination attempt on the Pope was merely an individual attack or part of a larger conspiracy. These two trials are of great importance not only in terms of Ağca's individual crime but also for understanding the political balances and intelligence wars of the 20th century.

Picture 60. An assassination, a trial, and a defiant hitman... Ağca disregarded not only the trigger but also justice: "Italy cannot judge me!" So who was really on trial? A man, or history itself?

The second trial of Mehmet Ali Ağca at the Rome Criminal Court became more than just a trial of an individual crime—it turned into a major event shaped by the geopolitical tensions and intelligence manipulations of the Cold War period. Ağca's actions were widely covered by the international media and attracted the attention and curiosity of the public.

Ağca's trial went beyond a simple individual criminal case and became a stage for the East-West struggle under the shadow of intelligence agencies such as the KGB and CIA.

Throughout the trial, Ağca's statements and his detention turned into an information war in which misinformation and truth were mixed at the international level. Both the Eastern Bloc and the West created narratives that supported their own interests through this incident, and thus Ağca, in a sense, became trapped between the manipulation strategies of the great powers.

The assassination attempt on the Pope had a wide impact in the international media, and every step of Ağca's trial was headlined. Both the Pope's health status and Ağca's court proceedings constantly attracted media attention, causing the incident to go beyond the borders of the Vatican and become a global issue. This interest led to the event being evaluated not just as an individual crime but as one with political and ideological consequences on a global scale.

Trials That Pushed the Limits of Justice
Rome: The Courtroom of History

Rome, the ancient city of justice and betrayal... Throughout history, from the Senate where Caesar was stabbed, to medieval trials, and Mussolini's court proceedings, this city has witnessed great reckonings.

Now, Rome's stone walls were bearing witness to yet another trial. Was Mehmet Ali Ağca the modern-day Brutus? Or was he an assassin who struck Caesar, only to be caught by the cold justice of history himself?

July 21... Four months after the assassination attempt... Courtroom of the 1st Rome Criminal Court...

The high-ceilinged, stone-walled hall of the 1st Rome Criminal Court was about to echo with weighty words that would go down in history. Prosecutors were preparing to present their evidence, while lawyers were ready to draw the sword of justice. Yet this trial carried much more than a simple legal process. Every word, every movement, carried hidden meanings, resonating within the shadows of the Cold War. In this courtroom, not only crime and punishment would be heard, but also the fates of nations and the whispers of secret services.

The Selected Jury: Witnesses of Justice or Players of History?

This historic trial rose not only on the shoulders of prosecutors and lawyers but also on those of jury members selected from the public. The six-person jury consisted of ordinary people from various parts of Italy. Among them were a rabbit keeper, an architect, a retired teacher, and a housewife. But beyond their ordinariness, what turned them into figures on Rome's historic judicial stage was the fact that they would determine Ağca's fate.

Each of them was facing a responsibility they had likely never encountered before. Their decisions would not only determine the punishment of one man but also the fate of the great powers lurking in the shadows of international politics.

Like the Roman senators who witnessed Caesar's assassination, these jury members knew they would become part of history.

Ağca's Transfer to Court and Security Measures

The day before the trial, a leading Italian newspaper published a striking headline:

"If some people armed Ağca and incited him to commit this assassination, they might now try to kill him in the courtroom."

This news not only raised debate over the court process but also caused a stir regarding Ağca's safety.

Ağca was brought from Rebibbia Prison to the courthouse under extraordinary security measures. The convoy, surrounded by armored vehicles, set off in the early morning hours. Snipers were stationed on rooftops, and the courthouse perimeter was completely secured. Ağca's entrance into the courtroom was closely followed by cameras and journalists.

As he was brought into the hall, his grey trousers and green shirt were carefully ironed; but Ağca's face was pale, and his body appeared exhausted. When placed inside the bulletproof glass booth, he fixed his eyes on a single point and did not look around. Dozens of journalists in the room observed his every move carefully, recording every detail of the courtroom.

Ağca's first words shocked everyone. Suddenly irritated by the constant photo-taking, he shouted at the reporters: "That's enough, enough!"

Placed in the specially prepared bulletproof glass enclosure in the courtroom, Ağca waited calmly and coolly for the court panel to take their seats—15 minutes in total. When the panel entered the room, Ağca stood up...

The First Indictment Against Ağca: List of Committed Crimes

The prosecution read out the indictment prepared against Ağca, listing the crimes he had committed. The most serious accusation, without a doubt, was the attempted assassination of Pope John Paul II. Additionally, the file included unauthorized use of a firearm in a public area, entering the country with a fake passport, and forging a student ID in the name of an Italian university. Each allegation would soon be weighed on the sharp scales of justice and etched into the memory of history.

Presiding judge Soverio Sortapici had the indictment read out by the prosecutor. One of the two interpreters who would serve during the trial, a Turkologist named Anna Mansala, translated the indictment into Turkish for Ağca. During its reading, Ağca remained calm and nodded in agreement at certain points.

Picture 61. A case shrouded in the shadows of justice. Judge, prosecutor, and lawyer were arguing; Ağca was challenging the court. But who was truly on trial? A single man, or a conspiracy hidden in the shadows?[20]

---

20 Source: Milliyet Newspaper dated 1981

After the indictment was read, Ağca's lawyer Pietro Davido took the floor, arguing that the Italian courts had no jurisdiction over an incident that occurred on Vatican territory and that authorization from the Italian Ministry of Justice was required. However, the prosecutor replied that under an agreement signed between Italy and the Vatican in 1929, crimes committed in the Vatican could be prosecuted in Italy. The court rejected the objection raised by Ağca and his lawyer on jurisdictional grounds and decided to proceed with the trial. While the two legal experts debated in Italian, Ağca watched them in confusion, trying to understand.

Dispute with State-Appointed Lawyer and Prosecutor
"The Italian court is finished for me!"

Ağca's state-appointed lawyer, Pietro Davido, attempted to determine a defense strategy throughout the tense trial. However, Ağca insisted on defending himself rather than listening to his lawyer. One of the moments when tensions peaked was a heated argument between the prosecutor and Ağca. As the prosecutor explained how Ağca carried out the assassination plan, Ağca suddenly interrupted, shouting: "You can't judge me without knowing the truth!"

The prosecutor calmly replied: "You're hiding the truth. You're trying to cover up the crime you committed!"

This exchange escalated, and the court panel struggled to calm the parties down. Despite the objections from Ağca and his lawyer, the court ruled to continue the proceedings.

Shortly after the trial resumed, Ağca cried out: "Is this

justice? How can a defense be made without allowing the accused to speak? There's torture in prison, pressure, and bans!" Ağca demanded to be judged by the Vatican and rejected being tried in an Italian court.

He also added: "For seventy days, we've been living under inhumane conditions."

"If the Vatican does not judge me, if I'm not extradited to Turkey or tried in an international court, I will continue my hunger strike. If the Italian government doesn't put an end to the inhumane practices in prison, I will condemn them under international law... Italy cannot judge me. I've given Italy five months. I started my hunger strike on December 20. The Italian court is finished for me. Thank you."

Ağca's stance became one of the most influential factors in the court, even causing the jury members to pause and reflect.

Final Verdict Session: A Silent Rebellion

Throughout the trial, Mehmet Ali Ağca occasionally had outbursts of anger. For the final session, he refused to attend, saying: "I have no business with the Italian court anymore."

Perhaps this was his greatest act of defense: silence.

On the final day, the courtroom was packed. Camera lights were flashing, the judges had taken their seats, and the jurors had opened their files. Everyone was waiting for Ağca's entrance. But the expected moment never came. He refused to step into the courtroom and chose to observe the court where his fate would be decided from afar.

Upon learning this, the presiding judge sent a written order to the prison. The response from the prison stated that Ağca was in his cell, listening to music and chatting with the guards. This news sent a cold breeze through the courtroom. The judge remarked: "The defendant preferred to spend time with music rather than await the judgment of justice," expressing both disappointment and the gravity of the situation.

The prosecutor demanded a life sentence for Ağca. His lawyer delivered a one-hour defense, claiming that Ağca saw himself as a "commando for the Islamic world" and added: "just like some of our devout Catholics…"

In his defense, lawyer Diovido asserted that according to the Italian Secret Intelligence Service, there was an assassination attempt on Ağca in Germany in 1980, and that certain circles found Ağca too talkative and tried to silence him by blowing up a car believed to be his.

However, Ağca stated that he had never been to West Germany, and the West German police issued similar statements.

In the remainder of the defense, Diovido referenced the Pope's statement after being shot: "I am praying for the brother who shot me and I sincerely forgive him."

He concluded by stating that "The shooting of the Pope also wounded him as a person and a Catholic," and lamented that in this extraordinary trial, "there wasn't much else he could do."

After Diovido's defense, the presiding judge Severino Santiopcihli and the six-member jury (including two women) retired to deliberate.

Ağca's absence from the final hearing led to many

speculations. Some newspapers highlighted the lingering dark corners of the case, saying: "Had he come to court, he might have spoken and revealed the names behind the scenes."

Life Imprisonment and the Final Verdict

The world held its breath outside, waiting for the court's decision. Ultimately, Ağca was sentenced to life imprisonment, including two years in solitary confinement, for the attempted murder of the Pope and two American women at the scene. In addition, he was sentenced to 12 years for crimes such as carrying illegal weapons, using a false identity, and entering the country illegally. The jury reached this decision after hours of deliberation. However, this verdict did not mean the case was closed. Many questions still lingered about Ağca's connections and the powers behind him.

The court regarded and assessed Ağca as an individual terrorist. The court's detailed ruling included the following summary:

"It must be stated clearly that this court, based on the evidence obtained, concludes that the young man from Malatya, after entering from Conciliazione Street and taking position near the columns on the right, acted alone when firing at the Pope, and that there was no one else camouflaged or hidden among the crowd. During the chaos of the moment, no one intervened to rescue him from the gendarmes or police. No one was seen attempting to take Ağca away from the scene, and there was no reason for suspicion in this regard. Given the insufficient evidence available, there is no choice but to hope for a deeper investigation to reveal all the circumstances that might identify other individuals sharing responsibility in this grave incident."

Could the mystery recorded in history ever be solved? Was the decision regarding Ağca a definitive victory for justice, or merely another veil of mystery echoing through the depths of history?

Perhaps Ağca was not just a suspect, but a symbol of the Cold War — a living enigma resonating on the world stage.

Mehmet Ali Ağca was placed in a cell within the stone walls of Rebbia Prison to serve his life sentence as decided by the court.

In a thirty-minute meeting with his lawyer upon arrival, Ağca stated that he did not recognize the Italian court or its decision, and would not appeal. He told his lawyer his reason for not appealing was due to "inhumane treatment by the Italian government and other authorities." As a result, Ağca, whose sentence was finalized, would spend the first two years of his punishment in solitary confinement. Despite the sentence, the Italian and Vatican press agreed that many questions about the attempt on the Pope's life remained unanswered.

And in time, the case would be reopened...

Picture 62 – 63. However, years later, Ağca was released after being pardoned by the Vatican. History has shown that sometimes even seemingly definitive decisions can change.

The Pope's Fate: A Second Attempt Under the Shadow of Prophecy

Fatima. May 13, 1982...

The Pope was making a pilgrimage to the city of Fatima, the center of secrets, to give thanks for surviving the assassination attempt by Mehmet Ali Ağca a year earlier.

Christian pilgrims, in joy and tears, embraced their Pope who had survived the attempt, as the courtyard of the holy site filled with prayers. Soon, would the stone walls of the Church add yet another secret to the ones they already concealed? As the flickering lights of candles danced in the howling wind, a voice echoed amid intertwined joy and sorrow:

"Death to the Pope! Death to the Second Vatican Council!"

The crowd was startled. Was history about to be rewritten again? But fate once more intervened. As the attacker was taken down by security, Fatima's prophecy remained unfulfilled. A Spanish priest named Juan Fernandez Krohn had attempted to attack the Pope.

Dressed in a robe, Fernandez Krohn emerged from the crowd, approached the Pope from behind, and attacked with the 40-cm bayonet of a Mauser rifle. Pope John Paul II survived the attack, and security forces neutralized and arrested Krohn.

Picture 64. Justice convicted him, but his faith remained unshaken. He remains blameless in his own conscience, a controversial figure in the eyes of history. Years later, Krohn would repeat the same words: "I regret nothing."

Imprisoned and sentenced under both church law and Portuguese criminal law for attempted murder, Krohn stated years later in an interview that, "I have no regrets, I see myself as sinful, but not guilty."

Regarding Ağca, he said: "He is anti-Christian and anti-Western. Despite this, John Paul II forgave him. But he never did that with me…"

A series of questions followed this incident:

Was there more to this failed assassination than mere coincidence — was it a message? Were these attacks part of a prophecy? Was the recurring date of May 13 a divine sign shaping the Pope's fate, or were there extraordinary forces behind the curtain? Was this simply the act of a fanatic, or part of a much larger reckoning within the Vatican?

Was the Pope truly a spiritual leader under God's protection, or a figure targeted by unknown powers?

But why May 13 — again?

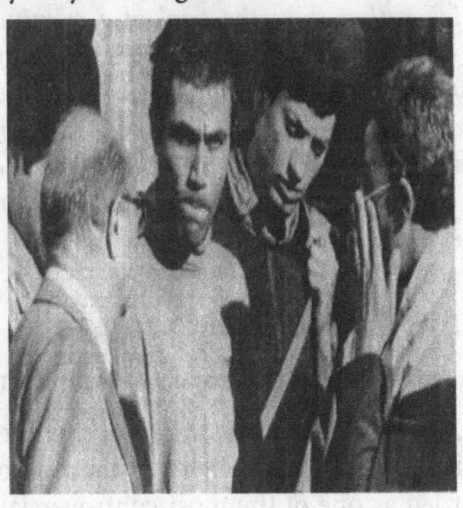

Picture 65-66. One Bullet, Two Blocks, an Eternal Secret: The Pope's assassination trial unfolded not in courtrooms, but in the intelligence battles of the Cold War. Mehmet Ali Ağca's trial, rather than the trial of a criminal, became a global showdown waged by two superpowers through media, intelligence, and political manipulation. Under the shadow of the CIA, the KGB, the P2 Masonic Lodge, the mafia, and the secret services, the identity of the true assassin, as well as the powers behind the scenes, would forever be debated.

The Trial of the Century: May 27, 1985

Mehmet Ali Ağca and the Pope Assassination Attempt

The May 13, 1981 assassination attempt on Pope John Paul II, the spiritual leader of the Catholic world, was recorded as one of the most controversial events in modern history. The verdict of the 1981 trial left many questions unanswered, and the court had expressed hope for a deeper investigation. Yet the reverberations of the incident continued, and everyone sought the true perpetrator behind the assassination attempt. Allegations arose that the attack by Mehmet Ali Ağca was more than a simple assassination — that it carried political and intelligence dimensions on an international scale.

Ağca's contradictory statements after the attempt fueled theories that the Soviet Union and Eastern Bloc countries were behind the attack.

And now the real trial was beginning.

To the prosecutor leading the investigation, Ağca initially gave the following statement:

"To protest the world's indifference to the murders of thousands of innocent people from Afghanistan to El Salvador at the hands of American and Soviet imperialist killers or their totalitarian allies, I felt compelled to kill the Pope. I held no personal grudge. My mission was to bring attention to fundamental issues that the world and Western media ignore. The UN must take a strong stance against international developments and abandon its passive, indecisive attitude. Especially, the veto powers of the US, UK, China, France, and the USSR must be revoked. A global peace and disarmament conference must be organized. A high-level peace and disarmament committee should be established under the UN framework, and an international propaganda campaign should mobilize public opinion. Committees should address hunger, health, torture, and human rights immediately. Action must be taken to prevent racial discrimination and religious wars. Developing countries should be granted a debt-free grace period until the year 2000."

Picture 67. The true question of history is not who gave the order, but why. The weapon left in Ağca's hand targeted not just one man, but the world order. Assassination was the signature of shadowy plots. That day, an assassination was on stage; behind the scenes, a collapsing world order was quietly crumbling.

Though sentenced to life imprisonment for shooting the Pope, Ağca later retracted his earlier claim that he acted alone. His pre-trial testimony led to a new indictment against seven suspects. He was also charged with smuggling the weapon used in the attack into Italy.

Italian Judge's Report and Second Shooter Allegations

This second trial relied on a comprehensive report prepared and submitted by Italian Judge Ilario Martella, outlining possible connections behind the attack. The report raised serious doubts that Ağca acted alone. Witnesses who heard multiple gunshots at St. Peter's Square that day strengthened these suspicions. The investigation thus expanded and took on an international dimension.

The case, started in 1981, had become highly complex due to Ağca's contradictory statements and international ties. The second trial was initiated to investigate Ağca's claim of a Bulgarian connection and a possible Soviet-backed conspiracy.

An Italian judge ruled that three Bulgarians and four Turks would stand trial for allegedly being involved in the May 13, 1981 assassination attempt on Pope John Paul II.

Defendants and Trial Process:

The trial began on May 27, 1985, and continued into 1986. During this period, Ağca was interrogated 128 times, and a 1,243-page indictment was prepared. There were 97 hearings, important witnesses were heard, and thousands of pages of case files were compiled.

One Bulgarian defendant, Sergei Antonov, 37, assistant manager of the Balkan Airlines office in Rome, had been detained since 1982. Two other Bulgarians, Todor Aivazov and Zhelyo Vassilev, who were embassy officials at the time and considered accomplices, had safely returned to Sofia shortly before Antonov's arrest. With no extradition agreement between Italy and Bulgaria, they could not be arrested.

Other defendants included Turkish citizen Ömer Bağcı, accused of smuggling Ağca's weapon into Italy, and Musa Serdar Çelebi, accused of facilitating contact between Ağca and Bulgarian officials. Çelebi was alleged to have funneled money to Ağca. According to prosecutors, Turkish mafia leader Bekir Çelenk had offered Ağca and his team $1.2 million for the assassination. However, Çelenk was in Bulgaria and could not be extradited. Two of the four Turkish defendants were also missing. Oral Çelik, allegedly the second gunman photographed fleeing the scene, remained at large.

Claims that Oral Çelik was present during the attack increased suspicions that Ağca had not acted alone. Ağca stated in questioning, "After my second shot, someone grabbed me hard and prevented me from continuing to fire." Prosecutors took this as strong evidence that the assassination was planned and executed by more than one person.

International Reactions to the Arrests: "NATO Conspiracy"

An "International Commission" was formed in Brussels concerning the trial. In its first statement, it protested Antonov's detention, claiming he was held based on baseless accusations in violation of Italian and international law.

The "International Association of Democratic Lawyers," including French, Indian, Belgian, and West German lawyers, harshly criticized Italian authorities for holding the Bulgarian citizen without proven charges.

The Bulgarian news agency BTA published a declaration, asserting the innocence of the three Bulgarians and demanding Antonov's release.

The Soviet news agency TASS sharply criticized Antonov's indictment:

"Prepared in cooperation with NATO and US intelligence, this case is an example of destructive efforts to increase international tension. It is a conspiracy to disgrace Bulgaria and other socialist countries."

Meanwhile, protests erupted in Sofia, with citizens demonstrating against the trial of their fellow countrymen.

The First Day of the Historic Trial...

May 27, 1985 – 9:45 a.m.

Nearly 450 journalists, including from TRT, as well as American and Bulgarian TV stations, were following the globally anticipated trial and transmitting updates instantly to their news centers. Additionally, correspondents from the Soviet Union and Bulgaria showed great interest in the case. The Kremlin even began broadcasting the trial live to Moscow via Novosti, setting up a special TV feed. American, Italian, and Bulgarian TV networks were filming the trial, while the four defendants watched the proceedings from separate barred cages that covered an entire wall of the courtroom. Each cage was guarded by three police officers, with additional police positioned in front of and behind each one.

Wearing a light pale blue suit and a light blue open-collared shirt, Ağca stood throughout the hearing in a sort of military stance, while the other defendants sat on benches. The trial was expected to have repercussions not only as a legal matter but also as a significant event in the political theater of the Cold War. Protests were held in Warsaw Pact countries against the trial, while Italian newspapers ran the story with huge headlines.

From Turkey, journalist Uğur Mumcu, author of the book Papa-Ağca-Mafia, followed the trial from start to finish. From time to time, the prosecution sought information from Mumcu during the investigation. Mumcu shared his impressions from the courtroom in his column in the newspaper Cumhuriyet:

"The lawyers are lined up like Roman gladiators. Thick files stand in front of each of them. They have been preparing for this trial for days, for weeks. They have dissected Ağca's statements and are waiting for the moment to question this Malatyan Jesus…"

The panel of judges consisted of eight people—two lawyers and six selected from among the public.

The trial was being held in the Foto Italiano sports hall, built by Italy's fascist leader Mussolini and previously used during the 1960 Rome Olympics, where 82 members of the Red Brigades had once been tried. Bulletproof sections and metal cages had been prepared for the defendants. Strict security measures were taken in front of the hall where the trial was to be held. As the trial began, two police helicopters flew above the building, and more than 500 police officers wearing bulletproof vests and carrying light machine guns patrolled the area. This was the first time such security measures were implemented in an Italian court.

In this trial where Ağca would appear both as a witness and a defendant, Bulgarian and Turkish citizens accused of being part of the assassination conspiracy were arrested and brought to court. Among the arrested Turks, the most notable was Musa Serdar Çelebi, president of the Federation of Democratic Idealist Associations of Europe. As Çelebi was brought into the courtroom, a group of 150-200 idealists gathered outside, chanting slogans in support of him. This group insulted the Turkish journalists covering the trial.

Ağca entered the courtroom first, followed by the most important defendant in the case, Sergei Ivanov Antonov. The 37-year-old Antonov was accused of accompanying Ağca and Oral Çelik to St. Peter's Square on the day of the armed attack. When brought to court, he appeared hopeless and exhausted. One of his lawyers, Adolfo Larussa, said, "Antonov is physically stressed, and this reflects in his mental state. He's having trouble concentrating."

The first day of the trial was spent in procedural debates. The defense lawyer for the Bulgarian defendants claimed that his clients had diplomatic immunity and could not be tried in Italy, requesting the case be dismissed for this reason. At the beginning of the trial, defense lawyer Manfredo Rossi asked the court to dismiss the charges against two Bulgarian citizens in Sofia on the grounds that they had diplomatic immunity. However, Judge Santiapichi rejected this request, stating, "An attempt on the Pope's life is not within the scope of a diplomat's duties," and added that Todor Ayvazov and Major Zhelyo Vassilev lost their immunity when they left Italy in 1982.

The prosecutor requested that the investigation be expanded to bring three Turkish citizens from various countries to Italy to testify. These individuals were Abdullah Çatlı, Yalçın Özbey, and Mehmet Şener. The court decided to recess for two and a half hours to evaluate these requests. During this time, a group of 150 idealists watching the trial stood together to salute their leader, Musa Serdar Çelebi, while a group of 60 people outside also shouted slogans in his favor.

At that moment, Ağca made his first shocking declaration, shouting in Turkish from his place and stunning everyone. In a very loud voice, he proclaimed that he was "Jesus Christ." As soon as the audience heard this, the courtroom erupted into chaos, and dozens of journalists turned their cameras toward Ağca.

He then continued in Italian: "You know who I am. I am Jesus the Prophet. In the name of the Almighty God, I declare the end of the world."

The courtroom descended into mayhem. The officials silenced Ağca, took him by the arm, and forcefully removed him. Five minutes later, with the return of the judicial panel, Ağca was brought back into the courtroom, and the trial resumed. The panel announced that it had rejected the defense's requests and that the trial would continue. Due to the chaos, the hearing was postponed until the afternoon.

Commenting on the developments, Prosecutor Marini expressed confidence and said about Ağca's statements:

"The lead witness's erratic outbursts will not harm the trial. These are merely performances for the journalists."

Afternoon – 4:30 p.m.

On the first day of the trial, the chaos continued. A technical malfunction in the sound system caused the session to be cut short.

The prosecutor demanded that Abdullah Çatlı and Oral Çelik be heard as witnesses and had a heated argument with the lawyer of the Bulgarian defendants.

The presiding judge called Mehmet Ali Ağca to testify, and Ağca was taken from his cage and seated in front of the judicial panel. He began answering questions about the origin of the weapon used in the assassination attempt.

In the indictment, read in Turkish, Ağca was charged with bringing firearms and ammunition into Italy for terrorist purposes in order to overthrow the democratic order. Ağca then said:

"I am mentally sound. I understand and interpret everything that has happened perfectly. They called me mad because of what I said earlier. I am not insane. I am normal. My mind works perfectly."

When Ağca stated that he did not need an interpreter and understood and spoke Italian very well, the judge said:

"You need to speak Turkish. Otherwise, Çelebi and

Bağcı won't understand you. But if you want, we can do a test run."

Then Ağca said: "For the sake of humanity, we are all here because of the assassination attempt on the Pope. Humanity is going through its greatest tragedy. Everyone knows this. Most of all, the Vatican knows it."

To this, the judge responded:

"Your thoughts don't concern me. Answer my questions," and asked when and from whom he got the weapon.

After answering in detail about Ömer Bağcı, Ağca again began to say, "For the sake of humanity..." but was interrupted by the judge repeating,

"Your thoughts don't concern me. Answer my questions."

The trial ended late in the evening. The first day of the trial was highly tense due to procedural disputes and Ağca's outbursts. The Italian press labeled the case "the trial of the century" and anticipated that the court would begin evaluating evidence and uncovering the backstory of the assassination in the coming days.

The first day of the trial turned into more of a spectacle than a legal process due to intense media attention and dramatic statements by the defendants.

The international media covering the trial headlined not the assassination-related testimonies, but rather Ağca's claims of being the Messiah: "Ağca Declares Himself the Messiah"

Such outbursts, expected to continue from Ağca, combined with claims that obscure the facts and his psychological state, would make it harder to understand the truth behind the assassination.

The Future of the Trial

While referred to as "the trial of the century," the coming days were expected to bring the court's assessment of evidence and possibly uncover the hidden side of the assassination. However, Ağca's erratic behavior and contradictory statements raised questions about his reliability as a witness. It became clear that the trial would not be limited to Ağca alone but marked the beginning of a major judicial process with potential international diplomatic implications.

This major trial, which began in a courtroom in Rome, seemed likely to continue capturing the world's attention for a long time.

Picture 69. *The finger that shook the world order with a single bullet was now declaring itself a symbol of salvation. Ağca's statement, "I am Jesus," obscured the political depth of the case and significantly weakened the possibility of directly exposing the larger structures behind the assassination. The truth would be lost in the labyrinth of mind games.*

The 1985 Trial: "Postpone the Hearing, Let the Vatican Reveal the Third Secret"

In the trial for the attempted assassination of Pope John Paul II, the session on May 28, 1985, drew attention with Mehmet Ali Ağca's striking statements. On the second day of the hearing, the court immediately proceeded to question Ağca. However, Prosecutor Antonio Morini claimed that Ağca was trying to send messages to certain parties and gain time, and instead requested that Ömer Bağcı, who was accused of providing the weapon to Ağca, be interrogated first.

Perhaps aware of the impact of his previous day's statements, Ağca this time used even more sensational expressions, declaring himself to be the "resurrected Prophet Jesus." Shouting in Italian, he said:

"I want to make statements. The assassination attempt in St. Peter's Square is related to the three secrets of Fatima. There are things I didn't tell Martella. The Pope assassination is related to the Virgin Mary's third message. As God's Messiah, I declared yesterday in court that the end of the world has come. You may think I'm crazy because of these words. I am not crazy. I'm very intelligent. I am the resurrected Prophet Jesus. He was announcing the end of the world. I have revealed this. In my conversation with the Pope, I informed him of these things. God showed me the death and crucifixion of Jesus again. Neither the Soviet Union nor America can stop the destruction of the world."

These words caused great astonishment in the courtroom. However, the presiding judge did not indulge Ağca's mystical rhetoric, saying, "These statements do not concern us. We are conducting a trial on behalf of the Italian state," and called on him to focus on actual evidence.

Ağca continued his speech, arguing that the private conversations he had with the Pope would help solve the case. Claiming that the Pope should "reveal the third secret of Fatima," Ağca gave an unexpected answer when the judge told him, "Then reveal this secret."

"I cannot reveal it today."

When the judge asked, "What are you waiting for?" Ağca replied, "I'm waiting for a message from the Vatican," and requested that the trial be postponed. But Judge Severino Santiapichi responded firmly:

"This is the Italian state, and I'm conducting this trial on behalf of the Italian people. We have nothing to do with the Vatican. I can't suspend the court just because you're waiting for a message from the Vatican."

With these words, the judge rejected Ağca's demands and ensured that the hearing continued. Ağca's mystical and conspiratorial rhetoric in court received wide coverage in the press, with debate arising over whether he truly believed what he said or whether it was part of a strategic ploy.

Ağca Crucifies the Italian Justice System from Day One

Although the world was riveted by this case—referred to as the "trial of the century"—the legal process had become something of a nightmare for the Italian judiciary from the very first day. The prosecution's case was based on Ağca's claims, made after spending the first year of his life sentence in solitary confinement, alleging a conspiracy involving the Bulgarians and Soviets.

According to the prosecution, the alleged motive behind the attempt on the life of the Polish-born Pope was to silence a charismatic supporter of the defiant Solidarity movement in Poland. But when Ağca took the witness stand, he failed to cooperate disastrously.

On the second day, Mehmet Ali Ağca once again drew all attention with his conduct in the courtroom. From behind the iron bars of the courtroom, he shouted in Italian: **"I am Jesus Christ! I am omnipotent! I declare the end of the world! The world will be destroyed!"**

This declaration created chaos in the courtroom and resulted in Ağca being removed from the court for disturbing the proceedings. As security forces escorted him out, a police officer reportedly said, **"The show is over."**

Ağca's Sabotage of the Hearing and the Judge's Reaction

Judge Santiapichi tried to persuade Ağca, who was brought back into the courtroom, to give rational answers. But Ağca replied:

"I can't answer. I want to continue tomorrow. I'm waiting for a response from the Vatican. If the Vatican denies me, I can't do anything. I can't continue."

When Chief Judge Santiapichi asked where he got the Browning 9mm pistol used in the assassination attempt, Ağca said:

"I'm sorry, I can't answer that today. That doesn't mean I'm refusing to answer questions."

However, even after a break, Ağca still refused to answer questions and was removed from the witness stand. After this, the judge took a recess to allow Ağca to make up his mind.

Ağca's second claim of being Jesus in court was met with joy by the lawyers of Musa Serdar Çelebi, by his supporters observing the trial, and by the Bulgarian defendants and their attorneys. The defense attorneys initially intended to request a psychological evaluation to determine whether Ağca was mentally fit but later abandoned the idea. Ağca's statements worked in their favor, casting doubt on his credibility and making their defense easier. His statements had become a lifeline for all of them. From that point on, every time Ağca spoke, the trial became more convoluted.

Picture 70. *The Trial of the Century: Mehmet Ali Ağca is in court, accused of an assassination attempt shrouded in international intrigue. Will the judge be able to uncover the truth in this case shrouded in mystery, or will the dark curtain never be lifted?*

Ağca's Strange Court Statements Continued Ağca's bizarre courtroom statements did not stop. Every statement he made became a factor influencing the course of the trial. During later hearings, he introduced himself as the reincarnated form of Jesus Christ, and continued to make mystical, apocalyptic declarations.

These kinds of remarks led to various speculations about Ağca's psychological state and raised doubts about the reliability of his testimony. Some analysts interpreted these remarks as part of a deliberate strategy. According to this view, Ağca was trying to present himself as mentally unstable, thereby preventing his testimony from being taken seriously.

However, this tactic did not prevent the court from continuing its investigation into the alleged Bulgarian connection.

The Bulgarian Trace (Pista Bulgara) and the Soviet Union's Stance

Although Ağca initially stated in his testimony that he carried out the assassination attempt on his own, he later claimed that Bulgaria had organized the attack. This claim evolved into a conspiracy theory, especially in the Western media, referred to as the "Bulgarian trace," and it was alleged to be connected to the Soviet Union's secret services. The allegations raised in court caused significant political tension between Eastern Bloc countries and the West.

In his statements, Ağca claimed that during his time in Bulgaria, he had made contact with the Bulgarian intelligence service. This led to a strong belief in Western countries that the Soviet Union was behind the assassination attempt. According to this theory, the Soviets organized the attempt to eliminate the threat posed by a Polish-born Pope to Communist regimes in Eastern Europe.

Picture 71. Bulgarian Sergey Antonov, accused of the 1981 assassination of Pope John Paul II, was acquitted in 1986 due to lack of evidence. However, the "Bulgarian trace" claim was long debated during the Cold War. The Pope's visit to Bulgaria in 2002 served as a symbolic response to these claims. Throughout history, the victors have written the story, while the vanquished have been forgotten; as Napoleon Bonaparte said, "History is written by the victors."

However, officials from Bulgaria and the Soviet Union categorically denied these allegations. The Soviet news agency Tass described the claims about the assassination attempt as part of a disinformation campaign conducted by the West against the Eastern Bloc. Similarly, the Bulgarian defense attorneys argued that Ağca's statements were contradictory and unreliable.

Intelligence Wars in Rome

The World-Shaking Conspiracy: The Assassination Attempt on Pope John Paul II and the Bulgaria–Soviet Covert Operation in Light of CIA Reports[21]

The assassination attempt on Pope John Paul II in St. Peter's Square in Rome on May 13, 1981, went down in history as one of the most striking and shadowy events of the 20th century. The identities of the powers behind this attack were debated for many years. Reports by the U.S. Central Intelligence Agency (CIA) offered striking information and analyses, especially regarding the possible roles of the Soviet Union and Bulgaria in this incident.

A Strange Mix of the Papal Assailant and Bulgarian Smuggling

An article prepared by the U.S. State Department's Bureau of Intelligence and Research on December 10, 1982, contained notable information about Mehmet Ali Ağca's connections with Bulgarian agents and Sofia-based major smuggling networks. According to the report, Ağca's contacts with Bulgarian officials in Rome were directly tied to the arms, drugs, and contraband trade conducted around the Vitosha Hotel in Sofia.

Following Bekir Çelenk's $1.2 million assassination offer to Ağca and his subsequent arrest by Bulgarian police, the deep links between smuggling and intelligence networks were revealed. The CIA and the State Department reported that due to economic hardships, Bulgaria deliberately tolerated these smuggling activities and even officially supported them to address its shortage of hard

---

21 United States Foreign Relations Papers, 1981–1988, Volume X, Eastern Europe.

currency. The report also included information about the use of Bulgaria's relations with Malta and its airlines in drug trafficking.[22]

Evidence of Soviet and Bulgarian Involvement

According to CIA reports, Soviet military intelligence (GRU) and Bulgarian military intelligence (RUMNO) were behind the Pope assassination attempt. After the Soviets rejected the direct implementation of the operation, the task was delegated to Bulgaria. The Bulgarians coordinated the assassination plan through their agent Bekir Çelenk, and Mehmet Ali Ağca was chosen to carry out the act.

In statements to Italian authorities, Ağca said he met with two Bulgarian military intelligence officers in Rome and that the operation was conducted under Çelenk's control. This information was confirmed in a classified memorandum sent to U.S. President Reagan on February 27, 1985.

Bulgaria's Concerns and Post-Attempt Plans

According to CIA reports, after the assassination attempt, Bulgaria prepared various assassination and poisoning plans to prevent individuals linked to the incident from testifying. The elimination of Sergey Antonov, a Bulgarian airline official arrested in Rome, and Bekir Çelenk, under protection in Sofia, was on the agenda. The CIA secretly warned Italian Prime Minister Bettino Craxi about these issues.

---

22 Foreign Relations of the United States, 1981–1988, Volume X, Eastern Europe: Papal Assault and Bulgarian Smuggling Are a Strange Mixture

Moments of Crisis in Sofia, Leaks, and Diplomatic Moves

Sofia entered a major crisis due to the assassination attempt and the subsequent international pressure. Bulgarian leadership feared the Italian trial process would damage the country's image. During this period, reports from the DS (Interior Intelligence Service) were leaked, and the press in Sofia began discussing security shortcomings. Domestic intelligence officials were questioned over flawed intelligence operations and uncontrolled foreign agent relationships.

KGB advisors were dispatched to Sofia to hold high-level crisis meetings. These meetings focused on the DS's failures and the risks arising from its connections with the Turkish mafia. In an attempt to correct its errors, Bulgaria began reorganizing its networks of espionage, smuggling, and propaganda.

State-controlled media in Sofia frequently emphasized that the CIA was conducting a provocation and that Ağca's statements were entirely manipulated. Suspicious news reports in Western media were immediately turned into anti-Western propaganda in the Bulgarian press. At the same time, articles and books defending Bulgaria in the case were published in Western countries. Propaganda activities aimed at French and Greek public opinion were organized by Bulgaria's embassies and intelligence cells abroad.

In October 1984, under Sofia's direction, the International Association of Democratic Lawyers convened in Athens and decided that the case should be reviewed by an independent international commission. This initiative aimed to influence Western public opinion and exert pressure on the legal process.

Reflections in the Western Press

The Western press—especially newspapers in the U.S., U.K., and Italy—published multifaceted stories about Bulgaria's involvement in the incident. The New York Times and The Washington Post included articles examining the role of Bulgarian intelligence following the release of CIA-sourced documents to the public. The Times and Le Monde ran analyses supporting Bulgarian complicity but highlighted the lack of conclusive evidence. These reports were carefully monitored in Sofia and cited line by line in domestic propaganda materials.

Tension Between Moscow and Sofia

The Soviet Union initially gave full support to Bulgaria. However, the unexpectedly large impact of the event and its escalation into an international matter caused new tensions between Moscow and Sofia. Soviet leader Yuri Andropov was both angry and disappointed with Bulgaria due to its careless intelligence and smuggling activities. According to CIA reports, Moscow wanted to be actively involved in finding a solution but was constrained by other international priorities.

Antonov's Situation and Sofia's Fears

Sergey Antonov's long detention, personal problems, and signs of psychological breakdown became a critical threat for Sofia. Bulgarian leaders were deeply concerned that Antonov might crack during the trial and provide testimony implicating Bulgaria. According to CIA reports, Antonov's resilience was a constant topic of discussion in Sofia, and plans to eliminate him quietly if necessary were considered.

Moreover, the risk that Antonov might leak information about espionage activities caused panic in Bulgaria. The Sofia administration devised multifaceted plans to extend the trial process if Antonov was found guilty, influence Western public opinion, and conduct counter-propaganda.

Sofia's Crisis Management and Projected Scenarios

CIA analyses revealed that Sofia would use diplomatic pressure, misinformation, media manipulation, and conciliatory gestures together to influence the trial process. In order to gain trust from the West, Sofia offered unexpected cooperation in various areas and hinted at sharing sensitive information about drug traffickers and certain terrorist organizations.

If Antonov were acquitted, it was expected that Sofia would launch a brief propaganda campaign against the U.S., but in the long run, would seek to rebuild relations in line with its economic and political interests. If Antonov were convicted, long appeals processes, harsh diplomatic pressure on Italy and Western governments, and public opinion manipulation were planned.

Antonov's Divorce Case

According to CIA reports and diplomatic correspondence, during Antonov's imprisonment, he experienced major personal issues in addition to psychological distress. While in prison in Italy for an extended period, Antonov's wife filed for divorce in Bulgaria. This case disturbed the state leadership and intelligence officials in Sofia. The divorce proceedings deepened Antonov's morale collapse, and Bulgarian intelligence began to worry that he might cooperate with Italian authorities and make confessions. In high-level meetings in Sofia, it was emphasized that Antonov's personal troubles and the divorce process weakened his resistance, and options such as postponing or softening the trial process through diplomatic intervention were considered.

February 27, 1985 Memorandum Sent to President Reagan by McFarlane

Memorandum No. 379, included in Foreign Relations of the United States, 1981–1988, Volume X, Eastern Europe, provided President Reagan with information on the possible roles of the Soviet Union and Bulgaria in the 1981 assassination attempt on Pope John Paul II. It stated that after Soviet military intelligence (GRU) declined to carry out the operation directly, the task was transferred to Bulgarian military intelligence, and long-time agent Bekir Çelenk was included in the plot by portraying him as a "right-wing fanatic." Çelenk then assigned Mehmet Ali Ağca to execute the assassination. The report also notes that Ağca gave statements to Italian authorities about Çelenk's role and his meetings with two Bulgarian military intelligence officers in Rome.

The Bulgarians, fearing that Antonov might admit the Bulgarian connection during the trial, planned to eliminate both him and Çelenk, who was under protection in Sofia. While Bulgarian intelligence devised a plan to kill Antonov with a slow-acting poison that would appear natural, Italian Prime Minister Bettino Craxi was secretly informed of this plot by the CIA.[23]

---

23 Reagan Library, System IV Intelligence Files, 1985, 400165. Top Secret; Sensitive. Prepared by deGraffenreid and Cannistraro, with a copy sent to Vice President Bush and annotated by President Reagen.

Picture 72. When the curtain rose, not only the hitmen but also the mafia lords and shadowy alliances appeared on stage. The bullets did not stop, for every mouth that spoke sealed other secrets with blood.

The crisis in Sofia was a deep intelligence and propaganda war that challenged not only Bulgaria's but also the Soviet Union's diplomatic stability. CIA reports reveal how complex and multi-layered this process was. The assassination attempt on Pope John Paul II remains one of the most sophisticated operations conceived in the dark corridors of the Cold War and continues to be an unresolved file in its entirety.

Defense Speech Delivered in Court by the Bulgarians' Lawyer Giuseppe Consolo

One of the lawyers representing the Bulgarian defendants, Giuseppe Consolo, frequently emphasized in his courtroom speeches that Ağca's statements were not reliable. Consolo reinforced his defense by saying, "Ağca himself has rejected seventy percent of his statements. If a witness admits that most of their testimony is false, how can we trust the rest of it?"

In addition, Consolo argued that there was no concrete evidence to support Ağca's claims and that all accusations were part of a political propaganda campaign backed by the Western media. Lawyer Consolo described Ağca's statements as "proof that he has misled the Italian judicial system for three years."

Prosecution Defended Ağca's Credibility

Ağca, the prosecution's main witness, had given detailed and sometimes contradictory statements about the involvement of Bulgarian secret services in the incident. Ağca was the most important witness for the Italian prosecutor, and at this point, the prosecution's case largely rested on his testimony. In a statement he made in June, Prosecutor Antonio Marini stated that Bulgaria could not act without the Soviet Union's approval. According to him, the rise of the Solidarity Movement in Poland and the Pope being Polish posed a significant threat to the Soviets and the Eastern Bloc.

The prosecutor rejected claims that the case relied solely on Ağca's testimony and emphasized that the information he provided was reliable. The prosecution insisted that Bulgaria, with the support of the Soviet Union, was behind the assassination attempt on the Polish-born Pope, but both the Soviet and Bulgarian governments had issued strong denials of these allegations.

Marini said of Ağca, "I don't believe he is insane," and added: "When he begins to tell the truth, he is extremely reliable."

During one hearing, 27-year-old Ağca said, "I am the reincarnated Jesus Christ. The days of this generation are numbered." Carefully continuing his speech, Ağca stated, "Neither the Americans nor the Soviets, no one will be spared. There will be great destruction." These statements left everyone in shock.

As a result, previous evaluations of Ağca's mental health were brought up again in court. The lawyers representing the Bulgarian defendants stated that when Ağca was arrested in 1979 in Turkey for the murder of a journalist, he had been examined by Turkish psychiatrists and found mentally sound and fit to stand trial. The Italian court had also accepted this evaluation. Therefore, the defense lawyers announced that they would not request a new mental health assessment. As the hearings continued, debates over Ağca's testimony and credibility persisted.

What Ağca Said in Court

Throughout the court proceedings, Ağca often gave contradictory statements and pointed to many different individuals and organizations during the trial. Some of his courtroom declarations included:

- "I am the Messiah" claim: Ağca repeatedly claimed to be the reincarnation of Jesus Christ and said the end of the world was near.

- Contradictory Statements on the Assassination's Organizers: Initially claiming that Bulgaria and the Soviet Union were behind the assassination attempt, Ağca later suggested that the CIA and Western intelligence agencies might also have been involved.

- Vatican and P2 Masonic Lodge: Ağca claimed in court that the P2 Masonic Lodge was behind the assassination and specifically pointed to Licio Gelli. He argued that P2 might have attempted the assassination to preserve the balance of power within the Vatican.

- Bulgarian Connection: He claimed that he had been hired by Bulgaria in 1981 to shoot the Pope and that he had been paid $1.2 million for it.

- Emanuela Orlandi Kidnapping Incident: Ağca suggested that the 1983 disappearance of Vatican employee Emanuela Orlandi was linked to the P2 Masonic Lodge and the criminal underworld. He said her kidnappers had promised to release her in exchange for Ağca's release.

- Concerns for His Own Safety: Ağca frequently expressed fear of being killed during the trial. He claimed that powerful forces wanted to silence him and that revealing the truth behind the assassination would endanger his life.

Ağca's Statements on the P2 Masonic Lodge
June 14, 1985 Hearing

Claims that Mehmet Ali Ağca's assassination attempt was not an individual act but part of a larger conspiracy involving international intelligence services and secret organizations were debated for years. During the trial, Ağca pointed to the P2 Masonic Lodge as one of the forces behind the assassination.

The P2 Masonic Lodge was founded in 1877 as part of the Grand Orient of Italy, but its Masonic charter was revoked in 1976. It began operating as an illegal organization in violation of Article 18 of the Italian Constitution, which bans secret societies. After being expelled from the Masonic charter in 1976, it transformed into a secret, radical right-wing, and anti-communist group. Under the leadership of Licio Gelli, P2 became associated with incidents such as the Banco Ambrosiano scandal tied to the Vatican, and the murders of Roberto Calvi and Mino Pecorelli.

P2 had deep ties to Italian politics, intelligence services, and the mafia, and was involved in corruption scandals that shook governments. It was also mentioned in Ağca's claims regarding the assassination attempt on Pope John Paul II. Linked to false passports, financial manipulations, and deep state structures, P2 went down in history as one of the Cold War's biggest political intrigues.

Bulgarian and Soviet officials claimed that people connected to "Masonic lodges" had reached out to Ağca in prison and may have influenced him to accuse the Soviet bloc in exchange for promises of release.

P2 Masonic Lodge and Assassination Claims

In his court statements, Ağca alleged that the P2 Masonic Lodge played a major role in planning the assassination. According to Ağca, P2 was connected to NATO and Italian intelligence agencies and was disturbed by the Pope's anti-communist policies. He said the assassination aimed both to shift the power dynamics within the Vatican and to influence the political games between the Western and Eastern Blocs.

In his claims, the name of P2's leader, Licio Gelli,[24] stood out. Ağca said that Gelli and the organization were uncomfortable with Pope John Paul II's reforms within the Vatican and his support for anti-communist efforts in the Eastern Bloc.

Additionally, he claimed that the kidnapping of Emanuela Orlandi in the Vatican was an operation orchestrated by P2 and that the incident was linked to financial scandals.

Stefano Delle Chiaie and the Legal Process

One of the important names mentioned in the assassination trial was Stefano Delle Chiaie, a far-right Italian figure. Allegedly linked directly to Ağca, Delle Chiaie was connected to paramilitary groups in Europe and Latin America.

According to testimony by Francesco Pazienza to U.S. customs officials, Delle Chiaie was seen in the U.S. with a Turk. This development drew the attention of Italian judge Ilario Martella, who was conducting the inves-

---

24 Licio Gelli: He has gone down in history as one of Italy's most controversial figures. He was the "grand master" of the illegal Masonic lodge Propaganda Due (P2), which was uncovered in 1981 and accused of collaborating with right-wing extremists and the mafia to undermine Italian governments. Gelli admitted that the P2 was a shadowy organization with deep connections to the Vatican, Italian intelligence services, and the world of international finance. In 1982, he was sentenced to 12 years in prison for fraud related to the death of Roberto Calvi, known as "God's Banker," who was found hanging under Blackfriars Bridge in London. However, he did not serve most of his sentence. He was also found guilty of obstructing the police investigation into the 1980 bombing at Bologna train station, which killed 85 people. He later escaped house arrest and sought refuge in Switzerland.

tigation. Pazienza was asked, "Was Delle Chiaie or the Grey Wolves directly involved in the assassination, or were they used as subcontractors?" Pazienza replied, "If I claimed to know about this, I would be lying. I don't know such a thing." Although this denial indicated that there was no concrete evidence directly linking Delle Chiaie to the assassination plot, it did not dispel the lingering doubts.

Picture 73. *"I am a fascist and I will die as a fascist,"* Gelli said at a press conference in 1999.

Gladio, P2 Masonic Lodge, and Intelligence Connections

Ağca's statements reignited the Gladio debates in Italy. Francesco Pazienza, a former Italian intelligence official imprisoned in the U.S., was one of the names mentioned in the Bologna train station bombing and the Pope assassination investigation.

Investigations in Rome alleged that Pazienza and other right-wing elements tried to create the perception that Bulgaria was behind the assassination. It was claimed that Pazienza visited Ağca in prison and encouraged him to use certain statements. However, Pazienza denied these accusations and claimed that it was entirely a political manipulation.

In the press following the trial, allegations emerged that Ağca had connections with the far-right Turkish organization Bozkurtlar (Gray Wolves). However, it was also claimed that he was not only affiliated with local organizations but also with international deep-state structures such as Gladio. Gladio was known as one of NATO's counter-guerrilla organizations established in Europe against the Soviet threat. Similar structures were said to exist in Turkey, and it was alleged that CIA agent Duane Clarridge played a role in coordinating these organizations. Ağca's escape from the military prison in Turkey was also claimed to have occurred under the shadow of these structures.

P2 Masonic Lodge and Alleged Vatican Connection

One of the most striking points in Ağca's statements was the alleged connection between the P2 Masonic Lodge and the Vatican. P2, one of the most powerful illegal Masonic structures of its time, had strong ties with intelligence services, the mafia, financial circles, and the political world.

Journalist Philip Willan, who followed the trial, claimed that P2 was directly connected to Ağca and argued that the assassination attempt was not just an individual act, but part of a grand conspiracy. P2 leader Licio Gelli was accused of planning a coup in Italy. He also drew attention with his connections to the Vatican bank and financial ties with Italian banker Roberto Calvi.

Pope Assassination, Roberto Calvi, and Allegations of Masonic-Style Execution

Another figure alleged to be directly connected to the Pope assassination was Italian banker Roberto Calvi. Calvi, who handled the Vatican's financial affairs, had close ties with the P2 Masonic Lodge. However, following the developments after the assassination, Calvi was found dead in London at Blackfriars Bridge in a manner said to be in line with Masonic rituals. A rope with a special Masonic knot was tied around his neck, and stones were placed on his feet. "Blackfriars Bridge" also means "Bridge of the Black Monks," a name that caught attention due to its symbolic overlap with P2.

The Pope assassination and Calvi's death once again revealed the dark, intertwined relationships of secret organizations. Could the disputes between P2 and the Vatican and their economic conflicts of interest have been one of the real motivations behind the assassination?

Picture 74. *There was law on the bench, but invisible laws ruled the courtroom. Even though Ağca's tongue was loosened, the silence of the system prevailed.*

Mehmet Ali Ağca's trial for the Pope assassination went down in history as one of the greatest examples of Cold War-era intelligence wars. It was claimed that the P2 Masonic Lodge, Gladio, and intelligence agencies were behind the assassination. Ağca's inconsistent statements and Pazienza's possible role in the assassination process remain topics of debate. The relationships of the P2 Masonic Lodge with the Vatican, Italian intelligence, and international financial circles further complicated the truth behind the assassination.

June 15, 1985 – Trial

On June 15, 1985, a critical hearing took place in the trial related to the assassination attempt on Pope John Paul II. Mehmet Ali Ağca testified once again in a Rome court, expanding his claims and presenting new connections. However, the inconsistencies in his testimony and the questionable credibility of his statements left both prosecutors and judges stunned.

Ağca's New Conspiracy Theories Regarding the Assassination

As in his previous testimonies, Ağca repeated that the Soviet Union, Bulgaria, and Turkish right-wing groups were behind the assassination attempt. This time, however, he claimed the attempt was not just an attack on the Vatican but part of a global conspiracy plan.

New Allegations:

- He suggested the Pope's assassination was a result of the Cold War between the Soviet Union and the Western world.

- He stated that individuals linked to the illegal Masonic lodge "Propaganda 2" (P2) in Italy were behind the scenes of the incident.
- He claimed the kidnapping of Vatican employee Emanuela Orlandi in 1983 was an operation intended to secure his release.
- He asserted that Licio Gelli, the former head of the P2 lodge, organized Orlandi's abduction and that this group wanted to use him as a tool within the Vatican.

Contradictions and Doubts in Court

Prosecutors and lawyers observed that Ağca's statements were inconsistent and increasingly evolved into a complex conspiracy theory. Chief Judge Severino Santiapichi asked several questions to clarify Ağca's statements, but Ağca often gave evasive answers or avoided the questions altogether.

His sensational claims about his own identity further weakened his credibility. He once again declared himself to be Jesus Christ and claimed that the Vatican and world order needed to recognize him. These statements raised serious concerns about his psychological state among the court and prosecutors. The fact that Ağca's new statements contradicted his earlier ones strengthened theories that his testimony may have been manipulated or influenced by external forces.

Defense attorneys of the defendants present at the hearing emphasized that Ağca's statements were unreliable and full of contradictions. Bulgarian and Soviet officials once again denied any involvement in the assassination plot, asserting that Ağca had been influenced by certain groups in prison and that a narrative aimed at blaming the Soviet Union was being constructed in the West.

Ağca's inability to provide clear information about the people involved in smuggling the weapon used in the assassination was another point that cast doubt on the truthfulness of his testimony. Furthermore, Licio Gelli's lawyer, Maurizio di Pietropaolo, stated that Ağca was mentally unwell and his allegations should not be taken seriously.

General Course and Outcome of the Trial

The June 15, 1985 hearing went down in history as a session that significantly questioned Ağca's credibility. His statements sparked serious doubts about whether they were part of an international conspiracy or merely products of his imagination.

This hearing reignited the debate over how reliable Ağca was as a witness in the Pope assassination case. His constantly shifting narrative made the trial even more complicated and obscured the truth behind the assassination attempt. In the subsequent process, the lack of any concrete evidence to support Ağca's claims further weakened his assertions.

Ağca's Bulgaria Allegation

One of the most notable claims made by Ağca in court was that the assassination was carried out by an organization linked to Bulgaria and the Turkish mafia. He said these groups specifically prepared him for the attack in Rome and that the Turkish mafia consistently supported him after breaking him out of prison in Istanbul.

However, inconsistencies were found in Ağca's testimony. During the trial, he claimed to personally know three Bulgarian officials involved in the plot. Before identifying them from a photo album, he gave detailed descriptions of each. Judges believed that such details could not have been learned from the media and took his words seriously. Nevertheless, defense lawyers suggested that Ağca could have learned these details from various sources and that his testimony may have been directed.

Ağca also mentioned a truck departing from the Bulgarian Embassy in Rome that was part of his planned escape. This truck was considered part of a plan by Bulgarian officials to help Ağca flee the country after the assassination. However, this claim could not be substantiated in court.

After the assassination attempt on Pope John Paul II, Mehmet Ali Ağca pointed to an international conspiracy in his courtroom statements. Having been serving a life sentence since 1981, Ağca hoped to gain a pardon by emphasizing the Bulgarian connection. But as the process continued, the forces behind the assassination appeared increasingly complex.

According to Ağca, the organizers were not just Bulgaria and the Soviets but also intelligence agencies and political interest groups in the Western world. He argued that no government—neither the Soviet Union, the U.S., nor the Vatican—wanted the Bulgarians to be convicted. Therefore, he claimed that a "political solution" was necessary for his safety and release. From that point on, the case became more obscure. Ağca began making contradictory statements that undermined his credibility without withdrawing his original confession. When cross-examined by Prosecutor Antonio Marini, Ağca admitted that some of his statements were true but later retracted them. His claim of being Jesus Christ created the impression that he was deliberately trying to mislead the court and divert attention elsewhere.

Soviet Union's Reaction During the Trial
Moscow-TASS: "This Slander Poisoning Relations with Italy Must End"

The official news agency TASS in Moscow responded strongly to the accusations against the Bulgarians, warning the Italian government:

"The Soviet Union expects this disgusting fabrication, which aims to poison the international atmosphere and damage relations between Italy, the USSR, and other socialist countries, to end. The sooner this happens, the better."

This marked the first official statement by the Soviet government since the beginning of the events related to the assassination attempt on the Pope. TASS's message was seen as a firm and official stance towards Italian authorities. Soviet officials regarded the Rome trial and Ağca's statements as "false allegations and a political provocation fabricated by Western intelligence services."

According to the TASS statement, the Soviet Union claimed that Ağca's statements were baseless and a "series of lies supported by Western intelligence services like the CIA."

The announcement marked a shift to a new phase in response to the recent intensification of media campaigns, especially following Judge Martella's investigation and the start of the Rome trial. Until then, Soviet denials of the trial's legitimacy had only appeared in press articles or through the newly formed "Solidarity with Antonov Committee" in Moscow. Now, the Soviets officially broke their silence.

This statement from the Soviet Union came at a critical stage of the trial and aimed to prevent the production of "new and terrifying accusations against countries."

The TASS statement emphasized that these accusations were completely unfounded and "directed by certain Western intelligence services," describing the trial as having "turned into a disgraceful legal process." It stressed that the court in Rome repeatedly presented "false testimony, slanders, and fabrications," which "provoked great anger among Soviet and international public opinion."

Moreover, TASS responded directly to Ağca's allegations against the Soviet Union, particularly those involving alleged contacts with Soviet diplomats in Sofia, firmly denying them.

The statement included: **"The absurd fantasies of such a pathological liar are being put on display. And yet, in Rome, he is provided a platform to spread these lies. It is also clear that this is being done because of support from certain overseas circles."**

At the end of its statement, TASS addressed the Italian government directly: **"Do the authorities in Rome not realize how damaging these accusations are to the country's reputation?"**

Emanuela Orlandi's Kidnapping and the Assassination Connection

Ağca claimed during the trial that the kidnapping of Emanuela Orlandi, the daughter of a Vatican employee, led his accomplices to use her against him. According to his statements, his accomplices claimed Orlandi's safety was contingent upon Ağca's release. Ağca said this incident prompted him to "tone down" his accusations against the Bulgarians. However, these claims could not be supported with concrete evidence. The news of Orlandi's abduction was published in Italy on June 25, 1983. Then, on June 28, Ağca said he wanted to meet with Judge Ilario Martella and admitted to fabricating the story of a meeting held at Sergei Antonov's apartment. This raised serious questions about the credibility of Ağca's statements.

Ağca's New Allegations Regarding Italian Intelligence and Mafia

Mehmet Ali Ağca claimed during his testimony that Francesco Pazienza, allegedly linked to Italian intelligence and the mafia, visited him in prison after the assassination. Ağca said Pazienza tried to persuade him to give statements blaming Bulgaria for the assassination attempt. However, Ağca later changed his statement again, claiming that his previous remarks about Bulgaria were made of his own will and that the country had no connection to the incident.

Another striking claim in Ağca's testimony was that at least three other people were involved in the assassination attempt besides himself. This brought up the possibility that the plot was organized by a wider network than previously thought.

Contradictions in Passport Photo

Ağca had previously said that he traveled to Bulgaria in 1980 using a fake passport. However, in his new testimony, he claimed that the photo on the passport was not his, though it contained his image. This contradiction was met with suspicion by the court. The claim of a passport with his photo but not belonging to him suggested either a deliberate distortion of facts or significant memory gaps.

Inconsistencies in the Escape Plan

Ağca gave different accounts of his escape plan at various times. Initially, he said the plan involved a train, a plane, and a BMW. Later in court, he said the escape vehicle was a Ford Granada rented from Hertz or Europcar. He also frequently changed his narrative regarding the people who helped him in Rome on the day of the assassination and their movements.

Contradictions About Weapon and Vehicle Use

Inconsistencies were also found in his statements about the weapon and escape vehicle. He claimed to have met other defendants for dinner four days before the assassination and left the weapons in the car. In earlier statements, he had said only two people attended the dinner. Also, his claim that the car keys were left in the ignition was considered illogical by the judges and jury.

Changing Narratives About the Plot's Origin

Ağca initially said the plot was organized by Bulgaria. Later, he included the Soviet Union and claimed that orders came from the Soviet Embassy in Bulgaria. Previously, he had dismissed this idea as a conspiracy theory. These changes raised suspicions that Ağca was intentionally altering his statements to serve a political agenda or strengthen his position. The changing narratives about the passport photo, escape plan, weapons, and forces behind the assassination reinforced the possibility that he distorted facts or manipulated information. During the trial, Ağca's inconsistencies were criticized by prosecutors and judges, and his reliability as a witness was widely questioned.

Germany Found No Evidence That Mehmet Ali Ağca Had Lived There

After the assassination attempt on Pope John Paul II, Ağca's movements in Europe and possible supporters were investigated. West German authorities stated that they found no concrete evidence that Ağca had lived in West Germany between his escape from prison in Istanbul in 1979 and his entry into Italy.

Statements from West Germany and Passport Inspection

West German Interior Ministry spokesperson Hendrik Vygen said that the passport Ağca carried in Italy had no German entry stamps and that there were no official records of him entering or exiting West Germany under any known alias. However, Vygen also acknowledged that they could not entirely rule out the possibility that Ağca had entered the country through secret means.

Connections with Right-Wing Turkish Groups

According to Turkish reports, right-wing Turkish groups in West Germany were allegedly in contact with Bonn's internal security agency. West German officials declined to comment on these claims. In the trial of former executives of Turkey's Nationalist Movement Party (MHP) in Ankara, evidence suggested that Ağca might have been connected with right-wing Turkish groups in Europe.

MHP and West German Intelligence Links

As part of the case, a petition was submitted containing a letter written by West German MHP official Enver Altaylı to former MHP leader Alparslan Türkeş. The letter, presented in court, named contacts within West German intelligence and suggested links between Turkish right-wing groups and intelligence services in West Germany.

One notable person mentioned in the letter was Hans-Eckhardt Kannapin, a member of the Christian Democratic Party serving in the Schwalmstadt region of southern Germany. The letter stated that Kannapin would attend a meeting in Cologne in May 1976 and would introduce Altaylı to the Turkish intelligence section in West Germany. However, since Kannapin died in 1980, these claims could not be definitively proven.

Allegations That Ağca May Have Been Hidden in West Germany

West German authorities also considered the possibility that Ağca might have been hiding within the large Turkish community in West Germany. Officials in Bonn stated that some informants had claimed at least 10 times that Ağca was under the protection of right-wing Turkish groups in the country. Following these allegations, Italian Interior Minister Virginio Rognoni met with German Interior Minister Gerhart Baum in Bonn to hold discussions on international terrorism and the assassination attempt.

Structure of Turkish Right-Wing Groups in Western Europe

In 1976, a Turkish court banned the overseas activities of the Nationalist Movement Party (MHP), but the party continued its activities under the new name

"Federation of Democratic Idealist Associations in Europe." Although this federation was officially claimed to be a cultural organization, the federation of worker and church organizations in West Germany accused it of being a front for far-right activities.

The president of the federation, Musa Serdar Çelebi, was tried in Rome in connection with the assassination attempt on the Pope.

Left-wing groups claimed that this federation harbored various far-right individuals, including Mehmet Ali Ağca. However, West German authorities stated that these accusations were not supported by any evidence.

West German officials announced that they had not found any concrete evidence indicating that Mehmet Ali Ağca had lived in West Germany, but they did not rule out the possibility that he may have entered the country through secret means. The allegations regarding the activities of right-wing Turkish groups in Western Europe and their connections with intelligence services remain unclear and largely speculative. Although arrests made in Germany related to right-wing groups suggest their presence, the matter of Mehmet Ali Ağca's movements within Europe and who may have supported him still remains uncertain.

June 24, 1985

"The Madman Act" I Am Jesus, I Raise the Dead

At the hearing held on June 24, Ağca continued to make statements that shocked everyone. In the trial entering its fifth week on Monday, the 27-year-old Ağca, the star witness of the prosecution, moved into what court reporters referred to as "the madman act" following hours of persistent questioning by Judge Severino Santiapichi.

Picture 75 - 76. Ağca's voice transcended the courtroom; his target was no longer just justice but the international balance of power. He had become a silent instrument of interstate bargaining.

Ağca in Court; "I tell you this: I will scientifically resurrect a man who is dead. The Vatican will recognize that I am Jesus Christ," said Ağca. "If you reject me, you, the people of the planet Earth, it will be the final collapse of this world," said Ağca, who had already been sentenced to life imprisonment for shooting and injuring the Pope. "This is the truth that (President) Reagan and the Kremlin must understand. I am a former terrorist, a criminal, but this is the truth," he said, and

added, "I am not a fraud or a madman. Believe me, this final generation of humanity will soon perish. One day, let me speak to humanity."

Clearly irritated by Ağca's mumbling attempts to avoid directly answering questions and his frequent changes to earlier statements, the judge firmly said, "Come on, Ağca, finally tell the truth, for everyone's benefit."

Wearing a sky-blue suit and an open-collared shirt, Ağca, in his shy testimony before the court, claimed that the third Turkish terrorist present in St. Peter's Square during the shooting of the Pope was Ömer Ay. In a previous hearing, Ağca had stated that he had never met the Turkish terrorist Ay, who had been arrested in West Germany and later extradited to Turkey, where he remains in custody. However, this time, Ağca said that the person he identified last week by the codename "Akif" was indeed Ömer Ay. Ağca said that Ay's planned role was to throw two hand grenades into the crowd in the square as "panic bombs" to allow the other two Turks to escape. But no panic bombs were thrown. According to the allegations, another terrorist named Oral Çelik was also present in the square as a backup, and Ömer Ay was also there. Ay is not among the defendants on trial, but the court was trying to bring him to the Rome court as a witness.

Ağca angered the judge again by changing his story about how he, Çelik, and Ömer Ay came to Rome a few days before the attack on the Pope, in early May 1981. Ağca had previously stated that they flew to Rome from Munich, Germany, but in this hearing, he told the judge they came by car.

With every word Ağca spoke, the case became more complicated.

Italian Prosecutor: Ağca Is Sabotaging the Trial

As the trial neared its conclusion, Prosecutor Antonio Marini claimed there was sufficient evidence that the assassination attempt was part of a Bulgarian and Soviet conspiracy, but that the state's key witness, Ağca, was trying to sabotage the trial. These claims by Marini were seen as one of the most critical stages of the case.

In the final session, Prosecutor Marini asserted that based on circumstantial evidence admissible in Italian court, Bulgaria was involved in the conspiracy. Meanwhile, the testimonies of two Turkish witnesses questioned by a court in Turkey were also added to the case. According to these witnesses, it was claimed that the Bulgarians paid Mehmet Ali Ağca for the Pope's assassination on the orders of Abuzer Uğurlu, a significant figure in the Turkish underworld. The prosecutor argued that this showed the Bulgarian secret service played a key role in the incident.

Defense Lawyers' Objections

Adolfo Larussa, the lawyer representing the Bulgarian defendants, argued that Marini first needed to prove the existence of a conspiracy and then examine each defendant's involvement individually. The defense argued that the claims were largely based on speculation and emphasized the lack of concrete and independent evidence.

Ağca's Testimony and the Course of the Case

Marini tried to explain the contradictory statements Ağca had made during the eight-month-long trial. Referring to Ağca's statements on November 5 in court, the prosecutor noted that while Ağca initially claimed he planned the assassination alone, he later began accusing Bulgaria. The prosecutor alleged that Ağca's accusations against the Bulgarians were part of a blackmail attempt to secure his escape from prison in Italy.

Marini also submitted the results of psychiatric tests conducted on Ağca in Turkey, rejecting claims about his mental health. According to the prosecutor, Ağca deliberately tried to destroy his own credibility over time and aimed to deliberately mislead the court.

The trial prosecutor continued to accuse Ağca of intentionally misleading the court and remained angry with him. At the beginning of the trial in May, Ağca had introduced himself as Jesus and predicted the end of the world, and was accused of deliberately trying to confuse the court. When the hearings resumed after the summer break, Ağca rarely attended the court sessions.

Prosecutor Marini also suggested that Ağca might be connected to the 1983 kidnapping of Emanuela Orlandi, the daughter of a Vatican employee. The kidnappers sent messages claiming they would guarantee the girl's safety in exchange for Ağca's release, which Marini considered a possible direct link to the assassination attempt.

According to Marini, in one of the hearings Ağca said, "Of course I failed, and I want to give up the double game," attempting to discredit both the Bulgarians and the Western media's portrayal of the Soviet Union and Bulgaria as the main actors of terrorism.

During his closing arguments, Prosecutor Antonio Marini emphasized the contradictions in Mehmet Ali Ağca's statements and the evidence of the conspiracy, trying to prove that Bulgaria and the Turkish underworld were behind the assassination attempt. However, the heavy reliance on witness testimony and the lack of solid evidence made the outcome of the case uncertain. Whether the final verdict would uncover the mysteries behind the Pope's assassination attempt or leave many questions unanswered would become clear in the coming days.

Ağca's Manipulation Strategy

After the assassination attempt on Pope John Paul II, Mehmet Ali Ağca drew attention with his statements and the way he used the media. He used the press both as a tool for manipulation and to give the impression of creating public support in his favour.

The American Press and Ağca's Letters:

In a letter dated August 5, 1983, it was mentioned that Ağca tried to establish contact with the American Embassy. Although the letter stated that the embassy had no contact with Ağca, he used the media to spread his story and create the impression of a relationship with the U.S.

In another letter dated September 18, 1982, he claimed

to have given the press officer at the American Embassy in Rome information about Soviet plans to overthrow the Ayatollah Khomeini's regime. This may have been an attempt to show proximity to America and to obtain some form of conditional protection or support.

Hope for Release and Media Strategy:

While in prison, Ağca adopted different approaches depending on political developments outside. At the time, he believed some circles were seeking a political solution rather than a legal one to get him out of prison, so he tried to influence the public agenda through the media to strengthen his position.

To support this strategy, he cited incidents such as Bulgaria taking two Italian tourists hostage in 1983–1984, suggesting a possible swap in exchange for the release of Bulgarian defendant Sergei I. Antonov.

Shaping Public Opinion and Playing Both Sides:

In court, Ağca continuously made contradictory statements, but used this as a strategic move. Phrases such as "I was only acting based on external conditions" and "I had to play all my cards" showed he was not cornered and was still trying to create bargaining power.

Ağca's attempts to give the impression that the American bureaucracy was interested in him show he was trying to influence public opinion through the media.

The Relevance of the Press and Ağca's Attitude:

Ağca's efforts to manipulate through the media showed that he closely followed newspapers and other media sources. However, when the judge referred to a report published in an Italian newspaper, Ağca could not hide his surprise and said, "Was it published?", revealing some gaps in the media narrative he sought to control.

Picture: 77. AGCA OFFERS TO PERFORM A RESURRECTION FOR REAGAN AND U.N. CHIEF. By John Tagliabue, Special To the New York Times. June 25, 1985

Mehmet Ali Ağca actively used and manipulated the press both for political and personal gain. He used the power of media in various strategies to shape his story, gain support from certain circles, and influence public opinion. However, over time, this strategy, riddled with contradictory statements and distortions of the truth, undermined his credibility and raised questions about whether he was truly a master manipulator.

One of the documents made public by the CIA in 2011 contains the extraordinary statements made by Mehmet Ali Ağca in court.[25] The document notes that Ağca declared himself the Messiah and offered to resurrect a dead person in front of Reagan and the UN Secretary-General. These statements raised questions about his psychological condition and his role in the assassination attempt. Ağca's varying testimonies increased doubts about whether he was truly part of an intelligence operation. In the documents released by the CIA, it is seen that Ağca's statements were contradictory and that he retracted some of his claims.

The Defendants' Behavior and State of Mind During the Trial

The mental state displayed by the defendants in court and their demeanor during the hearings were among the factors that influenced the course of the case. Particularly, Ağca's contradictory statements occasionally shook trust in the court, while other defendants also reacted differently during this historic trial.

Mehmet Ali Ağca: Contradictory Statements and Strange Behavior

During the hearings, Ağca at times described himself as "Jesus Christ," made mystical comments about world order, and shouted in court, significantly undermining his credibility. Prosecutors especially questioned whether Ağca's behavior was a deliberate strategy to sabotage the case.

---

25 Source: CIA-RDP90-00965R000706600018-7, Declassified CIA Documents, 2011." (See CIA-RDP90-00965R000706600018-7)."

Sergei Antonov: Confusion and a Defensive Stance

Sergei Antonov, the head of the Rome office of Bulgarian Airlines, was arrested for allegedly assisting in the assassination plot. In court, Antonov appeared tense and shaky, denying the charges against him. When questioned by the judge, he shouted in his defense: **"I've never seen this man (Ağca), never talked to him!"**

He frequently rubbed his hands, avoided eye contact, and spoke with a trembling voice, clearly showing the intense pressure and fear he was under. During his defense, the issue of Antonov's lack of English proficiency became a major point of contention. The judge questioned how an international airline executive could operate without knowing English. Antonov explained that he had learned some basic phrases by writing them in a notebook, but this explanation was found unsatisfactory.

Other Defendants: Shifting Between Fear and Anger

Different moods were observed among other defendants during the trial. While Ömer Bağcı and Musa Serdar Çelebi approached the court calmly, some defendants fluctuated between fear and anger. Defendants like Bekir Çelenk firmly denied the charges, but Italian authorities insisted that he provided financial support for the assassination plot. Oral Çelik and other defendants denied the allegations and attempted to present themselves as "victims of a conspiracy." However, due to the evidence and conflicting statements presented by the prosecution, their claims of innocence were called into question.

Ağca's Strategy in Court: Evasive Answers and Diversion Tactics

Initial Hearings: Calm and Manipulative

In the initial hearings, Mehmet Ali Ağca exhibited a very composed and calm attitude. Rather than displaying the panic or strong defense usually expected from an assassination suspect, Ağca appeared confident and manipulative.

Example:

When the judge asked Ağca how he had planned the assassination, Ağca did not give a clear answer; instead, he made statements implying that global powers were behind the assassination:

"This was not just my decision. It was planned by those who rule the world."

Guided and Contradictory Statements

When asked in court who had orchestrated the assassination, Ağca initially pointed to Bulgarian intelligence, but later failed to provide any concrete evidence to support this. In fact, he was eventually acquitted of the charges related to Bulgaria.

- In his first statement, he claimed that the KGB had supported him.
- In later statements, he suggested that the CIA might have been involved.
- In subsequent hearings, he changed his story again, claiming the assassination was entirely his own initiative.

Example:
Judge: "Who ordered this assassination?"
Ağca: "This wasn't something I could do alone. If I reveal

the truth, the world order will collapse."

One of his most notable strategies was continuously pointing to different organizations in court in an attempt to steer the prosecution's investigation.

Ağca's "Messiah" Claim: A Deliberate Tactic?

One of the most striking moments in the trial was when Ağca declared himself the "Messiah."

Example:

- During one hearing, he shouted, **"I am the Messiah, the end of the world is near!"**, stunning the court.

Was this a sign of psychological illness, or a calculated move to divert media attention? These statements helped portray him as unstable and enabled him to manipulate the court. If he were mentally unfit, it would also call into question the credibility of his other statements.

Legal Evaluation:

This outburst can be interpreted as one of the strategies a defendant might use to seek a reduced sentence through a psychological defense. Ağca's Italian lawyer made noteworthy comments regarding his mental health in an effort to influence the court. However, his later retraction of these claims suggests it may have all been a tactic.

Strategies to Prolong the Trial and Conceal the Truth

Ağca appeared intent on deliberately prolonging the trial. He avoided giving clear answers and presented a new story at each hearing. He constantly introduced new allegations to steer the investigation.

Example:
- In one of the 1985 hearings, he claimed that a secret Vatican conspiracy was behind the assassination.
- Later, without presenting any concrete evidence, he began accusing a different organization.

This behavior suggested he was simply trying to protect himself and was continually changing the narrative to hide the true perpetrators.

What Did Ağca's Court Strategy Reveal?
A review of Ağca's defense reveals several key conclusions:Throughout the trial, he continuously changed the narrative and tried to steer the case. When asked who incited him, he gave contradictory answers and failed to provide clear explanations. At times, he distracted attention by claiming to be the Messiah and employed psychological manipulation. He prolonged the trial with ever-changing allegations, but never provided real evidence to support them.

So what was the goal of these tactics?
- To protect the real accomplices?
- To cast doubt on his mental health and reduce his sentence?
- Or simply to manipulate the court, the media, and public opinion?

While these questions remain unanswered, Ağca's behavior in court indicated that he was acting in a calculated manner.

Deputy Prosecutor Niccolo Amoto, who investigated the case, ultimately stated:
"Ağca talks a lot but says nothing."

Mehmet Ali Ağca's Statements

Ağca's statements changed over time and became increasingly contradictory. From the very beginning, he claimed to have acted alone in the assassination attempt, but no one believed him. Over time, his statements emphasizing involvement in an international conspiracy became more prominent. However, some experts argue that Ağca's statements were influenced by intelligence services and that he spoke according to a pre-determined script after being captured.

Some notable statements include:

- "I was alone, but they didn't believe me."
- "I met with Bulgarian intelligence in Sofia and received support from them."
- "I'm sure I shot the Pope, but I couldn't continue because someone pulled me back."
- "Oral Çelik was part of the plan and was supposed to detonate a bomb, but he didn't."

These contradictory statements raise questions about whether Ağca was speaking on his own or was being guided according to a script.

Ağca's Belief That He Could Escape from Prison

Ağca believed he would not remain in prison for long after the assassination attempt. Several reasons supported this belief:

- **Intelligence Agency Games:** It is alleged that Ağca believed he would be protected according to a certain plan before or after the assassination.
- **Bribery or Swap Plans:** Ağca expressed that a large bribe could be paid to authorities for

his release or that he could be exchanged for someone who would be kidnapped.

- **Waiving His Appeal:** His decision not to appeal the life sentence handed down on July 22, 1981, showed his confidence that he would receive outside help.
- **Hunger Strike Threat:** On July 20, 1981, in court, he threatened to start a hunger strike within five months if his demands were not met, even specifying the date—December 20, 1981. This was interpreted as a signal sent to the outside world.

These findings indicate that Ağca believed he would receive external support and that, despite the failed assassination, a plan was in place to free him from prison.

Was Ağca a Lone Wolf?

The assassination attempt on Pope John Paul II was too complex to be viewed as the act of a single individual. However, whether Ağca acted alone remains a matter of debate. Some sources argue he was part of a conspiracy, while others claim he was manipulated and forced to speak according to a scenario by intelligence services after his arrest.

Although the Italian prosecution claimed Ağca was involved in a conspiracy, some experts disagreed. According to an alternative view, Ağca was indeed a lone attacker but was manipulated by intelligence agencies afterward and forced to follow a scripted narrative.

- **Changing Testimonies:** Ağca's varying statements over time suggest he may have been dictated a specific scenario.
- **Intelligence Wars:** It is claimed that during the

Cold War era, the assassination attempt was exploited by major powers for political purposes.
- **Manipulation Theory:** Ağca may have carried out the attack on the Vatican alone, but was later used as a political tool by intelligence agencies.

According to this perspective, Ağca was a lone wolf but was turned into a political weapon by intelligence services after the event. Especially the Western world used this assassination attempt as a propaganda tool against the Soviet Union and the Eastern Bloc. Pope John Paul II's Polish origin and his strong stance against the Soviet Union necessitated that the event be interpreted in the Cold War context. His support for the Solidarity (Solidarność) movement in Poland made the Soviets see this movement as a major threat.

Although the claims that the Soviet Union supported the assassination were strongly defended by the U.S. and Western media, they were never backed by solid evidence. Ağca's statements changed over time, and the true forces behind the assassination have still not been fully revealed. While the full identity of the actors behind the attempt remains unclear, considering the Gladio structure, Italian intelligence, and international political dynamics, the possibility that the event was part of a much larger operation rather than an individual act becomes more likely. The question of whether Mehmet Ali Ağca acted alone or was part of a manipulation process remains a controversial issue.

Outcome of the Pope Assassination Trial: Rulings and Detailed Judgments

Decision of the Italian Judiciary and the Reaction of Defense Lawyers

The defendants were accused of being accomplices of Ağca in the planning, procurement of weapons, and financing of the assassination. The indictment claimed that the assassination was not merely an individual act by Ağca, but an international conspiracy in which the Bulgarian secret service played a direct role.

The trial, involving seven Bulgarians and Turks accused of aiding Mehmet Ali Ağca in the assassination attempt on the Pope, was nearing its end. Prosecutor Antonio Marini presented his evidence related to the conspiracy and summarized his claims. Among the evidence were:

- Ağca's confession that the Bulgarians paid him for the assassination,

- Indirect evidence that Bulgarian agents in Rome planned the attack,

- Supporting testimonies from members of the Turkish-Bulgarian smuggling mafia.

Marini emphasized that the evidence for this conspiracy was obtained "independently of Ağca's statements." He warned the judge and jury not to be misled by "deceptive lies and intrigues." Marini also provided his interpretation of why Ağca gave contradictory statements in court. According to the prosecutor, at the beginning of the trial, Ağca declared himself to be Jesus and predicted the end of the world, trying to buy time for the Bulgarians to somehow rescue him. Previously, in June 1983, the daughter of a Vatican employee had been kidnapped, and ransom notes had demanded Ağca's release. This led Ağca to believe that the Bulgarians were still trying to save him. Prosecutor Marini quoted Ağca as saying: "They wanted to force me to retract my statements by accusing me. They wanted me to confuse the trial process, and my task was to undermine the credibility of the Western press." However, according to Marini, Ağca failed in this game and eventually said, "I want to stop this double game."

After a deliberation lasting 6.5 hours and a trial that spanned nearly four years, the Italian court announced its verdict on March 30, 1986: In what was called the "trial of the century" against the Kremlin, if it could have been proven that the Soviets were involved in the assassination of the Pope, East-West relations would have been seriously endangered. However, the 10-month trial of three Bulgarians and five Turks accused of attempting to assassinate Pope John Paul II fell apart without meeting expectations. The attempt to prove the "Bulgarian connection" collapsed due to insufficient evidence, weak prosecution work, and the bizarre behavior of the main witness, Mehmet Ali Ağca. One major shortcoming of the trial process was the provision of a Rome telephone directory to Ağca during the hearing, which gave him the opportunity to support his claims of personal connections with the Bulgarians.

Three Bulgarians and three Turks tried in connection with the assassination attempt on Pope John Paul II were acquitted by the Italian court due to lack of evidence. The court stated that the evidence presented was insufficient to definitively convict the defendants. However, this acquittal did not equate to full exoneration under Italian law; that is, the court ruled that the defendants could be either guilty or innocent, indicating it could not reach a definite conclusion. In the Italian legal system, such a decision is called "acquittal due to lack of evidence," which means not full proof of innocence, but rather that the available evidence is inadequate.

Defense lawyers argued that the Italian judiciary was too invested in the case and could not give up prosecuting the defendants. Defense attorney Giuseppe Consolo harshly criticized the court by saying, "They created this case and didn't know how to close it." Another prominent defense attorney, Adolfo Larussa, argued that the decision was a half-measure delivered under political pressure on the court.

Convicted Defendants and Sentences

Although an acquittal was given for conspiracy charges, the court ruled that two Turkish defendants were guilty of arms smuggling and illegal possession of weapons:

- **Mehmet Ali Ağca**: Previously sentenced to life imprisonment for attempting to assassinate Pope John Paul II. However, the court additionally sentenced him to 1 year in prison and 2 months in solitary confinement for helping illegally bring the weapon used in the assassination into Italy.

- **Ömer Bağcı**: Found to have supplied the weapon used by Ağca in the assassination, Bağcı was sentenced to 3 years in prison. However, since he was extradited from Switzerland solely on conspiracy charges, it was stated that this sentence could not be enforced.

The court stated that the defendants had the right to appeal. Prosecutor Antonio Marini announced that he would file an appeal for a review of the decisions concerning the Turkish defendants.

Verdict on Bulgarians and International Reactions
The three acquitted Bulgarian defendants were:

- **Sergei Antonov** (Head of the Rome Station of Bulgarian State Airlines)

- **Todor Aivasov** (Former cashier at the Bulgarian Embassy)

- **Zhelyo Vasilev** (Deputy military attaché at the embassy)

These three individuals were at the center of claims that the Bulgarian secret service played a role in the assassination plan. However, the court acquitted them, stating that Ağca's testimonies were inconsistent and unreliable. Yet, because the acquittal was under "acquittal due to lack of evidence" in Italian law, the court did not fully confirm the innocence of the defendants.

After being released, Sergei Antonov returned to Bulgaria, but the years spent in prison and the psychological pressure he was subjected to took a heavy toll. Doctors diagnosed him with "brain atrophy" and stated that his mental health was seriously damaged. He spent the rest of his life in isolation, living a quiet and withdrawn life. He was found dead in his home in Sofia in August 2007. Antonov's fate was shaped less by his choices and more by the political chess game of great powers. A book titled *The Roman Victim* was published in Bulgaria about him.

The Bulgarian government stated from the outset that it rejected the accusations and interpreted the court's decision as "proof of Bulgaria's innocence." The Bulgarian news agency BTA declared, "This case showed that the efforts of imperialist powers to discredit Bulgaria failed." In 1991, the Bulgarian government officially announced in the U.S. the establishment of an independent international commission that would grant unlimited access to archives in Bulgaria regarding the assassination attempt on the Pope.

Other Acquitted Turkish Defendants

- **Musa Serdar Çelebi**: One of the leaders of the ultranationalist movement in Europe, Çelebi was acquitted due to lack of evidence.
- **Oral Çelik**: Allegedly a second gunman in the assassination attempt, Çelik was tried in absentia and acquitted.
- **Bekir Çelenk**: Described as a Turkish mafia leader, Çelenk was accused of paying Ağca $1.25 million. However, the case was dropped when he died in prison in Turkey during the trial process.

Appeal Process

Mehmet Ali Ağca, through inconsistent and contradictory statements during the trial, weakened the prosecution's hand and caused the case to collapse at its foundation. Claiming to be Jesus Christ several times during the court proceedings, Ağca even declared that the end of the world was near. Such statements were among the factors that undermined the political and legal credibility of the trial.

Since the Italian court had not yet decided on the travel rights of the defendants, the acquitted defendants would not yet be allowed to leave Italy. It was expected that the prosecution would file appeals for some of the defendants. If the court accepted this appeal, the case could be reopened.

A Historical Drama or an International Game?

The case of Mehmet Ali Ağca should be considered not only as a matter of justice but also as a process shaped by the interests of major powers. His statements in court provide important clues not just about a legal proceeding, but about the behind-the-scenes of international balances and intelligence wars.

This case has taken its place in history as a striking example of how international law can be influenced by political interests and how the ideological rivalry of the Cold War impacted individual lives.

The court's decision did not end the debate, particularly since it could not reach a definitive judgment on whether Bulgaria was involved in the assassination attempt. While debates continued in Western countries on whether it was a Kremlin-backed operation, the Italian judiciary failed to reach a legal conclusion.

It was anticipated that diplomatic tensions might arise between the Vatican and Italy following the case. Additionally, countries aligned with Bulgaria and the Soviet Union continued to argue that the verdict was a result of Western anti-communist propaganda. All these developments showed that the case would remain not only a legal issue but also a political one.

"Operation Mockingbird"[26]

Paul B. Henze and Iona Andronov: The Master's Voice and Operation Mockingbird

The Cold War era was a period marked by intense intelligence warfare and propaganda activities. In this context, the mutual accusations between American intelligence expert Paul B. Henze and Soviet journalist Iona Andronov regarding the assassination attempt on the Pope are significant in understanding the information wars of the period. Additionally, the concept of "The Master's Voice" and "Operation Mockingbird," which denotes the CIA's influence over the media, are worth examining to understand the media's role in this struggle.

---

26 Operation Mockingbird: During the Cold War, the CIA engaged in manipulation of various media outlets to shape public opinion. Operation Mockingbird is known as a program in which the CIA took control of 25 major media outlets and journalists for propaganda purposes. As part of this operation, these media outlets broadcast news aligned with US foreign policy objectives and manipulated public opinion.

Picture 79 – 80. Cold War Spokespersons: Andronov and Henze ... The papal assassination trial has become more of an intelligence war than a courtroom. Iona Andronov, acting as the voice of the Soviets, accused the CIA, while Paul Henze argued that the Soviets were behind the assassination. One was a mask for the East, the other for the West. The papal assassination trial has moved from the courtroom to the media war between the intelligence agencies. Is it true? They were merely pawns in this war.

Paul B. Henze and Iona Andronov: The Assassination and Information Wars

Paul B. Henze is known as an intelligence expert connected to the U.S. Central Intelligence Agency (CIA). In his book *The Plot to Kill the Pope*, written about the 1981 assassination attempt on Pope John Paul II, he claimed that the Soviet Union and Bulgaria were behind the incident. Henze used various media outlets to get this thesis accepted by American and Western public opinion. On the other hand, Soviet journalist Iona Andronov, in his work *On the Wolf's Track*, accused Henze of being the planner of the assassination and claimed that the U.S. was involved in the event. According to Andronov, the assassination attempt was part of a psychological war waged by the U.S. to demonize Eastern Bloc countries. These mutual accusations serve as a critical example of the media wars and manipulation of information during the period.

The Spokesmen of the Pope Assassination and the Effect on Trials

The 1981 assassination attempt on Pope John Paul II was not just an attack but also the beginning of a media and propaganda war during the Cold War. American intelligence expert Paul Henze and Soviet journalist Iona Andronov practically became spokesmen of the assassination in an attempt to sway global opinion. Henze, an American intelligence expert and author, wrote *The Plot to Kill the Pope*, in which he claimed the Soviet Union and Bulgaria were behind the attack. Conversely, Soviet journalist Andronov, in *On the Wolf's Track*, accused Henze of orchestrating the attack and claimed the U.S. had a hand in it.

Paul Henze: Spokesman of the Western Bloc

Paul Henze[27] was an expert working for U.S. intelligence at the time, and his views on the assassination reflected the White House's stance. Following the assassination attempt, Henze proposed that it was planned by the Soviet Union and the KGB-backed Bulgarian intelligence service. This came to be known as the "Bulgarian Thesis." According to Henze's claims, Pope John Paul II was targeted by the Soviets for supporting the anti-communist Solidarity movement in Poland. The KGB allegedly supported and approved the assassination via the Bulgarian secret service and Mehmet Ali Ağca. The assassination was portrayed as part of the Soviets' strategy to maintain their influence in the West. This view was especially accepted and heavily promoted by the U.S. government and Western media, being used as a tool in the West's ideological war against the Soviets.

Iona Andronov:[28] Spokesman of the Eastern Bloc

Iona Andronov worked as a journalist for *Literaturnaya Gazeta*, one of the Soviet Union's prominent publications. At the time, the Soviet press dismissed the West's allegations regarding the Pope assassination as fabrications

---

27 Paul Henze (1924-2011) was an American historian, author, diplomat, and intelligence expert. He played a key role in US intelligence and foreign policy during the Cold War. He is particularly known for his connections with the CIA and his work on Turkey, the Caucasus, and Central Asia. In the post-Cold War era, he prepared reports on Turkey for think tanks like the RAND Corporation to consolidate Türkiye's position as a strategic ally of the US.

28 Iona Ionovich Andronov (1934-2024) – Journalist, Author, and Politician Iona Andronov began her career as a journalist and became a prominent investigative journalist in the Soviet Union. She is particularly known for her work on political and intelligence matters.

orchestrated by the CIA, with Andronov playing a key role in this propaganda effort. Newspapers were filled with news and articles supporting Andronov's thesis. According to Andronov, it wasn't the Soviets or Bulgaria behind the assassination, but Western intelligence services. Due to Ağca's connections with far-right groups, the plot traced back to the U.S. Andronov argued that the West was waging psychological warfare against the Soviets using the assassination. Through his published articles in the Soviet Union, Andronov became one of the leading figures shaping the Eastern Bloc's official response to Western accusations. He maintained that the CIA had the power to manipulate such assassinations and that evidence could be conveniently manufactured by the West.

The Pope Assassination Trials and the Struggle of Narratives

The narratives of Paul Henze and Iona Andronov directly influenced the trial process and public opinion regarding the Pope's assassination. In 1983, Mehmet Ali Ağca claimed in an Italian court that the Soviets and Bulgarians were behind the assassination. In 1985, a trial was launched against individuals allegedly connected to Bulgarian agents. However, in 1986, the Italian Court of Assizes acquitted the Bulgarian agents due to insufficient evidence. This ruling was seen as validating Andronov's thesis, as the court determined that Henze's "Bulgarian Thesis" lacked legal proof.

Paul Henze and Iona Andronov went down in history as figures who showed that the Pope's assassination was not merely an individual act but became part of a major propaganda war during the Cold War.

The West Won Propaganda, The East Won the Trial

In the propaganda war over the Pope's assassination, the Western Bloc won the psychological battle due to its more powerful and effective media influence. By the early 1980s, the Western public had been covertly persuaded that the Soviets were behind the assassination. The West succeeded in influencing public opinion and waging psychological warfare against the Soviets. The Eastern Bloc, on the other hand, came out clean from a legal perspective due to the acquittal of the Bulgarian agents and the absence of evidence in Soviet archives.

The West Won the Propaganda War: Through media influence
The East Won the Legal Battle: Due to the acquittal of the Bulgarians.

However, in propaganda wars, perception is often stronger than legal truths. The trial process surrounding this assassination went down in history as one of the Cold War's most impactful psychological operations.

What Was the Truth?

During the trials, no conclusive evidence was presented to prove that the Soviets orchestrated the assassination, but the U.S. and the Western Bloc continued to use Henze's claims for Cold War propaganda for years. Even today, the Pope assassination remains a historical example of how information wars and intelligence games unfold. Despite ongoing debates, Western propaganda victories have left a lingering public suspicion regarding Soviet involvement. In this context, intelligence-connected figures like Paul B. Henze influenced public opinion by using the media and framed specific events in line with their political agendas. Similarly, the Soviet Union engaged in the information war by using its own media outlets to accuse the West.

In conclusion, the mutual accusations between Paul B. Henze and Iona Andronov offer a significant example of how information became weaponized during the Cold War. In a process where media independence was questioned, concepts such as "The Master's Voice" and the CIA's "Operation Mockingbird" are essential to understanding the global dimensions of information wars. Media manipulation and propaganda activities continue to this day.

Mehmet Ali Ağca: CIA, the Bulgarian Link, and Assassination Allegations

Covert Action Magazine and an Alternative Perspective

After the assassination attempt, *Covert Action*, a major publication of the American alternative press, examined the issue in depth. The magazine claimed that the assassination was purely a "Turkish operation" and that the Bulgarians had no involvement. Writers in the magazine argued that the CIA used the incident to accuse the Soviet secret service, the KGB. Analysts such as Claire Sterling and Paul Henze, known to be linked to the CIA, supported the "Bulgarian Connection" theory, which was allegedly rooted in Cold War propaganda operations. *Covert Action* also claimed that the Italian judicial system and Judge Martella were pressured by the CIA.

The Bulgarian Connection and Lack of Evidence

Despite the "Bulgarian Connection" theory

gaining traction in the Western press, no concrete evidence was ever presented to prove a direct link between Ağca and Bulgarian agents. Western intelligence agencies' efforts to associate Bulgaria with the event were allegedly aimed at weakening the Soviet Union and the Eastern Bloc internationally. The magazine stated:

"The Bulgarian Connection thesis found great support in the West within the framework of Cold War ideology. However, no solid evidence was ever presented to link Ağca to the Bulgarians or the Bulgarians to the assassination."

Covert Action claimed the event was the result of a two-stage conspiracy:

1. The far-right Turkish group "Grey Wolves" helped Ağca escape from prison and provided financial and logistical support.
2. Italian intelligence, the CIA, and certain Western political forces ran an organized propaganda operation to link the assassination to Bulgaria.

Connections in Sofia and Missing Evidence

Although some reports suggested Ağca had been in Sofia, no definitive link to the assassination could be proven. Ağca admitted to having visited 12 countries besides Sofia, but noted that only Bulgaria was singled out. According to the magazine's analysis, the dominant belief in the West that "Bulgaria could not act independently of the Soviets" intensified focus on Bulgaria and raised suspicions of Kremlin involvement. However, there was no solid intelligence report confirming Ağca's stay in Bulgaria or a hotel record at the Vitosha Hotel.

The Geopolitical Dynamics Behind the Assassination

Western analysts claimed that Pope John Paul II was targeted by the Soviets for supporting the Solidarity movement in Poland. However, *Covert Action* questioned this assertion, emphasizing the lack of concrete evidence to support the idea that the Soviets directly approved such an initiative.

Picture 81. The Queen of Propaganda: Claire Sterling, a journalist and author who allegedly had close ties to the CIA, was one of the most ardent proponents of the "Bulgarian Connection" theory. She sought to prove that Soviet and Bulgarian intelligence were behind the assassination. But was her narrative true or a massive Cold War manipulation? That question still lingers in the shadows.

Claire Sterling, the CIA, and the Pope Assassination Case

An important American journalist closely followed Ağca's trials: Claire Sterling (1919–1995), known for her research on international crime syndicates, terrorism, and intelligence operations. In her book *The Terror Network*

(1980s), she claimed the Soviet Union had links to terrorist organizations worldwide. These claims caused a stir in the U.S. and helped shape Cold War propaganda in the West. Sterling also wrote *The Time of the Assassins*, alleging that the Soviet Union and Bulgaria were behind Mehmet Ali Ağca's assassination attempt on Pope John Paul II. The book sparked broad discussion in the West, though some critics claimed Sterling was engaged in CIA-backed propaganda.

Sterling's writings significantly influenced the Western public's understanding of the political context surrounding the assassination. Arguing that the Pope's Polish origins and support for the anti-communist "Solidarity" movement made him a Soviet target, she shaped public and judicial perspectives in Italy.

Sterling's Claims and Judicial Ambiguity

Sterling's writings contributed to elevating the Pope assassination case to an international issue. Claiming the Soviet Union and Eastern Bloc countries were behind the attempt, she aligned her narrative with Ağca's court testimony—but this was never fully substantiated with conclusive evidence. The jury stated that Ağca's statements were insufficient to fully reveal the background of the assassination. His testimony was inconsistent, and the possibility of manipulation by Western intelligence remained. In the end, a "suspicious" verdict was reached, and the true masterminds behind the assassination were never identified.

Sterling's Book *The Time of the Assassins*

Claire Sterling's *The Time of the Assassins* explores the assassination attempt on Pope John Paul II and its international connections. Sterling argues that Ağca did not act alone and was directed by Bulgarian intelligence and, indirectly, the Soviet Union. While she admits that direct evidence linking Moscow may not exist, she points to indirect evidence supporting the connection. The book follows a detective-story format and unfolds the narrative step by step. Though it presents significant claims about the assassination and its international links, the book relies more on interpretations and indirect clues than on definitive proof. Critics highlight its academic shortcomings and bias, questioning its credibility. While it can be considered a historical resource, it should be weighed against other perspectives.

Contradictions in Ağca's Testimony and CIA Links

Writers such as Edward Jay Epstein, Paul B. Henze, and Claire Sterling analyzed Ağca's statements to investigate the connections behind the assassination. Sterling and Henze argued that the attack was orchestrated by the Soviet Union and Bulgarian intelligence. They based their claims on three findings:

1. Ağca's escape from prison was supported by Turkish criminal networks.
2. These support groups were based in Bulgaria.
3. Bulgarian crime syndicates had ties to the Soviet Union.

However, Epstein and other critics emphasized that these arguments were based only on indirect links and lacked direct evidence. The CIA's inability to conclusively prove the Bulgarian connection rendered Sterling's theory controversial.

Picture 82. This article is compiled from documents released by the CIA under FOIA, Wall Street Journal articles, and international intelligence reports. The "Bulgarian Nexus" theory is considered one of the greatest intelligence battles of the Cold War. However, not all allegations related to the case have been definitively proven and are open to varying interpretations based on historical documents and deposition transcripts. For more information, the original documents can be viewed at the CIA Reading Room.

The Bulgarian Connection and CIA Documents: The Conspiracy Behind the Mehmet Ali Ağca Assassination Attempt

The "Bulgarian Connection" theory, which emerged

following the assassination attempt, led to one of the greatest intelligence crises of the Cold War era among the U.S., Soviet Union, and NATO countries. Documents published by the CIA contain striking details about the origins of this conspiracy.

The Bulgarian Connection Theory and CIA Documents

A CIA report[29] based on an article published in *The Wall Street Journal* on February 12, 1986, claims that Ağca carried out the assassination attempt with financial support from Bulgarian agents. Among the pieces of evidence presented by Prosecutor Antonio Marini during the trial were:

- Ağca's confession that he received money from Bulgarian agents,
- Indirect evidence suggesting that Bulgarian intelligence planned the assassination in Rome,
- Evidence indicating that the Turkish-Bulgarian mafia network contributed to the assassination process.

However, it is stated that these claims are largely based on indirect evidence and witness testimonies. Since Italian courts place greater emphasis on circumstantial evidence compared to U.S. courts, arguments supporting the Bulgarian link were more strongly emphasized in the trial.

Ağca's Contradictory Statements and Manipulations

Throughout the process, Mehmet Ali Ağca's statements constantly changed. At the start of the trial,

29 Source URL: https://www.cia.gov/readingroom/document/cia-rdp90-00965r000201340001-4Document Publication Date: February 10, 2012Sequence Number: 1Case Number: Publication Date: February 12, 1985Content Type: OPEN SOURCE

Ağca declared himself to be "Jesus" and later predicted the end of the world, claiming Bulgarian agents would try to save him. In 1983, Ağca also linked the kidnapping of a Vatican employee's daughter to the assassination trial, asserting that the Soviets and Bulgarians were trying to rescue him. However, over time, he changed these claims in contradictory ways.

According to Prosecutor Marini, Ağca's accomplices asked him to:

- Withdraw his accusations,
- Complicate the trial process,
- Discredit the Western media.

Reports also stated that Ağca declared, "I failed and want to abandon this double game."

The Soviet Union and Counter-Propaganda

After the assassination attempt, the Soviet Union and Eastern Bloc countries claimed that the incident was entirely a manipulation by the CIA and the West. Initially, the Soviet press argued that Ağca acted alone as a "fanatical anti-Christian," later suggesting he was a fascist linked to the Turkish ultranationalist group Grey Wolves.

The Soviets' final claim was that the CIA and Italian intelligence services directed Ağca to carry out the assassination and then coerced him into blaming the Bulgarians. This theory was based on Francesco Pazienza, a former agent of Italy's military intelligence service SISMI. Pazienza had been arrested in the U.S. on fraud charges and was awaiting extradition to Italy.

Pazienza and SISMI's Role

Francesco Pazienza, mentioned in CIA documents, was alleged by Soviet propaganda to be one of the key figures behind the assassination. In its January 15, 1986 edition, the Soviet newspaper *Literaturnaya Gazeta* claimed, "Before being arrested in the U.S., Pazienza hid important documents about the Pope assassination in Paris." In a January 29 interview with Pazienza, the same newspaper wrote that he was "reluctant to speak" in U.S. prison.

However, Western media and CIA sources dismissed these claims as "communist propaganda." From 1982 onward, Soviet and Bulgarian press reports claimed that Pazienza had visited Ağca in Ascoli Piceno Prison in Italy and directed him to accuse the Bulgarians.

Prosecutor Marini noted that French lawyer Christian Roulette wrote a book in 1984 alleging that Pazienza trained Ağca for the assassination, but that no concrete evidence supported these claims. According to Marini, such claims were examples of "large-scale manipulation."

Stefano Delle Chiaie and Deep Connections

Another figure mentioned during the trial was Italian neo-fascist terrorist Stefano Delle Chiaie. U.S. customs officials asked whether Delle Chiaie had been seen in the U.S. with a Turk, and this was recorded. However, CIA documents stated that there was no conclusive evidence of Delle Chiaie's direct involvement in the assassination plot.

Judge Ilario Martella asked Pazienza directly, "Did Stefano Delle Chiaie or the Grey Wolves have a direct role in the assassination attempt on the Pope, or were they just intermediaries?" Pazienza responded, "If I said I knew about that, I'd be lying—and I don't want to lie," thus evading the question.

Conclusion: Truth or Manipulation?

The Pope assassination case became one of the most striking examples of Cold War intelligence warfare. While CIA documents argued that Ağca carried out the attempt with support from Bulgarian agents, the Soviets insisted it was a CIA and Western-orchestrated conspiracy.

- Whether Bulgarian intelligence was truly behind the assassination remains unresolved.
- Ağca's ever-changing statements obscured the truth behind the attack.
- The roles of SISMI and the CIA in this incident remain controversial topics even today.
- Possible links between Bulgarian agents and Italian neo-fascist groups were never fully clarified.

In conclusion, the Pope assassination case continues to harbor many dark corners. Overshadowed by CIA and Soviet intelligence warfare, this case laid bare the influence of intelligence agencies on global politics.

Was the True Nature of the Assassination Revealed?

The case of the assassination attempt on Pope John Paul II went down in history as a complex trial entangled in international relations, intelligence wars, and ideological conflicts. Ağca's courtroom behavior and the defense strategies of the other defendants prevented the case from reaching a definitive conclusion. This trial can be seen not just as the prosecution of an assassination attempt but also as a reflection of Cold War power dynamics and political reckonings.

Ağca's contradictory statements and the differing psychological attitudes of the defendants increased the difficulties of the trial, and were among the main reasons the truth could not be fully revealed. Even today, the Pope assassination case remains a significant topic of political and intelligence-related debate. Ağca's statements before and during the trial were insufficient to fully uncover the truth behind the assassination. Though CIA-backed writers and researchers tried to prove the Bulgarian connection, they could not provide definitive evidence. Because Ağca's statements constantly shifted, it remains unclear which of his declarations were truthful.

Whether the Soviet Union or another intelligence agency was behind the attack is still an unanswered question. With his courtroom statements, Ağca wove a web of contradictions that only deepened the suspicions of prosecutors and judges.

The Trial Process and Investigative Barriers

The trial became even more complicated due to language barriers and international bureaucracy. The court traveled 24 times to countries like West Germany, the Netherlands, Turkey, Switzerland, and France to collect witness testimonies. With numerous witnesses and defendants speaking different languages—particularly Bulgarian and Turkish—the trial's progress was significantly hampered.

Presiding Judge Severino Santiapichi stated, "With nearly a hundred witnesses and defendants speaking three different languages in court, our work slowed down considerably." In one session in the Netherlands, the hearing had to be conducted in Turkish, Dutch, German, and Italian. The Italian judiciary viewed taking action against the alleged assassins as a matter of honor. Although the trial has now legally ended, many compelling questions remain unanswered.

Prosecutor Marini remarked, "This trial needed to happen."

Ağca's constantly changing statements and enigmatic demeanor led to differing views among observers. Some saw him as mentally unstable, while others described him as a strategic thinker with a calculating mind.

Prosecutor Marini highlighted Ağca's manipulative behavior by saying, "Ağca is not insane, but he pretended to be." Ağca's highly detailed knowledge about Antonov's lifestyle and family was seen as evidence by those supporting the Bulgarian connection.

The prosecutor expressed his frustration over the trial's inconclusive outcome with these words: "Ağca changed the cards on the table—our problem was that we could no longer trust his testimony."

Ağca spun a nearly inescapable web of contradictions with his courtroom statements. Another unresolved mystery of the trial was Ağca's behavior. While some observers considered him insane, others believed he was entirely sane.

Presiding Judge Severino Santiapichi commented on his intellect: "He has an extraordinary mind."

Ağca summarized his complex stance in court with these words: "I always told my own truth—not that it was the absolute truth."

Regardless of the legal outcome, public doubts and debates persist. Writer Claire Sterling remarked, "There are two verdicts in this case: the legal one and the historical one," highlighting the importance of historical assessments alongside the court's legal proceedings.

Despite the case's closure, the true facts behind the Pope John Paul II assassination attempt remain unclear. In the shadow of international intelligence games and Cold War power plays, the full truth may never come to light.

Picture 83. *Following the military coup of September 12, 1980, numerous political murders and incidents were tried as part of the Nationalist Movement Party (MHP) and Nationalist Organizations Trial. The case has gone down in history as one of the most significant examples of the political tensions and conflicts of the period being brought to justice.*

The Papal Assassination Trial Continues Amid the MHP and Idealist Organizations Case Opened in Ankara

While the trial for the papal assassination, referred to in Italy as the "Trial of the Century," was ongoing, political parties in Turkey had been shut down and party leaders arrested as a result of the September 12 military coup. Among the arrested leaders was the head of the Nationalist Movement Party (MHP), Alparslan Türkeş. The indictment prepared by the military prosecutor under martial law had been accepted by the court.

In the 945-page indictment prepared by the prosecution, it was alleged that the MHP and its affiliated Idealist (Ülkücü) associations aimed to dominate the state through armed actions. The accusations against the party, which was said to have played a role in the political terror incidents that shook Turkey for years, turned into official investigations following the military coup of September 1980.

The indictment included the statement: "Armed fascist and racist gangs established within the MHP have acted to dominate the state through illegal means." Furthermore, the party leader and 219 senior members were to be tried with demands for the death penalty. The hearings of the trial, which went down in history as the MHP and Idealist Organizations Case, had begun.

The Nationalist Movement Party (MHP), allegedly linked to Mehmet Ali Ağca's assassination attempt against Pope John Paul II, was accused by military prosecutors in Turkey of seeking to establish a fascist dictatorship through force. The MHP indictment stated that the party was structured in line with fascist parties in Europe, with an extreme nationalist, authoritarian, and violently anti-communist ideology.

The Abdi İpekçi Assassination and Ağca's Connection:

Although Mehmet Ali Ağca, the defendant in the papal assassination, was not directly mentioned in the indictment, the murder of journalist Abdi İpekçi was considered a significant element of the case. After escaping from a military prison in Istanbul and going abroad, it was claimed that Ağca had been smuggled out by MHP supporters. Regarding the İpekçi assassination, it was alleged that Ağca went to the MHP's district headquarters in Istanbul after the murder and handed over the weapon to Mehmet Şener of the MHP organization.

The indictment stated that the MHP was divided into two main branches: the political wing that sought power through legal means and the paramilitary Idealist groups that organized acts of violence. It was claimed that party leader Alparslan Türkeş aimed for a fascist dictatorship, advocated the principle of a "strong state," and did not believe in democratic processes. Party documents reportedly stated that it attempted to infiltrate key government sectors to seize control and established secret terror cells under the pretense of protecting Turkey from communism. The indictment included the statement: "The MHP is a gang acting under the guise of a political party, using reactionary, separatist, and violent methods."

Prosecutors alleged that the MHP and the Idealist movement planned and executed the murders of leftist labor leader Kemal Türkler and Adana security chief Cevat Yurdakul. Charges also included attempting to change the constitutional order through violence and establish a one-man rule.

Türkeş's background was also included in the indictment, stating that he had led the 1960 coup and then continued his political career. It was emphasized that during his significant roles in the coalition governments of Süleyman Demirel between 1975 and 1978, the MHP had strongly established itself within security units and educational institutions.

Comparison of the MHP with Nazi Germany:

The indictment described the MHP's ideology as "nationalist populism," but claimed that in reality, it resembled National Socialism (Nazism). It stated that the party's doctrine was based on the "Nine Lights" principles and argued that these principles, like those in Nazi Germany, promoted an ultra-nationalist and authoritarian regime. It also noted that the youth organizations within the party resembled the propaganda methods used in Hitler's Germany and Mussolini's Italy.

The indictment quoted writings by party leader Türkeş in which he stated that "the Turkish nation is superior to other nations," asserting that the party's doctrine was shaped on a racist foundation.

The indictment, prepared by military prosecutors after the coup, characterized the Nationalist Movement Party as an organization aiming to dominate the state through illegal means, utilizing paramilitary forces, and seeking to establish a fascist regime. The trial process of party leader Alparslan Türkeş and 219 senior members, who were to be tried with demands for the death penalty, was considered a significant turning point for Turkey's political structure and security policies. The outcomes of the indictment had profound effects on Turkey's political future.

Türkeş's Reaction to Ağca in Court

During the 1981 trial of the MHP and Idealist Organizations, MHP leader Alparslan Türkeş made significant statements about Mehmet Ali Ağca. Türkeş argued in court that Ağca had no connection with the MHP and did not act under the party's orders or directives. Specifically regarding Ağca's assassination attempt and crimes, he stated clearly: "Mehmet Ali Ağca is not a member of our organization. He has no ties to our party."

Türkeş claimed that Ağca's assassination attempt on Pope John Paul II and other crimes contained international connections and that these events were being used to smear the MHP. In his court defense, Türkeş stated: "Ağca was smuggled abroad and used by various intelligence organizations," emphasizing that the incident was more related to international forces than domestic ones.

These statements further inflamed the debate over whether Ağca was merely an individual actor or part of a larger conspiracy.

Picture 84. Alparslan Türkeş lashed out at the prosecutor in the MHP and Nationalist Organizations Case: "Is this court a court of law or a political showdown? We did not collaborate with traitors; we fought for the survival of the country! If you are looking for culprits, look to those who plunged the country into chaos! You may convict us, but you can never execute our ideas. Nationalists are the sons of this country; no one has the right to stain their blood!" These words, echoing in the courtroom, revealed the political tensions of the time and Türkeş's resolute stance.

Mehmet Ali Ağca's Connection to the MHP: Reactions and Analysis

After his assassination attempt on Pope John Paul II on May 13, 1981, Mehmet Ali Ağca made contradictory statements and gave varying testimonies regarding his connections to different groups. His potential links to the Nationalist Movement Party (MHP) and the Idealist movement were repeatedly questioned by historians, journalists, and security authorities. However, Ağca often gave evasive and inconsistent responses on this issue.

Ağca's Possible Ties with the MHP

In his youth, Ağca was involved with the Idealist movement and was accused of assassinating left-wing journalist Abdi İpekçi in 1979. At the time, the MHP and Idealist movement were associated with political violence in Turkey, which reinforced claims of Ağca's links with these circles. Allegations that he received organizational support during his prison escape, departure from the country, and the path to the papal assassination remained on the agenda.

Ağca's Reaction to Allegations of Ties with the MHP

During interrogations following the papal assassination, Ağca gave highly variable and inconsistent answers when asked about his connection to the MHP. While he initially did not deny his past ties with the MHP and the Idealist movement, in later statements he completely denied such affiliations and claimed he acted independently.

Especially during interrogations and in some interviews with the press, he angrily responded to such questions, saying:

- "I am not affiliated with any organization; I acted entirely on my own."
- "These allegations are a deliberately fabricated propaganda."
- "I have no ties with the MHP; this is a complete lie."
- "I am not an ideological militant; I am someone who acts independently."

Despite these strong denials, evidence that Ağca was once active in the Idealist movement and operated within an organized structure cannot be overlooked.

Alparslan Türkeş's Reaction in Court and Ağca's Response

The allegations regarding Mehmet Ali Ağca's connection to the MHP also came onto the agenda of Alparslan Türkeş, the founder and leader of the Nationalist Movement Party (MHP). After the military coup, during the court proceedings in 1981, when he was asked questions about Ağca and the Ülkücü (Idealist)

movement, Türkeş firmly denied these claims. In his courtroom defense, he stated the following:
- "Mehmet Ali Ağca is not a member of our organization. He has no connection with our movement."
- "The Ülkücü movement has never supported terrorism. Ağca committed an individual crime."

These statements by Türkeş were interpreted as part of an effort to prevent the MHP from being associated with the assassination. However, Ağca's reaction in court on this matter also drew attention. In response to Türkeş's statements, Ağca said the following:
- "I did not act on behalf of anyone."
- "I did not allow anyone to use me."
- "I have no ties with the MHP."

However, findings that Ağca had previously been part of the Ülkücü movement and had connections with some former MHP members brought his statements into question.

Inconsistent Statements and Strategic Evasion: Ağca's contradictory statements suggest that he adopted a strategic stance both during the trial and in his interactions with the media. In the political climate of the time, being associated with the MHP and the Ülkücü movement could have led to certain consequences, and thus Ağca tried to portray himself as an "independent actor" by denying or giving ambiguous answers about such connections. This was seen as an attempt to shape his own position during the legal process and in the eyes of the public.

Picture 85. Historic Hearing in Rome Court: Mehmet Ali Ağca and Abdullah Çatlı testify amidst the shadow of an assassination and shady dealings. This trial, shaped in the deep recesses of the Cold War, bore the marks of intelligence warfare and international conspiracies.

The issue of Mehmet Ali Ağca's connection with the MHP and the Ülkücü movement continues to remain a controversial subject. Although there is strong evidence that he had relations with these circles in the past, his occasional denial of such connections or his contradictory statements have made it difficult to clearly understand the forces behind the assassination. Ağca's responses raise the question of whether his actions were merely a strategy to save himself or an effort to reinforce the claim that he was truly an independent operative. However, existing historical data suggests that it would have been difficult for him to carry out such large-scale operations without the support of a certain organization.

Ağca and Çatlı: Two Names Reunited at the Rome Court

Mehmet Ali Ağca and Abdullah Çatlı are two figures who caused significant public debate in Turkey and internationally during the last quarter of the 20th century. Mehmet Ali Ağca became globally known for his attempted assassination of Pope John Paul II on May 13, 1981, while Abdullah Çatlı was prominent for his role in the Turkish nationalist movement and his alleged links to the deep state. Çatlı was known as a key figure within the Ülkücü (Idealist) movement in Turkey. Brought to court by the efforts of Italian prosecutor Antonio Marini, Çatlı became one of the individuals who changed the course of the case with his testimony. In 1985, as part of the investigation conducted by Italian prosecutor Antonio Marini, Çatlı was brought face-to-face with Ağca in court. This confrontation became a turning point in the trial.

The Court Process and Çatlı's Testimony

Abdullah Çatlı testified as a witness in the Pope assassination case on September 16, 1985. In his testimony, Çatlı suggested that Ağca could be a Bulgarian agent and proposed that there might be an international conspiracy behind the assassination. He also stated that Oral Çelik, who was accused in the case, was not involved in the incident, and claimed that Ağca acted independently of the crimes he had committed in Turkey.

The Confrontation Between Ağca and Çatlı

According to the statements of Italian prosecutor Antonio Marini, when Ağca and Çatlı came face-to-face in the courtroom, a strange tension filled the atmosphere. Çatlı's commanding presence cast doubt on Ağca's testimony and led to scrutiny of some of the claims presented by the prosecution. The courtroom confrontation between Ağca and Çatlı became one of the most notable moments of the Pope assassination trial. Çatlı's composed and resolute demeanor, the impact he had in the courtroom, and the respect Ağca showed toward him revealed that this process was not only a legal battle but also a psychological one. This encounter between the two figures resonated deeply in both Turkish and international public opinion, prompting deeper investigation into the complex relationships behind the incident. The event is considered not only an assassination trial but also a significant turning point in the international politics of the period and the alleged deep state structures in Turkey.

Çatlı's Testimony and the Course of the Case

Abdullah Çatlı's testimony became a critical turning point in the case. It led to a verdict of insufficient evidence for defendants like Oral Çelik. Çatlı weakened some of the earlier claims about the planning process of the assassination and revealed inconsistencies in the evidence presented to the court.

1. **Acquittal of Oral Çelik:** Çatlı's testimony increased doubts about Oral Çelik's role in the Pope assassination conspiracy. As a result, the court acquitted Çelik due to lack of evidence.

2. **Weakening of the Bulgarian Connection:** Çatlı cast doubt on the theory that the assassination was an operation connected to

the Eastern Bloc. While it had previously been claimed that Bulgarian intelligence was behind the attack, the information provided by Çatlı indicated there was insufficient evidence to support this claim.

3. **Çatlı's "Leader" Persona:** Çatlı's calm, impressive, and authoritative demeanor in court had a profound psychological effect on both the defendants and the court panel.

Post-Trial Repercussions

Abdullah Çatlı's testimony in court was recorded as one of the most significant turning points in the Pope assassination case. His composed demeanor and strong statements not only led to Oral Çelik's acquittal but also seriously undermined Ağca's credibility and changed the course of the trial.

This encounter further solidified Çatlı's position in the criminal underworld. He became a figure not only known in Turkey but also associated with international crime and intelligence networks. Mehmet Ali Ağca, on the other hand, emerged from this trial as an even more complex character in the public eye. While the Pope assassination case still holds unresolved mysteries, Çatlı's role in court went down in history as one of the most significant moments in this complex trial.

The Assassination Plot Against Lech Walesa: Was Lech Walesa the Next Target After the Pope? Ağca's Confessions Changed Everything!

Lech Walesa, the founder and leader of the Solidarity Movement in Poland, came into the spotlight in 1980 due to claims of an assassination plot against him. However, years later, the Italian judiciary decided not to prosecute six individuals in connection with these claims. The allegations were linked to the attack on Pope John Paul II, with Mehmet Ali Ağca at the center of the case.

Background of the Case

Mehmet Ali Ağca, who was convicted for the attempted assassination of Pope John Paul II, claimed in his secret statements given in 1982 and 1983 that there was a planned conspiracy to assassinate Lech Walesa, one of Poland's most important opposition figures at the time. Ağca alleged that Bulgarian intelligence and some European figures were involved in this conspiracy.

The Defendants and Allegations

While Italian judge Ilario Martella continued the trial process against three Bulgarians and four Turks involved in the Pope's attempted assassination, he decided to halt the prosecution regarding the Lech Walesa assassination allegations. According to Ağca's statements, the individuals involved in the alleged conspiracy were:

- Sergei I. Antonov (former director of Bulgarian Airlines' Rome office)
- Todor S. Aivasov (Bulgarian official)
- Zhelyo K. Vasilev (Bulgarian official)
- Luigi Scricciolo (Italian trade union leader)
- Ivan Donchev (Bulgarian diplomat)
- Salvatore Scordo (another Italian trade union leader)

Among these, only Sergei Antonov was taken into custody; the other Bulgarians were in Bulgaria. In his initial statements, Ağca claimed these individuals were involved in a plot to assassinate Lech Walesa.

Ağca's Retraction and the Court Ruling

Mehmet Ali Ağca later retracted his statements regarding the Lech Walesa assassination. He explained that although he believed there was a plan to assassinate the Polish labor leader, he had made false claims about the individuals' roles in the plot to strengthen the accusations against the Bulgarians. This development marked a major turning point in the trial and once again called Ağca's credibility into question.

The Court's Decision and Its Impact

Judge Martella, in his 1,243-page report—of which 13 pages were made public—decided not to initiate legal proceedings against five defendants on charges of "massacre and illegal possession and transport of explosives." Additionally, the "massacre charge" against Salvatore Scordo was also dropped. As a result, all suspects related to the alleged Lech Walesa assassination plot were acquitted.

This ruling resonated strongly in the political atmosphere of the time and within the context of the Cold War. The judicial process conducted in Italy sparked debate on how socialist regimes in Eastern Europe were allegedly involved in assassinations and covert operations. However, the court's ruling demonstrated that the assassination allegations could not be legally substantiated.

The Lech Walesa assassination claims, which had

emerged in connection with the attempt on Pope John Paul II, did not lead to a legal conclusion due to lack of concrete evidence. The inconsistencies in Mehmet Ali Ağca's statements undermined trust in the court and led to the defendants' acquittal. This case went down in history as a significant part of the discussions surrounding international relations and the activities of secret services during the Cold War period.

İpekçi Murder Interrogation in the Rome Court

During the 7th session of the trial regarding the assassination attempt on the Pope in Rome, the murder of Abdi İpekçi resurfaced during the interrogation of Mehmet Ali Ağca. Ağca's statements had a wide impact in the Turkish press of the time and revealed the complex network of relationships behind the murder.

Picture 86. Ağca did not remain silent, he whispered: It would not be one man who would burn, but a whole system.

While answering Judge Santiapichi's questions

during the hearing, Ağca stated that he did not commit the İpekçi murder himself, but that he took responsibility to protect and silence those who did. According to his claim, there was an organized team of 50–60 people behind the murder, with high-level connections within the group. One of Ağca's most striking statements was: "If I talk, many will get hurt." With these words, he implied that if he revealed the truth, many important people in Turkey would suffer consequences.

Another prominent detail in the trial was Ağca's insistence that he "couldn't even hurt a lizard," reiterating that he did not directly commit the crime. However, it was understood that he assumed responsibility to protect the larger organization behind the scenes.

One notable element of Ağca's testimony was the logistics and firearms preparations related to the murder. He stated that they obtained a total of four weapons, two of which were Browning 9 mm guns. He said that these weapons were procured by Oral Çelik and his team, and that the money was used for "terrorist acts."

In his statements, he also emphasized that the event was not limited to Turkey and was part of a broader plan involving Bulgaria, Switzerland, and other European countries. This demonstrated that the murder had international dimensions.

During the trial, Ağca stated that the İpekçi murder was multi-faceted and complex, and that he received support from the organization behind the scenes during his prison escape plan. He even said that if he spoke, this organization of 50–60 people would be exposed and would cause a major political earthquake.

Meeting in Ankara, Connection with Abdullah Çatlı, and Going to the Faculty of Economics

Ağca said that when he first came to Ankara, he met prominent figures including Abuzer Uğurlu and Abdullah Çatlı through the Ülkü Ocakları (Idealist Hearths). These connections strengthened his position within the organization. Ağca stated that through these circles, he received guidance and participated in various actions. Although he first enrolled at Ankara University's Faculty of Political Sciences, he later transferred to the Faculty of Economics, saying that his education proceeded as part of ideological training and organizational development. He emphasized that the university environment had turned into a field where the youth branches of the nationalist movement actively operated.

Ağca stated that during his initial time in Ankara, he first made contact with the Ülkü Ocakları and joined the Grey Wolves, one of Turkey's most influential paramilitary organizations. He noted that during this period, he had the opportunity to meet figures like Abuzer Uğurlu, Abdullah Çatlı, and Oral Çelik directly. Ağca said that under their guidance, he received both ideological and practical training. During his time in Ankara, he participated in various propaganda and planning meetings at the center of the Ülkü Ocakları. He mentioned that although he initially enrolled in the Faculty of Political Sciences, his educational process took a back seat to his activities. He later transferred to the Faculty of Economics, but emphasized that he viewed the faculty not for education but as a center for organization and action. He stated that the university environment was used for ideological polarization and organizational structuring, and that most action planning was conducted there.

Crossing into Iran via Erzurum

In his testimony in Rome, Mehmet Ali Ağca also shared details of his plan to leave Turkey. As part of the escape plan, he crossed into Iran via Erzurum. Through connections within the nationalist structure that supported him in Erzurum, fake documents and necessary arrangements were made to ensure a smooth border crossing. At this stage, he said that with the help of Abuzer Uğurlu and other key figures, he was directed toward the Iranian border. Ağca stated that he was transported by land to Erzurum, then crossed into Iran with the help of contact persons waiting at the border, and was later directed to Bulgaria as the second stage of the plan. The claim that Turkish security authorities were aware of this process once again pointed to the possible links to dark networks within the state.

Meanwhile, one of the defendants, Ömer Bağcı, was also interrogated during the trial. Bağcı provided detailed information about the smuggling activities he carried out abroad with Ağca and their connections. This indicated that Ağca was not just a lone actor but operated within a broad criminal network.

Name of Former Minister of Customs and Monopolies Tuncay Mataracı

Later in the trial, Mehmet Ali Ağca claimed that under the influence and guidance of Abuzer Uğurlu, former Minister of Customs and Monopolies Tuncay Mataracı also took part in his escape plan. Ağca said that the escape to Bulgaria was organized under Mataracı's instructions and that he was assisted in crossing the border. These statements raised serious allegations about the involvement of political figures of the time. Ağca said that Turkish security authorities were aware of his escape to Bulgaria, which is why he first went to Iran and then crossed back through Turkey to reach Bulgaria.

These claims sparked serious suspicions about the links between the deep state, politicians, and paramilitary forces in Turkey. The government and opposition at the time had to approach Ağca's statements with caution. The mention of former Minister Tuncay Mataracı's name strengthened allegations that some high-level state officials were connected with organized crime and illegal organizations. This ignited a major debate in the public about the reliability of the state and the integrity of the political system. In particular, the media and political opposition demanded a deep investigation and the exposure of the people behind the scenes.

Mataracı's Imprisonment and Reaction

However, as an important detail, it was known that Tuncay Mataracı was in prison at that time. Therefore, the claims made by Ağca during the trial were seriously debated in the press and among the public. Mataracı's imprisonment raised questions about the truthfulness of Ağca's statements and his motivations. This led to commentary that the issue might not only be political but also psychological and manipulative.

Tuncay Mataracı, who was in Kayseri Prison, reacted strongly to Ağca's claims. In response to Ağca's statement that "he helped me escape abroad," Mataracı told the media, "I won't even respond to such a crazy claim." This reaction showed how much Ağca's allegations were questioned and how their seriousness was debated in public. Mataracı's response sparked major debates in political circles and the media about the credibility of the incident.

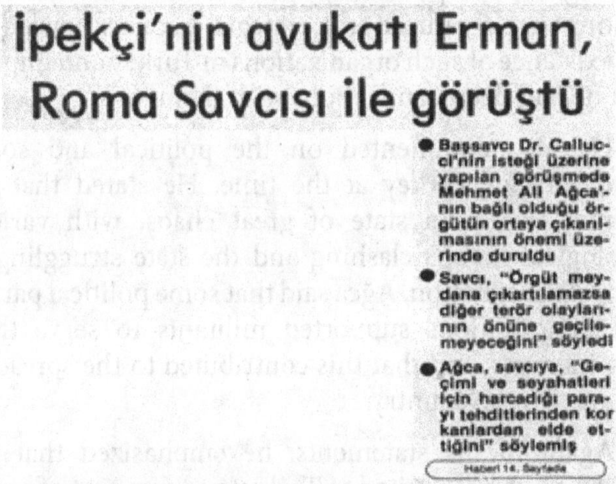

İpekçi'nin avukatı Erman, Roma Savcısı ile görüştü

- Başsavcı Dr. Callucci'nin isteği üzerine yapılan görüşmede Mehmet Ali Ağca'nın bağlı olduğu örgütün ortaya çıkarılmasının önemi üzerinde duruldu
- Savcı, "Örgüt meydana çıkartılamazsa diğer terör olaylarının önüne geçilemeyeceğini" söyledi
- Ağca, savcıya, "Geçimi ve seyahatleri için harcadığı parayı tehditlerinden korkanlardan elde ettiğini" söylemiş

Haberi 14. Sayfada

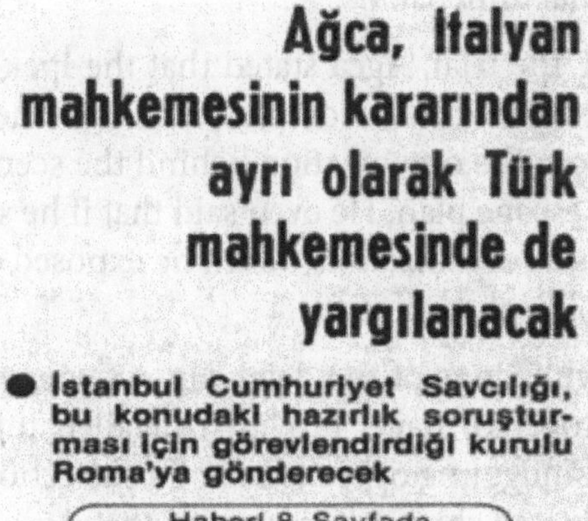

Ağca, İtalyan mahkemesinin kararından ayrı olarak Türk mahkemesinde de yargılanacak

- İstanbul Cumhuriyet Savcılığı, bu konudaki hazırlık soruşturması için görevlendirdiği kurulu Roma'ya gönderecek

Haberi 8. Sayfada

Picture 87- 88.

Ağca stated during the trial that he saw himself as part of the paramilitary group known as the Grey Wolves. He claimed that the group acted according to specific ideological and political goals and that some of their actions were organized and strategic. Ağca acknowledged the existence of such organizations in Turkey and implied that he had deep connections with them.

He also commented on the political and social conditions in Turkey at the time. He stated that the country was in a state of great chaos, with various ideological groups clashing and the state struggling to control the situation. Ağca said that some political parties and organizations supported militants to serve their own interests, and that this contributed to the spread of violence in the country.

Again in his statements, he emphasized that the incident was not limited to Turkey and was part of a plan carried out through Bulgaria, Switzerland, and other European countries. This revealed that the murder had international dimensions.

During the trial, Ağca stated that the İpekçi murder was multi-layered and complex, and that he received support from the organization behind the scenes during his prison escape plan. He even said that if he spoke, this 50–60 person organization would be exposed and cause a major political earthquake.

Meanwhile, one of the defendants, Ömer Bağcı, was also interrogated. Bağcı provided detailed information about the smuggling operations and connections he and Ağca conducted abroad. This proved that Ağca was not a lone actor but operated within a wide criminal network.

In conclusion, the statements made by Mehmet Ali Ağca during the trial and the newspaper reports of the time revealed that the İpekçi murder was not merely an individual act but involved deep state connections, international intelligence links, and a complex terrorist network. Ağca's remark, "If I talk, many big shots will burn," clearly showed how dangerously shrouded in secrecy the murder was within the political climate of the time.

Picture 89. *The courtroom has become the new frontier, not of justice, but of conflicts of interest. Ağca's trial was not a search for truth, but a battle over perception.*

The Impact of the Papal Assassination Attempt on Italian Politics

During the Cold War era, Italy held a significant strategic position. At that time, Italy was caught in the grip of both the United States and the Soviet Union. Although the country was a member of NATO and thus part of the Western bloc, it was also in an environment where the Communist Party maintained a strong presence. The tense atmosphere of the Cold War reflected itself in Italian political life and influenced the background of the papal assassination attempt.

At that time in Italy, there were significant political tensions between communists and right-wing groups. The occurrence of the assassination attempt in this context highlights the impact of the political and cultural atmosphere in Italian society. The attempt further deepened the existing political polarization in Italy.

In Italy, the ruling Christian Democratic Party used the assassination attempt on the Pope as an argument against the communist threat, which further increased political tensions between the left and the right. The incident had profound effects not only on the Vatican and the Christian world but also on Italy's domestic politics, justice system, and international relations. The assassination attempt became a sensitive topic in Italy's international diplomatic relations. Possible Bulgarian and Soviet connections behind the incident brought the tensions of the Cold War into Italy's foreign policy. While maintaining close ties with the West, Italy also had to manage this delicate process with the Eastern Bloc. Discussions about the possible influence of the Communist bloc in the background of the assassination further strengthened Italy's ties with NATO and the United States. Italy reaffirmed its commitment to the Western alliance during this process.

The assassination attempt had a significant impact on public security and counter-terrorism efforts in Italy. The event led to debates over secret organizations within the state, such as "Gladio," as well as clashes between extreme right- and left-wing groups.

The Italian government took stricter measures especially against foreign terrorist activities. In this scope, security policies were tightened and the powers of security forces were increased. The incident led to a revision and update of Italy's anti-terrorism laws. Activities of far-right and far-left groups began to be monitored more closely.

Did Ağca Destroy the Italian Left?

The ruling Christian Democratic Party in Italy (Democrazia Cristiana – DC) interpreted the assassination attempt on the Pope as an attack on Italian democracy and the West and used it effectively. When claims that the Soviets were behind the assassination attempt gained traction, the Italian Communist Party (PCI) found itself in a difficult position.

At that time, the PCI was following a policy known as "Eurocommunism,"[30] independent from the Soviets. However, the papal assassination attempt reinforced the perception that the communists had not entirely severed ties with Soviet influence. As a result, the PCI gradually weakened throughout the 1980s, losing votes in elections, in parallel with the global decline of the left.

Although no direct link between the event and Italian leftist movements could be proven, it triggered a series

---

30 Eurocommunism emerged theoretically in the early 1970s (1975-1977) and spread among communist parties in Western Europe. However, it was predicated on independence from the Soviet Union through events such as the 1956 Hungarian Uprising and the 1968 Prague Spring. In 1977, the Italian, Spanish, and French Communist Parties held a meeting in Madrid to officially declare Eurocommunism. This meeting was a major turning point in Eurocommunism and symbolized a definitive break with the Soviet Union.

of developments that led to the weakening of the PCI and increased pressure on far-left groups. The credibility of the Italian Communist Party was shaken, and the party gradually lost power. Repression of extreme leftist terrorist policies increased, and groups like the Red Brigades came under pressure. After the Cold War, anti-communist propaganda gained strength in Italy, and the social support for leftist parties declined. By the 1990s, the Italian left had entered a serious decline, and the Communist Party disbanded. In 1991, the Italian Communist Party (PCI) dissolved itself and transformed into the "Democratic Left Party" (PDS).

The bullets fired from Ağca's gun went down in political history as an event that accelerated the transformation and downfall of the Italian left.

The Impact of the Case on Italy's Justice System

The judicial process of Mehmet Ali Ağca placed great pressure on Italy's justice system. Claims of possible international connections behind the assassination required Italian judicial authorities to conduct extensive investigations. Theories about Bulgarian secret services and Soviet ties were emphasized, and arrests were made in this direction.

Ağca's defences in the Italian court generally contained distracting elements. Legally, it can be observed that he gave evasive answers to some key questions and tried to manipulate the court process. There were contradictions between his 1983 testimony and the statements he gave to the press in the 2000s. In one, he claimed he had planned the assassination alone, while in another, he pointed to an international conspiracy. These contradictions raised serious questions about what he actually knew and what he might have been hiding. Ağca's statements in court were of a nature that could have revealed the forces behind the assassination process. However, these statements changed over time and sometimes became contradictory.

During the trials, the public awaited answers to these questions: Was Ağca really telling what he knew, or was he being directed as part of a larger plot? Were the changes in his statements due to external pressures or personal interests?

The assassination attempt became a test for the effectiveness and impartiality of Italy's justice system in both national and international public opinion. Debates about judicial reform arose to ensure the independence of the courts and the proper delivery of justice. The Italian media produced extensive reports investigating both local and international connections after the assassination attempt. The media focused on the hidden powers behind the event and possible international conspiracies, which increased public awareness and led to widespread speculation. The assassination attempt and the subsequent trial process had a destabilizing effect on public trust in state institutions and the justice system in Italy. Eventually, there emerged a public concern that the true forces behind the assassination had not been fully revealed by the end of the trials.

The papal assassination attempt led to major changes in the country's security, justice, and foreign policy areas. The event deeply affected not only Italy's domestic politics but also its international relations and security strategies.

The Final Act of the Cold War: The Fall of the Evil Empire

Ronald Reagan's "Evil Empire" Speech

The Cold War was one of the most defining periods of ideological, military, and economic rivalry between the United States and the Soviet Union throughout the 20th century. In the 1980s, this rivalry entered a new phase with U.S. President Ronald Reagan's aggressive anti-communist rhetoric. His speech on March 8, 1983, to the National Association of Evangelicals, known as the "Evil Empire" speech, sharpened the ideological struggle of the Cold War. He virtually declared the Soviet Union a "Evil Empire" with a moralistic approach.[31]

Background and Reagan's Strategy

Having survived an assassination attempt in 1981, Reagan—like the Pope—saw the Soviet Union as the main threat to the U.S. and the Western world. Up until that time, U.S. administrations had tried to maintain peace through dialogue and diplomacy with the Soviets. However, Reagan believed it was now necessary to confront Soviet global expansionism with an interventionist tone. He particularly aimed to wear down the Soviet Union through a strategy that involved increasing U.S. military and economic power.

"Evil Empire" Definition

In the conference, Reagan defined the Soviet Union as a morally "evil" regime. He described the Soviet system

---

31 A Brief History of the 20th Century, Sina Akşin, Türkiye İş Bankası Publications, 3rd Edition 2015, Page 441

as totalitarian, violating human rights, suppressing religious freedoms, and being an imperialist expansionist structure. Throughout his speech, he emphasized that the West—and especially the U.S.—was the representative of "truth and goodness" guided by God.

Religious and Moral Emphasis

One of the most notable aspects of Reagan's speech was its religious emphasis. He based America's founding values on religious references and said that the American people's faith in God was the guarantee of freedom. This religious emphasis was intensified by portraying the Soviets as an atheist regime.

In his speech, Reagan stated, "America is good. And if America ceases to be good, America will cease to be great," aiming to remind the American people of their national identity through moral and religious foundations. At the same time, he claimed that the Soviet system was synonymous with evil and that communism had morally failed.

Reagan argued that the U.S. should increase its military power and respond to Soviet expansionism "in the language of strength." With the phrase "peace can only be achieved through strength," he underlined the inadequacy of containment policies and the need for a more active U.S. stance. His administration at the time incited an arms race to economically strain the Soviets, calculating that they could not bear the burden.

Connection Between the Papal Assassination Attempt and the Speech

A notable aspect of this speech is that it occurred two

years after the 1981 assassination attempt on Pope John Paul II. It was claimed that the Soviet-backed Bulgarian intelligence was behind the attempt. This reinforced the belief in the West that the Soviet Union supported international terrorism. Reagan's designation of the USSR as the "Evil Empire" indirectly relates to the assassination attempt.

It is known that Reagan and Pope John Paul II maintained solidarity against communism throughout the Cold War. As a Polish-born leader, the Pope directly defended religious and democratic freedoms in Soviet-influenced countries, encouraging anti-Soviet movements. Reagan's speech, when evaluated alongside the Pope's survival of the 1981 assassination and his intensified anti-Soviet rhetoric, can be seen as part of efforts to form a united front in the West against communism.

The Reagan Doctrine and the Course of the Cold War

Reagan's "Evil Empire" speech reflected a policy aimed at increasing military, economic, and moral pressure on the Soviet Union, hardening the rhetoric of the Cold War. This speech was also a signal of a shift toward a more active and interventionist U.S. policy.

Reagan's policies contributed to the weakening of the Soviet economy and ultimately the end of the Cold War. The fall of the Berlin Wall in 1989 and the collapse of the Soviet Union in 1991 are cited as evidence that Reagan's tough rhetoric and strategy were effective. However, this tough stance also brought fears of nuclear war.

Ronald Reagan's "Evil Empire" speech represented a major ideological and political battle, even if not on a hot battlefield. The papal assassination attempt and Reagan's speech are considered key links in a period when the West was united against the Soviet Union. This speech was not just the rhetoric of a leader, but also one of the foundations of the strategy that led to the U.S. victory in the Cold War.

The Papal Assassination Attempt and the Collapse of the Soviets: From a Spark to the Fall of an Empire

The assassination attempt on Pope John Paul II in 1981 at St. Peter's Square was not only an attack on a religious leader's life but also went down in history as one of the first sparks of the Soviet Union's collapse. After Mehmet Ali Ağca's attack, claims that the incident was linked to the Soviet-backed Bulgarian intelligence resonated in the Western world. This assassination attempt not only strengthened relations between the Vatican and the U.S., but also energized anti-communist movements.

The Retreat of the Communist Threat in Poland and Italy

Pope John Paul II, as a Polish-born leader, initially became a spiritual and later a political figure in the Eastern Bloc under Soviet influence. The Solidarity (Solidarność) movement that emerged in Poland against the communist regime gained strength with the Pope's open support and became one of the largest civil resistance movements challenging the Soviet regime. The collapse of the communist regime in Poland in 1989 was the beginning of a domino effect in Eastern Europe.

In Italy, the assassination attempt became a factor that shook the Soviet influence in Western Europe. The

Italian Communist Party, which was strong at the time, lost public trust due to alleged links to the assassination. This event accelerated the decline of Soviet-aligned movements in Western Europe.

Reagan and the Vatican: A Joint Force Against the Soviets

Following the papal assassination attempt, the relationship between U.S. President Ronald Reagan and Pope John Paul II grew even closer. The two formed a spiritual and political alliance against the Soviet Union. In his 1983 "Evil Empire" speech, Reagan defined the Soviet Union as a threat to humanity's values and emphasized the moral superiority of the West. This rhetoric enabled the Vatican and the U.S. to present a joint anti-communist stance.

This joint attitude from Reagan and the Pope provided moral and financial support to the Solidarity movement in Poland and encouraged civil movements against other communist regimes in Eastern Europe. This joint struggle undermined the ideological foundations of the Soviet Union and called into question the legitimacy of the regime.

Conclusion: From an Assassination Attempt to the Fall of an Empire

The assassination attempt on Pope John Paul II, although seemingly a singular event, became a turning point that changed the balance of the Cold War. The decline of the communist threat in Italy and Poland led to the loss of international prestige for the Soviet Union and its internal weakening.

This strategic partnership between Reagan and the

Vatican cornered the Soviet Union both morally and politically and accelerated the process leading to its collapse in 1991. The Pope's spiritual leadership and Reagan's firm political stance contributed to the end of the Cold War in favor of the West.

This event is remembered as one of the most striking examples in history of how an assassination attempt can lead to a major geopolitical transformation.

Secret Meeting
Alone with the Pope:
Rebibbia Prison,
December 27, 1983 – Rome – 3:00 PM

On a cold December day, as the heavy iron gates of Rome's Rebibbia Prison opened, the silence inside was broken only by echoing footsteps. Amid the respectful gazes of the guards, a man walked through the stone corridors of the prison—Pope John Paul II, the spiritual leader of the Catholic world.

Picture 90. An assassin and his target face to face behind bars... A fate written with a bullet was reshaped in the silence of a pardon. Pope John Paul II held Ağca's hand as he tried to kill him. Justice or mercy? Even time held its breath at this meeting.

Opposite him, waiting eagerly, was Mehmet Ali Ağca, the man who had carried out one of the most significant assassination attempts in Vatican history. Under dim lighting, a narrow room with an old table and two chairs was set as the stage for this historic encounter. The marks left by time on the walls merged with the shadows of rusted iron bars, and the heavy smell of the cell carried the weight of years spent inside.

Just four days after the shooting in St. Peter's Square on May 13, 1981, the Pope had publicly forgiven his attacker from his hospital bed. This meeting was the act that put his forgiveness into practice. Since the day Ağca shot the Pope, the two men had never been this close. Vatican spokesman Father Pastore reported that Ağca was not handcuffed or otherwise restrained during the meeting, describing the setting as reminiscent of a confessional, far from hatred or anger.

According to a Vatican official, when the Pope arrived to meet Mr. Ağca, the latter kissed the Pope's ring and, when asked by John Paul if he was feeling well, replied yes. During their whispered conversation, the Pope held Ağca's hands in his own several times.

Pope John Paul II and Mehmet Ali Ağca spoke quietly in the prison cell for about 22 minutes. After the meeting, the Pope told journalists, "What we said to each other will remain a secret between us," adding, "I spoke to him like a brother I have forgiven and trust." Later

Vatican statements emphasized that the Pope placed great spiritual significance on this meeting.

Media Reaction and Coverage of the Event

The meeting between the Pope and Mehmet Ali Ağca reverberated through the global press as a grand gesture by a spiritual leader who forgave a young assassin. International media approached the story from various perspectives:

- *The New York Times* and *The Guardian* described the meeting as an embodiment of Christian forgiveness, calling it a "spiritual demonstration of peace."
- *La Repubblica* and *Le Monde* took a more political angle, highlighting alleged Soviet or Bulgarian intelligence links behind the assassination attempt and speculating on whether the Pope questioned Ağca about these during the meeting.
- *Corriere della Sera* and *Il Giornale* called the act of forgiveness "a triumph of the Christian world," while some left-wing outlets labeled the meeting a "political maneuver by the Vatican."

More sensational media speculated that Ağca might use the private conversation to make new claims and suggested that the Vatican had been cautious to avoid bringing up topics like the Fatima Prophecy.

Some viewed the Pope's act of forgiveness as a "historic gesture of humanity," while others saw it as a "moral obligation." But around the world, the event was marked not as a regular news story, but as a historic moment.

The Political and Diplomatic Dimensions of the Meeting

This meeting also revealed the Vatican's role in global politics during the Cold War. At the time, Western media widely speculated that the Soviet Union was behind the assassination attempt. The Pope's meeting with Ağca only intensified such suspicions. Some analysts argued that the meeting was not only spiritually significant for the Catholic world, but also deeply meaningful in the realm of international diplomacy.

While the Vatican presented the meeting as a message of peace and reconciliation, some political commentators saw the Pope's gesture of forgiveness as a strategic move to increase the Vatican's influence over the Eastern Bloc. The meeting showed that the Catholic Church was not just a religious institution, but also a diplomatic actor.

Mehmet Ali Ağca's Statements and Speculations

Years later, Mehmet Ali Ağca claimed that his conversation with the Pope had dimensions not included in the Vatican's official narrative. According to Ağca, topics such as the Third Secret of Fatima and how the Vatican interpreted it were discussed.

In his 1996 book *La Mia Verità* (*My Truth*), Ağca wrote: "I asked the Pope: 'What is the Third Secret of Fatima?' The Pope said nothing and preferred to remain silent about this mysterious secret. Then I asked, 'When will the Third Secret of Fatima be revealed?' The Pope replied, 'After Sister Lucia's death.' When I asked, 'Why after her death?' he answered, 'Because Sister Lucia wishes it so.' That was the end of our conversation."

These statements fueled further speculation that the

Vatican had not disclosed the full truth about the Fatima Prophecy. Theories emerged within the Catholic world and academic circles suggesting that the Vatican had deliberately concealed the entire content of the Third Secret of Fatima.

This historic encounter made global headlines and was interpreted in many different ways. The Pope's declaration of forgiveness won widespread praise in the Catholic world and once again highlighted the importance of forgiveness in Christian belief.

At the same time, the meeting carried political implications. It occurred during the Cold War, a time when the powers behind the assassination attempt were still shrouded in uncertainty. The meeting, therefore, had significance beyond a religious encounter—it symbolized a step toward global peace and international diplomacy. This moment in Rebibbia became part of history with both spiritual and political weight.

While emphasizing the religious and human dimensions of forgiveness and reconciliation, the Pope's meeting with Ağca continues to provoke debate due to its international political impact. Ağca's claims and the speculations surrounding the Fatima Prophecy have led some to see the encounter not just as a story of forgiveness, but also as a conversation behind closed doors about one of the Vatican's greatest secrets. Yet only the Pope and Ağca truly know what was said between them.

Mehmet Ali Ağca's Extradition to Turkey: A Journey Wrapped in Secrets

Pope John Paul II's 1983 prison visit and forgiveness of Ağca paved the way for his future release and extradition to Turkey. Ağca's release and extradition revealed a complex story deeply embedded in history.

This process was more than the extradition of a criminal—it was a challenging endeavor involving international law, diplomacy, and public persuasion. Ağca's journey, which began with the 1981 assassination attempt, evolved into a tale where justice and mystery were intertwined.

Mehmet Ali Ağca's Release Document and a Historical Turning Point

To the Directorate of Ancona Prison...

Under this heading, a signature was quietly made on June 13, 2000—its echoes would last for years. This document was not merely a legal order but a sealing of the final pages of a long story shrouded in the shadows of the past.

Signed by Deputy Prosecutor Giuseppe Saieva of the Rome Republic Prosecutor's Office, the document was swiftly sent to the Ancona Prison Directorate in great secrecy on June 13, 2000. This document not only recorded a historical event but also demonstrated the interweaving of law and politics.

The June 13, 2000 release order from the Rome Prosecutor's Office marked the final step in the legal process following the highly debated assassination attempt. It declared the end of Ağca's 19-year imprisonment.

The document presented in our book clearly outlines the legal order for Mehmet Ali Ağca's release from prison and represents a point where national and international law closely intersected. His freedom was returned not just by serving time, but through shifting political balances and international negotiations. The iron gates of Ancona Prison were preparing to release a man they had long held. History was quietly turning the last page of a chapter.

On June 13, 2000, the release order signed by Deputy Prosecutor Giuseppe Saieva was more than a legal mandate—it was a decree marking the end of an era. As law and politics danced on a delicate thread, the decision became the key to unlocking a historical lock.

And that day, the heavy iron doors of Ancona Prison creaked open. The sound pierced through years of silence. Mehmet Ali Ağca stepped forward, bearing the deep marks time had left on his face. He was no longer just a prisoner. He was a symbol, a mystery, the name of an unknown. When the June sun touched skin that hadn't felt it in years, he paused. Was it mercy, or the cold hand of a forgotten truth?

Ağca stepped out from the shadow of his past. The years spent behind bars had ended—for now. But the world waiting for him outside was no longer the same… Those doors would open, but the man walking through them would not be the same Ağca. The marks of the past weighed on his shoulders, while the eyes of the world cast shadows upon him.

And the moment came… Outside: journalists, cameras, questions. The entire world searched for answers in his eyes. But one thing was certain: that day, it was not just a man who was released. History once again set out to rewrite its own fate.

An era had ended. But the real story was only beginning... The weight of the years lost behind prison walls had not yet lifted from his shoulders. Would the world still see him with the same eyes? Or would he assume an entirely new role and take a step down the path destiny had laid for him? Sometimes, time can be a greater prison than captivity. Perhaps for him, true imprisonment was only beginning...

The Document's Historical Background

During Ağca's trial in the Italian courts, global public opinion, the Vatican, and international political and intelligence circles remained occupied for years with theories and debates. Ağca was eventually sentenced to life in prison in 1981 for the attempted assassination.

The release document sent to the prison was a legal order for Ağca's release following partial completion of his sentence and a presidential pardon.

Legal Details

The document stated that Mehmet Ali Ağca's release was decided under the following conditions:

1. He would be released immediately if he was not under arrest for any other case.
2. His sentence had been reduced and pardoned by presidential decree.
3. The release was conditional: if Ağca committed an intentional crime within 10 years or received a new prison sentence of more than six months, the pardon would be nullified.

This release document held both legal and political

importance. The conditional nature of the pardon reflected the delicate balance of international law and diplomatic relations. Ağca's release was closely followed by the media and public, sparking new debates to uncover the story's hidden layers.

Turkey's Request

While Ağca was imprisoned in Italy for the assassination attempt, Turkey sought justice of its own. Ağca had also deeply marked Turkey's memory through the assassination of journalist Abdi İpekçi and other serious crimes.

Turkey made diplomatic efforts for years to secure Ağca's extradition. Turkish authorities questioned him in the Italian prison at various times, and Turkish journalists had the opportunity to interview him, keeping him in the public eye.

In 1983, Pope John Paul II visited Ağca in Rebibbia Prison and declared that he had forgiven him. Following this, Italian judicial authorities reviewed Ağca's life sentence and raised the possibility of extradition to Turkey.

Turkey requested Ağca's extradition due to the İpekçi assassination and other crimes. Under international law, extradition depends on the seriousness of the crime, the legal system of the requesting country, and protection of the individual's rights.

Negotiations between Italy and Turkey intensified in the 1990s. Turkish officials guaranteed that Ağca would receive a fair trial and would not be sentenced to death. This was a key condition under international law, as many European countries refuse to extradite individuals who might face capital punishment.

Return in the Shadow of Mystery and Secrets

The extradition process of Mehmet Ali Ağca went down in history as a striking example from the perspective of international law and diplomacy. However, this process was not merely a legal matter, but a story that left deep marks in humanity's collective memory. One of Italy's leading newspapers, *La Repubblica*, commented on Ağca's extradition with the following words: ***"The assassin of the Pope took his secrets with him. He is now in a Turkish prison."***

Indeed, Ağca left behind countless question marks. Who were the forces behind the assassination attempt? How far did Ağca's connections reach? These questions still await answers in the dark pages of history.

Mehmet Ali Ağca's extradition to Turkey was not merely the delivery of a criminal to justice, but a striking example of how international legal mechanisms and diplomatic processes function. This process, which began with the 1979 assassination of Abdi İpekçi, gained an international dimension with the 1981 assassination attempt on Pope John Paul II. Ağca's extradition was the product of a complex and multi-sided negotiation where law, diplomacy, and human rights were discussed together. The incident attracted the attention not only of the Vatican, Italy, and Turkey but also of governments on a global scale. Legally, this situation presented a complex case due to a person being convicted of serious crimes in two separate countries.

The Extradition Process: Balancing Diplomacy and Security

On June 18, 2000, with the pardon decree approved

by the Italian President, Mehmet Ali Ağca's extradition to Turkey was carried out. The operation, conducted under intense security measures between the Italian and Turkish Interpol offices, stood out as an example of international legal and diplomatic cooperation.

Ağca was transported from Ancona Airport to Turkey on a Casa-type military transport plane belonging to the Turkish Air Force. During the extradition, one of the fundamental principles of international law—prohibition of double jeopardy—was observed. According to this principle, Ağca could not be retried in Turkey for crimes for which he had already been convicted in Italy. However, he could still be sentenced for crimes committed in Turkey.

By 2000, Turkey's extradition requests had begun to yield results. Ağca's extradition was finalized through confidential diplomatic negotiations between Italian and Turkish authorities. In this process, both Italy's judicial procedures and Ağca's security were of critical importance.

Turkish Interpol formed a special three-member team to initiate the extradition process. With the Italian President's approval of Ağca's pardon, the path for his return to Turkey was opened. The aircraft chosen for this operation was known more for its safety than speed—since even a minor setback could have turned this into a historic diplomatic crisis.

Reactions of the Italian Press to Ağca's Extradition

Ağca's pardon and extradition process received widespread attention in Italy. The country's leading newspapers covered the event from various angles:

- *La Repubblica:* "The assassin of Pope John Paul

II took his secrets with him. Now in a Turkish prison."

- *Corriere della Sera:* "Ali Ağca is pardoned and now in Turkey. The terrorist must complete his sentence for murder in his own country."
- *Il Messaggero:* "The former Grey Wolf has been extradited to Turkey. This was the Pope's wish."

The press especially emphasized the contradictions in Ağca's statements and the still-unresolved mysteries behind the assassination. This fueled criticisms that the pardon may have helped conceal the truth.

Statements by Chief Prosecutor Antonio Marini

Antonio Marini, Chief Prosecutor of the Rome Court of Appeal who led the investigation into the Pope's assassination attempt for 15 years, made the following striking remarks about Ağca: **"Mehmet Ali Ağca told dozens of lies. He deceived us, the Pope, the Italian justice system, the Fatima legend—even God."**

Marini expressed that Ağca constantly manipulated the justice system and avoided revealing the truth. His statement reignited debates in Italy following Ağca's pardon and extradition.

Political and Social Impact in Italy

The pardon and extradition of Mehmet Ali Ağca left a deep impression in Italy. The event went down in history not just as the consequence of an assassination attempt, but as an episode caught between international law, religious values, and diplomacy.

For many in Italy, this was a process where the

boundaries of the law were pushed, and political interests took precedence. While the Pope's pardon was praised as a symbol of tolerance and peace, the secrets and lies left behind by Ağca cast a shadow over the whole process.

The Role of International Law and Diplomacy

The extradition process of Mehmet Ali Ağca remains an important case in demonstrating how international legal mechanisms operate. In this process, international criminal law, extradition agreements, and human rights law played a central role. Italy considered the following elements during the extradition to Turkey:

- **Guarantee of Fair Trial:** Turkey committed to conducting Ağca's trial in accordance with international standards.
- **Ban on the Death Penalty:** Under the European Convention on Human Rights, it was guaranteed that Ağca would not face capital punishment.
- **Diplomatic Cooperation:** The talks between Turkey and Italy ensured the extradition process was handled with sensitivity.

Return to Turkey: The Interrogation of Justice

When Mehmet Ali Ağca arrived in Turkey on June 13, 2000, he faced not only prison walls but also a long legal process for the Abdi İpekçi assassination and other crimes. He began serving time in prisons in Kırklareli and Maltepe. Throughout this period, public debate around Ağca's extradition and sentencing continued intensely. International law also played a role here—his prison time in Italy was factored into the recalculation of his total sentence in Turkey.

Ağca was initially released in 2006. However, following an objection by then-Justice Minister Cemil Çiçek, he was returned to prison shortly after a brief period of freedom. This controversial decision sparked legal debate and accusations of double standards against Ağca.

By 2010, having completed his sentence in Turkey, Ağca was conditionally released. He now stepped into a world where he could no longer avoid confronting his past. After his release, he frequently appeared in the media, making statements about his past and drawing renewed attention. But did any of these explanations truly shed light on the mysteries behind the assassination attempts?

Perhaps some secrets are doomed to remain sealed in eternal silence...

Abolition of the Death Penalty in Turkey in 1984

In 1984, the application of the death penalty was effectively halted in Turkey, and it was formally abolished in 2002. Ağca's escape at the time meant that the death sentence initially imposed on him was never carried out. Nevertheless, the sentence revealed the seriousness of the assassination and provided insight into the Turkish justice system's approach at the time.

Political Dimension and Debates

The death sentence handed to Mehmet Ali Ağca was debated for years both legally and politically. Allegations about powerful backers behind Ağca raised suspicions that the case was targeting more than just one individual—it hinted at a broader organization.

This process is remembered as a reflection of the complex pursuit of justice overshadowed by Turkey's right-left conflict, political assassinations, and deep state structures in the 1970s. The trial and sentencing of Mehmet Ali Ağca remain one of the most striking cases in Turkish legal history.

Rahşan Amnesty and Mehmet Ali Ağca

The general amnesty law passed in 2000, known in Turkey as the "Rahşan Amnesty," enabled the reduction or release of many prisoners' sentences. Named after Rahşan Ecevit, wife of then Deputy Prime Minister Bülent Ecevit, the amnesty aimed to reduce prison overcrowding and restore social peace. One of the most high-profile beneficiaries of this law was Mehmet Ali Ağca, who had assassinated journalist Abdi İpekçi in 1979.

After being extradited to Turkey in 2000, Ağca was imprisoned again for the İpekçi assassination and other crimes. However, the Rahşan Amnesty triggered a series of developments that led to a reduction in Ağca's sentence and ultimately his release. His sentence was recalculated due to several reasons, which generated controversy:

1. **Sentence Reduction:** Although Ağca's crimes were officially excluded from the amnesty's scope, he indirectly benefited from sentence reductions.

2. **Time Served in Italy:** His prison time in Italy was added to his sentence in Turkey, leading to recalculations that contributed to his release.

3. **Release and Debates:** His release in 2006 provoked public backlash. However, due to legal gaps, he was quickly returned to prison.

Final Release in 2010

Mehmet Ali Ağca was finally conditionally released on January 18, 2010. Although the Rahşan Amnesty did not directly apply to him, the legal framework and sentence reductions it created accelerated his release.

Picture 92 – 93. "Divine secrets hidden within a letter... Fate burning in a hitman's eyes... Fatima's prophecy and Ağca's bullet met on the same line. Time was sealed, history was written in blood..."

Ağca's Cry from Prison to the Pope: "Reveal the Third Secret"

After the assassination attempt on the Pope on May 13—a date foretold in prophecies—Mehmet Ali Ağca described the incident in his testimony before the Roman courts as an **"inevitable fate"** and invited the Pope to reveal the Third Secret of Fatima.

At the time, Ağca's outcry made headlines, with interpretations suggesting he was mentally unstable or deliberately trying to create that impression. However, the Vatican would later demonstrate that this was not merely a delusion by eventually disclosing the secret.

Years after the event, Ağca—who had been extradited from Italy to Turkey and was serving his sentence in Kartal Prison—sent a get-well message to Pope John Paul during his treatment for a flu infection, thanking him for revealing the Third Secret and urging him to reveal the rest of it as well.

"You and I are both in the agony of fulfilling a universal plan. I wish you a speedy recovery. I am grateful that you revealed the Third Secret of Fatima on May 13, 2000. Now, you must also confirm the divine truth that the end of the world is near," he said.

Italian newspapers headlined the message as "Strange and Encrypted Messages to the Vatican from Ağca."

Picture 94. In Fatima, the Pope met with Sister Lucia, the only survivor of the three little shepherds to whom the Virgin Mary appeared in 1917.

Time Sealed in Blood

The Third Secret of Fatima and the Vatican's Surrender

Vatican, April 19, 2000…

In the misty mornings of 1917, in the humble village of Fatima, Portugal, a curtain was drawn open before the eyes of three small children… Years ago, the sky had spoken in its own language, and mysterious words had fallen to earth from the pen of Sister Lucia. These mysterious words were sealed deep within time, awaiting the moment they would be revealed by destiny's call. Sister Lucia stated that the envelope containing the Third Secret, which she delivered to the Vatican, should not be opened before 1960. She emphasized this date because she believed the message in the secret would not be understood before then.

When 1960 arrived, Pope John XXIII had the secret opened and reviewed its contents. However, he decided not to share it with the public, reasoning that the content could have a massive global impact. Thus, the Third Secret continued to be stored in the Vatican's secret archives for 83 years.

And the Third Secret manifested itself on a day the world witnessed in horror.

May 13, 1981... A gunshot echoed in St. Peter's Square and a divine intervention... As a bullet from Mehmet Ali Ağca's cold weapon struck the body of Pope John Paul II, the secret of Fatima was sealed with blood. The Pope survived, but humanity felt the cold breath of a prophecy on its neck.

Time passed, the era changed. And the Vatican finally unlocked the sealed moment. That ancient secret, kept hidden for 83 years, would be revealed in 2000. The Vatican was now preparing to lift the final seal.

Pope John Paul II was a leader who placed great importance on the Fatima prophecies, particularly the Third Secret. The assassination attempt on May 13, 1981, led the Pope to make a direct connection with this prophecy. Miraculously surviving the attempt by Mehmet Ali Ağca, the Pope declared that he owed his life to the protection of the Virgin Mary.

Following this event, the Pope began to study the Fatima prophecies more closely and, in 1984, held a ceremony titled "Consecration of the World to the Immaculate Heart of Mary." He wished to directly communicate with Sister Lucia to better understand the contents of the Third Secret. The Pope sent Archbishop Tarcisio Bertone, Secretary of the Congregation for the Doctrine of the Faith, to speak with Sister Lucia about the Third Secret of Fatima. The Vatican placed high importance on obtaining a clear interpretation of the final secret and greatly valued Lucia's views. In this context, on

April 27, 2000, Archbishop Tarcisio Bertone and Bishop Serafim de Sousa Ferreira e Silva of Leiria-Fatima held a private meeting with Sister Lucia.

Archbishop Bertone was tasked with asking Sister Lucia questions about the third part of the secret. The Pope wished for Lucia to speak sincerely and openly on the matter.

The Meeting with Sister Lucia

This meeting took place at the Saint Teresa Carmelite convent where Sister Lucia lived. A letter signed by Pope John Paul II was delivered to her. The Pope's letter was crucial in understanding how the Third Secret was interpreted and approached by the Vatican. Lucia received the letter with great honor and said she would answer all questions with an open heart.

In his letter, the Pope expressed his deep belief in the Fatima prophecy and emphasized that Lucia, the only surviving child witness of the apparitions, possessed invaluable knowledge. The Pope's letter contained key messages highlighting his devotion to the Fatima Prophecies and especially the Third Secret. In the letter, the Pope stated:

"I greet you with the holy joy of Easter. You should know that I pursue the divine light directed at the Church and all humanity through the peace message of the Risen Jesus. As a witness to the sacred moments in Fatima, I want to learn how you interpret the Fatima Prophecy. Your testimony, in the light of this message that is important for the Church and humanity, holds great value for us."

This letter was delivered personally to Lucia by Archbishop Bertone. With tears in her eyes, Lucia received the letter and expressed her respect for the Pope. Archbishop Bertone presented her with the sealed envelope containing the Third Secret of Fatima. Lucia immediately recognized the letter inside as being in her own handwriting and confirmed its authenticity.

During the meeting, Lucia explained the Third Secret of Fatima and its connection to the Pope with the following words:

"I saw the white-robed bishop suffering. He was under attack and surrounded by the prayers of the faithful. We didn't know who he was, but now we understand that this prophecy was fulfilled in you. What happened in St. Peter's Square in 1981 was a reflection of this holy message."

Lucia also emphasized that the message of Fatima did not merely recount past events but also shed light on the future. According to her, the Third Secret was a divine roadmap showing the trials the Church would face and how believers could stand firm through prayer. In the meeting, Lucia noted that the Third Secret resembled other prophetic visions in Church history and that it described the struggle of atheistic Communism against the Church and the martyrdoms of faith that occurred during that period.

Lucia said that in the vision, they saw the white-robed bishop (the Pope) suffering and being attacked, though they did not know which Pope it was. However, after the assassination attempt on May 13, 1981, she stated that the vision pointed to an attack on the Pope.

Lucia also clarified that the Virgin Mary had not instructed her not to reveal the secret before 1960; she herself chose that date because she believed the content wouldn't be fully understood before then. Nevertheless, she stressed that interpreting the secret was the responsibility of the Pope, not hers.

The Vatican's Disclosure Process and Cardinal Sodano's Announcement

In the process of revealing the Third Secret of Fatima to the public, the Vatican followed a careful path. During Pope John Paul II's visit to Fatima on May 13, 2000, Vatican Secretary of State Cardinal Angelo Sodano made an official announcement about the Third Secret.

According to Sodano's remarks, the central theme of the Fatima vision was the Church's struggle of faith and the persecutions endured throughout the 20th century. This vision was interpreted as a symbolic prophecy describing the war that atheist systems waged against the Church and the martyrs of that era. The scene showing the white-robed bishop being shot and falling was directly linked to the assassination attempt on Pope John Paul II. The idea was expressed that a mother's hand had guided the bullet's path.

Following this announcement, the Vatican published the full text of the Third Secret and emphasized that it contained a call to protect Christian faith, to prayer, and to repentance.

The Importance of the Period Before the Revelation of the Third Secret

The period leading up to the revelation of Fatima's Third Secret demonstrates the Vatican's profound concern with this matter and the personal faith of Pope John Paul II. After the assassination attempt, the Pope began to study the secret more closely, and his meetings with Sister Lucia contributed to the unveiling of its mystery.

And thus: The Vatican had lifted the final seal.

LETTER FROM POPE JOHN PAUL II TO SISTER LUCIA[32]

(Original Text)

Coimbra Monastery
To Sister Maria Lucia

With the great joy of Easter, I greet you with the words the Risen Jesus spoke to His disciples: "Peace be with you!"

I will be pleased to meet with you on the long-awaited day of the canonization of Francisco and Jacinta. God willing, I will celebrate this day on May 13 this year.

As there will only be time for a brief greeting on that day and no opportunity for a conversation, I am sending His Excellency Archbishop Tarcisio Bertone, Secretary of the Congregation for the Doctrine of the Faith, to speak with you. This is the Congregation that works most closely with the Pope in defending the true Catholic faith, and as you know, since 1957 it has kept your handwritten letter containing the third part of the "secret" revealed on July 13, 1917, in Cova da Iria, Fatima.

Archbishop Bertone, accompanied by His Excellency Bishop Serafim de Sousa Ferreira e Silva, Bishop of Leiria, will come on my behalf and ask you some questions about the interpretation of the "third part of the secret."

Sister Maria Lucia, you may speak openly and sincerely with Archbishop Bertone; he will convey your answers directly to me.

---

32 https://www.vatican.va/roman_curia/congregations/cfaith/documents/rc_con_cfaith_doc_20000626_message-fatima_en.html

I fervently pray to the Mother of the Risen Lord for you, Sister, for the Coimbra Community, and for the entire Church. May Mary, the Mother of pilgrim humanity, always keep us united with her beloved Son and our Brother, Jesus, Lord of life and glory.

With my special Apostolic Blessing,

IOANNES PAULUS

Picture 95. And the curtain of time was parted... The silent witnesses of time came together... Pope John Paul II met with Lucia de Santos, a 93-year-old Carmelite nun and bearer of the mysteries of the Virgin Mary. Secrets were whispered, and time sealed this moment—just like the fate written by Ağca's bullet...

Pope John Paul II's Letter to Sister Lucia and the Third Secret of Fatima
The Vatican's Silence and the Process of Disclosure

For years, a hidden secret was finally coming to light. The Third Secret of Fatima had been regarded as one of the greatest mysteries of the Catholic world, known for decades only to the highest authorities of the Church. But this mystical seal was being broken at the request of Pope John Paul II, and the truths kept in the deep archives of the Vatican were being presented to humanity.

According to the Vatican, the Third Secret of Fatima referred to events occurring since the mid-20th century and contained the Virgin Mary's call to humanity for conversion and repentance. On the day in 2000 when Francisco and Jacinta Marto were canonized, the Church decided to share the text of the Third Secret with the world. The revelations resonated deeply within the Catholic faith and went down in history as one of the most important mystical prophecies of humanity.

The Secret and the Assassination Attempt

On June 26, 2000, Cardinal Joseph Ratzinger revealed the content of the Third Secret before a large gathering of journalists. According to the Cardinal's statement, the Third Secret was directly linked to the assassination attempt on Pope John Paul II on May 13, 1981.

The attack by Mehmet Ali Ağca was, in the eyes of the Vatican and believers, a terrifying confirmation of the Fatima prophecy. The prophecy described a "bishop dressed in white" being attacked, falling to the ground among the people, and being surrounded by the prayers of the faithful. The assassination attempt in 1981 seemed to exactly fulfill this prophecy. Pope John Paul II believed this event was no coincidence and attributed his survival to the miraculous intervention of the Virgin Mary. After the attempt, one of the bullets that struck him was placed in the crown of the statue of the Virgin Mary in Fatima.

This act became a symbol of the deep faith in the Fatima message and the Pope's submission before the holy prophecy.

Ratzinger's Statements and Debates over the Secret

Cardinal Joseph Ratzinger emphasized that the Third Secret did not refer only to a specific historical event but also pointed to great trials the Church might face in the future. According to him, the vision of the bishop in white being attacked represented not only the assassination attempt on Pope John Paul II, but also the persecutions the Church had experienced and would continue to experience over time.

Ratzinger stressed that the Third Secret should not be interpreted as an apocalyptic scenario. Instead, he stated that the message of Fatima was a call for the transformation of humanity through prayer, repentance, and faith. In his statements, the Cardinal said:

"The message of Fatima contains God's love for the world and His warning to humanity. The Third Secret shows how important human free will and the power of prayer are. God's plan does not change, but if humanity repents and is transformed, some catastrophes can be avoided."

However, even these statements did not dispel all doubts. Some Catholic circles believed the Vatican had not fully disclosed the secret. There were claims that only part of the message had been revealed and that the real content was still being hidden. Speculations especially emerged that the secret revealed a great global catastrophe or major corruption within the Church.

Reactions of the World Media and the Catholic World

The revelation of the Third Secret caused a great stir around the world. International media emphasized that the Vatican's long-awaited disclosure of this secret was one of the greatest religious events of modern times. Major newspapers such as *The New York Times*, *The Guardian*, and *Le Monde* gave extensive coverage to the connection between the Fatima prophecy and the assassination attempt. While some media questioned why the Vatican had kept the prophecy hidden for so long, others claimed the Church was now adopting a more transparent policy.

Within the Catholic world, reactions varied. Many believers thought the revelation of the Third Secret affirmed the holiness of the Church and Pope John Paul II. Faith in Fatima especially grew stronger, and ceremonies of devotion to the Virgin Mary increased. However, some conservative Catholic circles claimed that the Vatican had not fully disclosed the real text and was still hiding key details.

A significant rise in pilgrimages to Fatima was also observed. Portugal's Fatima region drew many more visitors after the disclosure of the Third Secret, with people offering prayers in the holy site, trying to understand the message of the prophecy.

Revealed and Unrevealed Secrets

The Fatima prophecy went down in history as one of the greatest religious mysteries of modern times. Its direct link to the assassination attempt on Pope John Paul II showed that the prophecy was not only connected to the past, but also relevant to the living.

With the disclosure of the Third Secret, the Vatican

emphasized that this prophecy should no longer be a source of fear, but rather a call to prayer and repentance for believers. Yet some questions remained unanswered. Was the secret of Fatima truly and fully revealed? Or was the Vatican still concealing a truth humanity was not ready to know?

Whatever the answer, the whispers of Fatima would never vanish—they would continue to echo through the depths of time…

The Italian Press Focuses on Mehmet Ali Ağca

Following the Vatican's revelation of the Third Secret of Fatima, all eyes in Italy turned once again to Mehmet Ali Ağca. Having drawn global attention for his assassination attempt on Pope John Paul II, Ağca was now being considered in a religious and mystical context. The Catholic world's recognition of the assassination attempt as the fulfillment of the Third Secret of Fatima echoed widely in the Italian press.

The Secret of Fatima and Ağca

Italian newspapers brought Ağca's case and past statements back into public discussion after the Vatican's announcements. Interpreting the assassination attempt as part of a divine destiny, Ağca had for years made statements linking it to the Fatima prophecy. After the 1981 attack, he persistently said, "The Pope must reveal the Third Secret of Fatima," but his words were not taken seriously at the time. However, with the Vatican's official statement, these remarks began to be viewed in a new light.

Headlines of the Italian Press

One of Italy's leading newspapers, *Corriere Della Sera*, highlighted Ağca's words: "It was the devil who put the gun in my hand." The paper wrote that Ağca planned to go to the town of Fatima and pray once he was released. *La Repubblica* ran the headline: "I was only a tool used by fate; the Pope must now save me." These statements showed that Ağca viewed the assassination not as a personal act, but as part of a divine plan, portraying himself as a victim within that context.

Angry Reaction and Allegations of Manipulation Regarding the Third Secret of Fatima

Mehmet Ali Ağca's Reaction and Open Letter Following the revelation of the Third Secret, Mehmet Ali Ağca—who was at the center of the secret—did not remain silent. In an open letter he wrote from prison on June 27, 2000, he made harsh criticisms of the Vatican, the Third Secret of Fatima, and the dynamics of religious-political power. Ağca's letter contained severe criticisms of the Vatican's authority, controversies surrounding the Fatima prophecy, and eschatological references. Ağca claimed that the Fatima Prophecy was not merely a religious phenomenon but also used as a political tool. According to him, the Vatican had not revealed the true prophecy and instead adopted a narrative that served the Church's interests. While some circles took these claims seriously, they were widely criticized in the Catholic world and international media.

The Third Secret of Fatima and Mehmet Ali Ağca

The Third Secret of Fatima emerged as one of the Vatican's greatest mysteries of the 20th century. As Ağca noted in his letter, the secret was revealed in connection with the assassination attempt on Pope John Paul II on May 13, 2000. However, Ağca asserted that this explanation was a manipulation serving the Vatican's political and religious interests. According to him, the real Secret of Fatima had been altered, and a significant truth concerning human history had been concealed. This accusation was a strong criticism of the Vatican's efforts to control historical events using religious doctrine. Ağca's open letter dated June 27, 2000, attracted attention with harsh criticisms of how the Third Secret was disclosed and accusations of manipulation directed at the Vatican. He claimed that the Vatican had deliberately distorted the secret and associated it with the papal assassination attempt to hide the truth. According to him, the Vatican had changed the true meaning of the Third Secret in order to control divine truth.

Cardinal Ratzinger in Historical and Political Context

Cardinal Joseph Ratzinger stood out as one of the most powerful figures representing the Vatican's religious authority. Ağca accused Ratzinger of distorting the truth and manipulating collective memory. This accusation was tied to Ratzinger's role in the disclosure of the Fatima Secret and his symbolic representation of the Vatican's overall policies. Ağca's statement, "Use the truth as you wish; people's memory forgets," forms the basis of his criticism of Ratzinger. This highlights the dangers that arise when religious authority merges with political power.

Mysticism and Sister Lucia's Message

Another notable detail in Ağca's letter is a message he

claimed to have received from Sister Lucia: "Welcome to the world, Mehmet Ali Ağca, you may be the awaited final Messiah." This statement takes the letter from a religious context into an eschatological discussion. Ağca's claim could be interpreted as an attempt to position himself as part of a divine plan. However, such statements opened a controversial and questioning space around Ağca. This illustrates how mystical and religious themes become entangled with political contexts.

Vatican, Manipulation, and Divine Truths

One of the main themes of the letter is the assertion that divine truths cannot be obstructed by man-made manipulations. Ağca states, "There is no power in the heavens or the earth that can prevent the victory of divine truths," expressing his belief that the Vatican's efforts are in vain. This emphasis symbolizes the resistance of individual faith against religious authorities. It also serves as a challenge to the boundaries of the Vatican's controlled religious discourse.

Ağca's reaction to the Vatican through Cardinal Ratzinger is not merely a personal critique. It encompasses a broader questioning of the Vatican's religious and political authority. He argued that the Vatican reinterpreted religious messages to serve its own interests and, in doing so, manipulated the truth. The accusation that the Vatican turned divine truths into a political power game forms the foundation of Ağca's criticisms. Through Sister Lucia's message, Ağca positions himself as a religious figure and, in this context, challenges the Vatican. In conclusion, Mehmet Ali Ağca's letter is a significant document shedding light on the controversies surrounding the Third Secret of Fatima and strong criticisms of the Vatican. This text, which reveals the struggle between divine and political truths, is a valuable resource for those who wish to examine historical events from a different perspective.

Debates About the Third Secret – The Church's Doctrinal Crisis and Controversies

Pope Ratzinger's statements on the Third Secret disturbed other circles as well, and many Christian clergy openly stated that they did not believe in the official explanation. Monsignor Corrado Balducci, one of the Vatican's exorcist priests, said, "It's very hard to see the Pope's assassination attempt in the document that reveals the Third Secret of Fatima." The demonologist Monsignor Balducci expressed "disappointment," and emphasized inconsistencies between the statements of Cardinal Sodano and Cardinal Ratzinger. Balducci went further, asking, "What happened to the other parts of the prophecy? What about the sections concerning the doctrinal crisis of the Church and World War III?" In this sense, debates about whether the final prophecy concerned Ağca are still ongoing. On the other hand, the Third Secret of Fatima, long debated in the Catholic world and interpreted both symbolically and prophetically, triggered various crises and questions within the Church's doctrinal structure and authority. The main points of these debates can be summarized as follows:

1. Mystery and Uncertainty:

Critics argued that the Church gave incomplete information during the disclosure process and interpreted the text inadequately, while some theologians emphasized that the secret itself was a symbolic warning.

2. Doctrinal and Prophetic Debates:

The Church's official doctrines are tightly woven with the foundations of faith and divine revelation. The content of the Third Secret, with claims of prophetic elements, was considered by some to be contrary to or weakening the Church's doctrines. This, especially in the context of modern criticisms and crises of faith, increased questions about the Church's authority and was interpreted by some as a sign of a doctrinal crisis.

3. Political and Social Implications:

The interpretation of the Third Secret was not only a theological issue but also became linked with the Church's role in the Cold War era and the post-war world order, as well as with social uncertainty and political tensions. Some critics claimed that the Church sought to use the Third Secret as a warning about modern crises or as a defense mechanism.

4. The Church's Response and Official Statements:

The Vatican made official statements in an attempt to give hope to believers and keep prophetic elements away from overly speculative interpretations. However, these statements were seen as insufficient by some, who criticized the Church for displaying a weak stance against modern criticisms, thus undermining its internal authority.

The debates surrounding the Third Secret of Fatima are seen as part of a crisis that reexamines the boundaries of Church doctrine, the place of prophecy and symbolism within modern belief systems, and the Church's authority in the contemporary world. These debates continue to deeply affect both the Church's role in the modern world and the perceptions of its followers, in both theological and socio-political dimensions.

The Papal Assassination and the Mystery of the Third Bullet

The 1981 assassination attempt on Pope John Paul II continues to generate controversy. The assailant, Mehmet Ali Ağca, fired three shots at the Pope in St. Peter's Square, Vatican City, yet details of the incident have remained the subject of speculation for years. A recent dimension was added to these debates by the book *"Kill the Pope: The Truth Behind the Attack on John Paul II"* written by Italian journalist Marco Ansaldo and Turkish journalist Yasemin Taşkın.

Published in Italy, the book—authored by La Repubblica's Turkey and Vatican expert Marco Ansaldo and his Turkish journalist wife Yasemin Taşkın—introduced a new angle. The authors claimed that on May 13, 1981, Pope John Paul II was shot three times, but the Vatican had secretly hidden a third bullet that hit the Pope's podium during the attack.

The Mystery of the Third Bullet

One of the most striking claims in the book is that the Vatican concealed a third bullet that hit the Pope's podium during the incident. According to the authors, Vatican security forces retrieved the bullet after the attack and hid it until 1984. Later, it was placed at the Marian shrine in Fatima, Portugal, during a ceremony honoring the Pope. However, the bullet was never independently examined or subjected to ballistic tests.

According to the authors, if such an examination had been conducted, it could have been determined whether the bullet came from Ağca's gun, possibly providing concrete evidence of a second assassin.

This claim challenges the view that the assassination attempt was carried out solely by Mehmet Ali Ağca. The mystery of the third bullet rekindles theories of potential accomplices and deeper conspiracies behind the incident.

The Fatima Prophecy and the Assassination Connection

Following the assassination, many experts, prosecutors, and authors linked the event to the belief that the Virgin Mary appeared to three children in Fatima, Portugal on May 13, 1917. The date of the attack on the Pope coinciding with this was seen as part of the prophecy. However, journalist Yasemin Taşkın argues that Ağca's notes contained crucial information that discredits this connection. According to her, May 13 was chosen merely by coincidence and the assassination had no relation to the Fatima Prophecy. This view suggests that the attack was a planned assassination attempt rather than a divine prophecy, sparking new debates.

Ağca's Striking Statements

After the assassination, Mehmet Ali Ağca frequently made headlines with his statements. In interviews, he portrayed himself as a mystical figure and even caused major controversy by claiming, "I am the reincarnation of Jesus Christ." Ağca referenced John 10:20 from the Bible, stating, "Two thousand years later, the same story is repeating with me." As the central figure of the Third Secret, Mehmet Ali Ağca concluded all these debates in his characteristic style: "You see, I believe I am the reincarnation of Jesus Christ. Read this passage. John 10:20: 'Many of them said, He is demon-possessed and raving mad. Why listen to him?' Here, two thousand years later, the same story repeats—with me."

Picture 96. Following the death of Pope John Paul II, Catholics gathered in the Vatican pray with deep sorrow (2005).

Death of the Pope

Canonization of the Pope of the Secret

With the end of the Cold War, a new world order was established, and the Pope, as the victor of this war, continued his papal duties for many years. As the 2000s approached, Pope John Paul II, who had ascended to the papacy at the age of 58, had grown old and was battling severe Parkinson's disease. On April 2, 2005, Pope John Paul II passed away in the Vatican.

Picture 97. The Cold War spiritual leader bids farewell: Pope John Paul II's death was not just the loss of a religious leader, but also the end of his silent struggle against communism. As millions mourn, the diplomacy and secrets behind the scenes remain to be unraveled.

His funeral became one of the most attended religious ceremonies in history. In the heart of the Vatican, in St. Peter's Square, hundreds of thousands of people gathered in prayer and tears. The narrow streets of Rome echoed with the voices of Christian pilgrims from around the world. Especially Polish pilgrims had flocked to the square before sunrise to celebrate the canonization of Pope John Paul II. Red and white Polish flags waved in the square from the early morning hours. Thousands of people filling the streets and avenues of the Vatican shouted, "Santo Subito!" ("Make him a saint immediately!"). And their wish was granted. On April 27, 2014, history was made. When Pope Francis read the canonization formula in Latin, the crowd held its breath. At the moment he said, **"After due reflection, consultation, and prayer for divine assistance, we declare and define that Saint John XXIII and John Paul II are saints..."** everyone in the square was living a moment of history. Pope Francis declared his predecessors, Pope John XXIII and Pope John Paul II, as saints. Pope John Paul II was elevated to sainthood in the very square where he had been the target of Ağca's bullets.

Leaders Who Attended the Ceremony and Its Significance

This major event also brought world leaders together in the Vatican. Kings, queens, presidents, and prime ministers from over 90 countries attended the ceremony. Jewish leaders from countries such as the United States, Israel, Italy, Argentina, and Poland were present to honor the contributions of Pope John and Pope Paul to Catholic-Jewish relations. This ceremony was a strong reflection of the continuity of the papacy and served as a demonstration of the Vatican's status as a universal power.

The Sacred Relics of Pope John Paul II

Before his canonization, many of Pope John Paul II's sacred relics began to be displayed around the world. One of the most striking of these was the blood-stained and bullet-pierced undergarment he wore during the assassination attempt on May 13, 1981. Years later, the bloodied shirt he wore during the attack was preserved as one of the most important relics in the process of his canonization.

This undergarment is kept in the Regina Mundi Church in Rome and is visited with great reverence by Christian pilgrims. During the canonization process, the Vatican made a special exception to standard procedures by allowing the global distribution of Pope John Paul II's relics. Many churches in Poland house samples of his blood, locks of hair, and personal belongings. These relics are considered concrete evidence of his sanctity and his service to the Church.

The Secret Letter Pope John Paul II Wrote to Mehmet Ali Ağca but Never Sent

Poland's leading newspaper *Rzeczpospolita* revealed that, in the personal archives of Pope John Paul II opened after his death, there was a letter written to Mehmet Ali Ağca that was never sent. According to the report, in the letter the Pope asked Ağca, "While we both believe in the same God, why did you shoot me?"

It is believed that the letter was written between May 1981 and December 1983. The Pope's former secretary, Archbishop Stanisław Dziwisz, confirmed that the letter was never sent to Ağca and was not shown to anyone else.

This secret letter reflects the Pope's thoughts about Ağca and his deep questions regarding the assassination attempt. However, rather than sharing the letter with the public, the Pope chose to meet Ağca face-to-face, and the dialogue between them left a mark on history. This event is remembered in the Catholic world and in global history as a moment that reinforced the Pope's message of forgiveness and humanity.

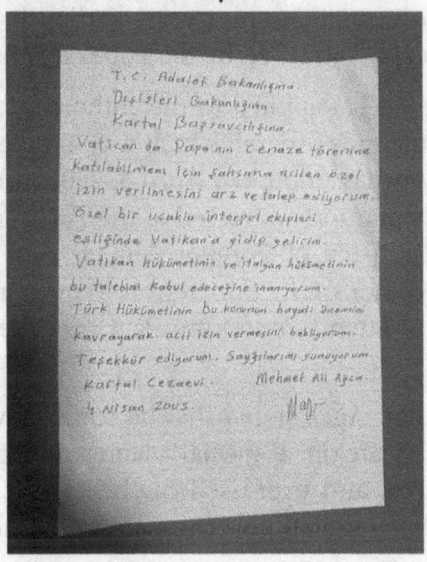

Picture 98. Mysterious words overshadowed by history: The secrets surrounding Pope John Paul II, whom Mehmet Ali Ağca called "my brother and my friend," have still not been fully elucidated. An assassination attempt, a pardon, and a mystical connection that followed... This incident, set in the dark pages of the Cold War, continues to be a story fraught with mystery, stretching from the Vatican to Istanbul.

Ağca's Condolence Message and Request to Attend the Funeral

Following the death of the Pope on April 2, 2005, Mehmet Ali Ağca, who was in prison at the time, issued a message of condolence. After the death of Pope John Paul II on April 2, 2005, Mehmet Ali Ağca's brother, Adnan Ağca, made a statement on behalf of the family, expressing their deep sorrow over the Pope's passing and saying they saw him as a friend. This was a particularly striking statement coming from someone who had attempted to assassinate him years earlier. It said, "My brother is deeply saddened by the Pope's death."

Moreover, Ağca applied to the authorities in Turkey to attend the Pope's funeral, which was to be held in the Vatican on April 8, 2005. On April 4, 2005, Mehmet Ali Ağca wrote a petition addressed to the Turkish Ministry of Justice, Ministry of Foreign Affairs, and the Chief Public Prosecutor's Office in Kartal, requesting special permission to attend Pope John Paul II's funeral in the Vatican.

In his letter, Ağca stated that he could travel to and from the Vatican on a special plane accompanied by Interpol teams, and expressed his belief that both the Vatican and the Italian governments would accept this request. He also expressed his expectation that the Turkish government would recognize the importance of the matter and urgently grant permission.

This request was quite notable as it demonstrated Ağca's desire to attend the funeral of Pope John Paul II, the man he had attempted to assassinate in 1981. Ağca's application was interpreted as part of a shift in his attitude toward the Pope and a message he wanted to convey to the public. However, his request to attend the funeral sparked major legal and diplomatic debate. After the assassination attempt in 1981, Ağca spent many years in prison and was extradited to Turkey in 2000, where he was sentenced to 17 years for previous crimes. In this context, his request to attend the funeral was denied due to both legal barriers and public controversy.

Picture 99 – 100. "The Opera Musical" recreated the historic encounter between Pope John Paul II and Mehmet Ali Ağca in an endless sea of melodies. From the secrets of Fatima to the shadow of the assassination, from the divine echo of pardon to the stage... "The Opera Musical" whispers through melodies the unsolvable knot of fate between Pope John Paul II and Mehmet Ali Ağca.

The Musical That Begins with Ağca's Assassination Attempt on the Pope

After Pope John Paul II was declared a saint, his life was brought to the stage as a musical titled *Karol Wojtyla: The True Story*. This special musical began with the sound of gunshots symbolizing Mehmet Ali Ağca's assassination attempt on the Pope and portrayed the Pope drifting between life and death. The production was staged at the Brancaccio Theatre in Rome and received great interest. The musical opened with a captivating depiction of the assassination moment—two gunshots followed by flying doves. It showed the actor playing Ağca trying to flee, being stopped by the public, and the Pope's struggle between life and death in the hospital scene.

The story continued with the Pope's childhood and youth in Poland. The musical deeply explored the story of Karol Wojtyla, a child born and raised in Wadowice who had a passion for theater. Directed by Duccio Forzano, the musical's original music and lyrics were composed by Israeli singer Noa. Rather than focusing on Karol Wojtyla's spiritual identity as a Pope who led the Catholic world for 27 years, the musical aimed to highlight his human side and private life. It covered in detail Wojtyla's emphasis on education and religious belief, his childhood and youth in Poland, and the process of being elected

Pope. His struggle against Nazism and Communism, as well as his interests in theater and sports, were also significant elements brought to life on stage.

The Third Secret and Ağca in the Pope's Book *Memory and Identity*

Pope John Paul II's 2005 book *Memory and Identity* is a theological and philosophical work that deals with topics such as humanity, freedom, evil, historical processes, and Christian teachings. The main theme of the book is the exploration of humanity's relationship with God through moral values and freedom. In the book, the Pope also discusses World War II, Poland's experience under communist rule, and events during his own papacy. He made mention of the assassin who tried to kill him. In particular, he described the 1981 assassination attempt by Mehmet Ali Ağca as a "divine intervention."

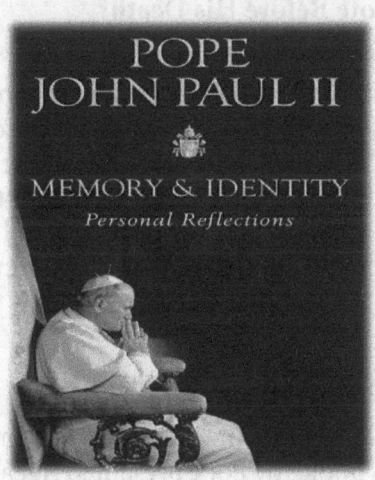

Picture 101. Memory and Identity... In these pages, Pope John Paul II recounts his faith, the history he lived through, and the events that shaped him. A leader's personal journey, or a testament to the conscience of humanity?

The Pope related Ağca's assassination attempt to the Third Secret of Fatima, expressing that the event was an example of God's intervention in human history.

In the Book, the Pope Said the Following About Ağca and the Third Secret: "The intended victim had survived. How could this be? The interesting thing is that this astonishment led him to religious questions. He wanted to know about the Fatima secret and what that secret actually was; this was his main curiosity. Perhaps those persistent questions showed that he had truly grasped something important. Ali Ağca had felt that there was a higher power beyond his own, beyond the power to shoot and kill. Then he began to seek it. I hope he found it, and I pray for that."

Why Did the Pope Include Mehmet Ali Ağca in the Book He Wrote Before His Death?

The Pope chose to address this issue in his book because the Third Secret of Fatima and Mehmet Ali Ağca's actions did not remain merely a historical or individual tragedy, but also became symbols of the ideological, psychological, and social conflicts of the modern world. From a secular perspective, several reasons can be suggested for why he included this discussion in his work:

Examination of Memory and Identity:

While examining the concepts of memory and identity in his book, the Pope presented Ağca's actions and the questions that arose from them as an example of how individuals and societies confront their own histories, beliefs, and identities. In this context, the issue of the Third Secret of Fatima is considered not only a mystical prophecy, but also part of the conflicts of memory, unspoken secrets, and personal transformations.

The lack of transparency and mysterious practices the Vatican and the Church have faced throughout history led the Pope to re-examine both his own identity and that of the institution. The contradictions reflected through Ağca's actions and the Third Secret of Fatima gave the Pope a platform to discuss the inconsistencies between power dynamics within the Church, hidden secrets, and the public image projected.

The dialogue in the Pope's book also emphasized that Ağca had entered a process of seeking a higher power and meaning beyond physical strength. This is presented as part of a universal story about how both personal tragedies and societal crises can lead to individual transformations.

In conclusion, the Pope's addressing of this topic in his book goes beyond a mere recounting of a past event or a simple narrative. It presents a deep inquiry into how fundamental issues brought by modernity—such as faith, identity, transparency, and transformation—are confronted. In this way, the reader is offered a chance to reassess these complex matters on both personal and societal levels.

Picture 102. A face, a lost life, and an unsolved mystery... Emanuela Orlandi disappeared into the shadows of the Vatican, leaving only questions. Are the posters raised in hands demanding justice the cry of a riddle that remains unanswered? Posters Raised in Hands Awaiting Justice: A Scream from an Unanswered Riddle?

The Vatican's Endless Mystery and International Intrigues
The Unsolved Riddle

Emanuela Orlandi stands at the center of a disappearance case considered one of the greatest mysteries in Vatican history. On June 22, 1983, at just 15 years old, Orlandi mysteriously vanished within the Vatican, and over the years her case has become the subject of international conspiracies, intelligence games, and religious debates. This incident serves as a critical key to understanding the Vatican's dark side and the complex geopolitical balances of the Cold War era.

A Life Lost Inside the Vatican Emanuela Orlandi was the daughter of Ercole Orlandi, who held a senior position in the Vatican. She was among the few Vatican citizens living with her family within the walls of the Vatican. On the day she disappeared, she left home to attend a music school in Rome but never returned. When Emanuela, who grew up within the Vatican's high walls, stepped out with her flute case, everything seemed like an ordinary day. However, that day, her name would become part of one of history's greatest missing person cases. Though different witnesses claimed she boarded a bus, approached a BMW, or spoke with unidentified individuals, Emanuela has never been found. Eyewitnesses reported that Orlandi boarded a public bus and chatted with a red-haired woman trying to persuade her to sell cosmetics. Other witnesses claimed to have seen the young girl getting into a car. These statements gave rise to strong suspicions of abduction. Despite intense search efforts by her family and authorities following her disappearance, no concrete clues were found, and the case gradually escalated into an international crisis. Her disappearance would later become more than just a criminal case—it became part of a vast riddle involving the Vatican's inner world, the dark dealings of the Italian mafia, and international intelligence operations. Her vanishing became one of the Vatican's deepest secrets. This event, occurring shortly after the assassination attempt on the Pope, shocked Italy.

Long-standing conspiracies and intrigues involving the mafia, intelligence agencies, and high-level Vatican officials were triggered by Orlandi's disappearance. This case emerged not merely as a missing person event but as a puzzle intersecting intelligence agencies, Vatican deep structures, mafia organizations, and global power dynamics. The connection to Mehmet Ali Ağca's assassination attempt on Pope John Paul II, the Vatican

Bank scandals, and shadowy religious groups like Opus Dei has trapped the Emanuela Orlandi case within a veil of mystery.

Emanuela Orlandi's disappearance in the Vatican's shadow is not only the loss of a young girl but also the beginning of an international enigma. On that summer day in 1983, as Orlandi's footsteps vanished into the quiet alleys of Rome, she left behind unanswered questions and a deep uncertainty.

The International Dimension of the Case

Emanuela Orlandi's disappearance quickly evolved from a legal case concerning the Vatican and Italy into an international intrigue. Various theories associated with this disappearance suggested the case was linked to the following details:

- **Vatican Bank and Mafia Connection:** At the time, claims arose that the Vatican Bank was involved in money laundering activities. It was suggested that Orlandi was kidnapped as a form of pressure regarding these operations. The Italian mafia was alleged to have been involved in the disappearance due to debts owed by the Vatican Bank.

- **Papal Assassination Attempt and Cold War Link:** Mehmet Ali Ağca's attempted assassination of Pope John Paul II was linked to the Orlandi case. Ağca claimed that Orlandi was kidnapped by the KGB and used as blackmail against the Vatican. Theories proposed that during the Cold War, the KGB and Bulgarian intelligence may have carried out such operations in response to the Pope's anti-communist stance. This theory added even more mystery to the assassination attempt.

- **Western Intelligence Agencies:** Due to alleged links to the kidnapping, attention once again turned to Mehmet Ali Ağca. Ağca put forward new claims, asserting that Western intelligence services had knowledge of the incident and were keeping it as a "state secret."

Picture 103 – 104. A missing young girl, an unsolved mystery, and the assassin's triggerman...Mehmet Ali Ağca establishes a connection between Emanuela Orlandi's disappearance and the deep shadows of the Vatican. What was the truth? A conspiracy, or a hidden truth?

Mehmet Ali Ağca's Claims and His Letter

In a letter dated June 27, 2000, written from prison, Ağca claimed that Emanuela Orlandi had been abducted by the KGB and taken to Russia. According to him, Orlandi and another young girl named Mirella Gregory are alive and being held under the control of former KGB agents. Ağca described the incident as a blackmail operation against the Vatican. However, no concrete evidence was presented to support these claims, and the letter was largely seen as speculative.

Religious and Political Implications of the Incident

- **The Vatican's Responsibility**: The Vatican faced intense criticism for its silence regarding the Orlandi case. Her disappearance once again raised questions about transparency and accountability within the Vatican.

- **International Relations**: The incident affected the international reputation of both the Vatican and Italy, adding a new dimension to the tensions between Cold War-era blocs.

- **Public Opinion and Human Rights**: The Orlandi family's pursuit of justice revealed that this was not merely a missing persons case, but also a matter of human rights violations.

The mystery surrounding Emanuela Orlandi remains

one of the darkest unresolved chapters in the Vatican's history. Due to Ağca's claims, the incident has become an international intrigue and political showdown. The Orlandi case continues to be significant as it demonstrates how religion, politics, and intelligence games can become deeply intertwined.

Emanuela as a Hostage: The Mehmet Ali Ağca Theory
Orlandi's abduction became even more complex with the claim that it was a bargaining tool for the release of Mehmet Ali Ağca, who attempted to assassinate Pope John Paul II in 1981. In a 1985 interview with Italian RAI TV, Ağca claimed that Emanuela had been abducted by the "Bulgarian branch of the Grey Wolves movement" and was still alive.

However, over the years, the inconsistencies in Ağca's statements made the case even more confusing and cast doubt on the credibility of his remarks. In his most recent interview in 2023 with the Italian newspaper *Corriere della Sera*, he made new claims:

- "I swear before God that Emanuela Orlandi is alive."
- "Emanuela is in Turkey, but naturally not in my hands, and I don't know her exact address. If the Vatican and Italian governments listen to me, I can help ensure her release."
- "No country, institution, or intelligence agency was involved in her abduction. She was kidnapped only so that I could be released from prison."

These statements once again raised the question of whether the incident was part of an international intelligence war.

Mehmet Ali Ağca's Letter

Despite making numerous statements over the years, Ağca also wrote a letter in 2000 regarding Emanuela Orlandi's disappearance, in which he stated: "I, Ali Ağca, swear before God that Emanuela Orlandi is alive. No country, no intelligence agency is involved in this matter. Emanuela was kidnapped solely for my release from prison. If the Italian government and the Vatican cooperate, we can ensure her release."

While these claims reinforced the possibility that Orlandi might still be alive, due to Ağca's past inconsistent statements, the letter was also met with scepticism.

Vatican, Mafia, and Money Laundering Allegations

Another strong theory suggested that Orlandi was a victim of illicit financial dealings between the Vatican Bank and the Italian mafia. Enrico "Renatino" De Pedis, a leader of the Rome-based Banda della Magliana mafia organization, was allegedly connected to the Vatican Bank. The gang may have kidnapped Emanuela because they could not collect their debts from the Vatican.

In 2012, De Pedis's tomb was opened, and bones not belonging to him were found. However, investigations revealed that these remains did not belong to Emanuela. This raised further questions about whether the mafia used her abduction as a message to the Vatican.

Horrific Allegation: Sex Trafficking Ring Within the Vatican

In 2012, Vatican chief exorcist Father Gabriele Amorth claimed that Orlandi may have fallen victim to pedophile rings within the Vatican. According to

Amorth, she was kidnapped for sex parties organized by a group of high-ranking Vatican officials. He claimed: "This crime was committed with the involvement of the Vatican police and some embassy staff. The girl was sexually abused and then killed."

This disturbing allegation gained more weight when documents about scandals inside the Vatican came to light and the Pope acknowledged in 2019 that some nuns had been victims of abuse.

Investigations Reopened

In January 2023, the Vatican reopened its investigation into Orlandi's disappearance, while Rome's Chief Prosecutor launched a separate case in May. On March 23, 2023, the Italian Chamber of Deputies approved a proposal to form a parliamentary commission to investigate the disappearances of Emanuela Orlandi and Mirella Gregori, who vanished under mysterious circumstances 40 years ago. This reignited public interest and led to greater attention from authorities.

Can the Emanuela Orlandi Case Be Solved?

Every new development in the Orlandi case reveals how intricate and convoluted it is. Trapped between the deep structures of the Vatican, the Italian mafia, and international intelligence agencies, this is not just a missing persons case—it reflects a global power struggle.

Ağca's claims, the mafia's financial entanglements, dark allegations within the Vatican, and intelligence wars have made solving the case exceedingly difficult. However, the new investigations launched in 2023 may finally bring answers about Orlandi's fate.

While the truth still appears hidden in the shadows, there remains a chance these dark secrets could eventually come to light. But will the Vatican and global powers truly allow the truth to emerge? Was Emanuela really a hostage for Ağca's release, or was this story a diversion meant to mislead the public? Ağca's references to the Vatican, CIA, and other intelligence agencies have only added more layers of ambiguity.

The Vatican's Strategy: Silence and Ambiguity

The Vatican remained silent for years about the Orlandi case. But the reopening of the file in 2023 broke this silence. While appearing to support the investigation, the Vatican also seemed to work behind the scenes to control the narrative. This dual approach has been interpreted as an effort to protect the Church's reputation and cover up internal connections.

Was Emanuela's disappearance a source of shame or a tool for blackmail? This question still remains unanswered. The Vatican's long-standing policy of silence has fueled suspicions that it sought to manipulate the case for its own interests. The Church's scandal-ridden history suggests that Orlandi's disappearance could be part of a larger systemic issue.

Why Can't the Case Be Solved?
The Orlandi case has been pulled in many directions over the decades, and each new investigation has only added to the uncertainty. Why has it remained unsolved? The case involves the Vatican, international intelligence agencies, mafia groups, and inter-state power dynamics. Each entity seeks to protect its own position, obscuring the truth.

As a sovereign state, the Vatican is governed by its own laws, which can hinder independent investigations. The Church's internal dynamics and diplomatic ties have led to the concealment of certain facts. Witnesses who emerged at different times gave conflicting and inconsistent accounts, leading the investigation into dead ends. Figures like Ağca, whose statements constantly changed, further complicated the search for truth. Over time, physical evidence has been lost or destroyed. Opened graves and examined documents have only raised more questions.

For the Catholic world, this case has the potential to spark a major crisis. As such, the Vatican is managing the situation carefully and implementing control mechanisms to prevent further escalation.

Legal Evaluation: The Emanuela Orlandi Case
Legally, Orlandi's disappearance is complex and multifaceted. Several key legal points must be considered:

- **International Law and the Crime of Abduction**: If it is proven that Orlandi was abducted and held, it would fall under the category of forced disappearance and would be evaluated under the UN's Convention for the Protection of All Persons from Enforced Disappearance. However, because the Vatican is a sovereign state, international legal procedures cannot be directly applied. In 1983, when Orlandi disappeared, Italy did not have well-developed legal provisions for such crimes. Today, institutions like the European Court of Human Rights (ECHR) could investigate the matter.

Medieval Darkness in a Modern World

How can a child disappear without a trace in an age of such advanced technology? How can the Vatican still provide no clear explanation for the disappearance of one of its own? How can graves be opened, documents examined, yet the result is always a void? How can powerful institutions, states, and religious authorities ignore the disappearance of a child?

According to the Italian public, the case is not just about Emanuela's disappearance but about the loss of human dignity. And if the Vatican can solve other mysteries, why not this one?

Ağca and Öcalan: Two Prisoners, Two Stories

Throughout history, assassinations have not only been seen as individual actions but also as parts of larger power struggles and intelligence wars. The attempted assassination of Pope John Paul II is one such case. Years later, in a completely different context, PKK leader Abdullah Öcalan wrote a letter to the Pope expressing his thoughts about Ağca and the assassination attempt, adding a new dimension to the event. Öcalan's letter contained critiques of both Ağca and international power dynamics, as well as Turkey's internal politics.

Mehmet Ali Ağca and Abdullah Öcalan

Despite differing ideologies and contexts, Ağca and Öcalan intersect as figures in the world of international law and diplomacy. Ağca was imprisoned in Italy for many years due to his assassination attempt on the Pope. Öcalan, as the PKK leader, also aimed to establish diplomatic relations in Europe and sought indirect contact with the Vatican.

Why Are Ağca and Öcalan Important Figures?

1. **International Political Impact:**
   - Ağca's assassination attempt caused global uproar during the Cold War and sparked numerous theories related to espionage and covert operations.
   - Öcalan, as the head of the PKK, has been central to debates on terrorism, diplomacy, and regional stability for decades.

2. **Global Media Focus:**
   - Ağca remained in the media spotlight for years after the assassination attempt and continued making public statements from prison.
   - Öcalan's capture in 1999 led to major international discussions on law, human rights, and counterterrorism.

3. **Representatives of Opposing Ideologies:**
   - Ağca came from a nationalist and anti-communist background, while Öcalan emerged as the leader of a leftist movement. Despite ideological opposition, both became entangled in global power politics.

4. **Involvement of Major Powers:**
   - Ağca's actions and the ensuing investigation involved global players like the USSR, Bulgaria, the U.S., and the Vatican.

- Öcalan became the focus of involvement from Middle Eastern powers, intelligence agencies, and European governments.

Mehmet Ali Ağca's Criticism of Öcalan
From prison, Ağca harshly criticized Abdullah Öcalan, focusing on two points:

1. **Rejecting Öcalan as a Freedom Fighter**:
   - Ağca claimed Öcalan and the PKK were tools of major powers and could not be seen as a true liberation movement. He saw Öcalan as an agent rather than a revolutionary.
2. **Öcalan's Surrender and Compromises**:
   - Ağca criticized Öcalan for surrendering in 1999 and believed a real leader should never give in. He argued that Öcalan's prison strategies were weak and inconsistent.

Picture 105. Two different cases, the same fate: One emerged with an assassination, the other with a rebellion; were Ağca and Öcalan merely namesakes of the global chess game?

Apo's Letter of Complaint to the Pope About Ağca

The assassination attempt on Pope John Paul II by Mehmet Ali Ağca in 1981 was an event that resonated significantly in the world of international politics and intelligence. Years later, the reemergence of this incident in a letter written by PKK leader Abdullah Öcalan to the Pope was recorded as a striking development. In his letter, Öcalan argued that the assassination should not be regarded merely as an individual act, but rather as part of a broader and more systematic plan.

Öcalan's Evaluation of the Assassination Attempt

In the letter to the Pope, Öcalan stated that Mehmet Ali Ağca did not reveal the truth and that the assassination should not be evaluated as an isolated incident. According to him, this event was more than an individual action—it was part of international power struggles and intelligence wars. He specifically criticized Turkey's political structure, claiming that "Ağca was released from prison by General Nurettin Ersin, one of the generals behind the 1980 coup." This claim aligns with theories suggesting the assassination was directed by Turkey's deep state or international intelligence agencies.

In the letter, Öcalan questioned the forces behind the assassination and proposed that Mehmet Ali Ağca was a proxy. Parallel to his own political stance and narrative concerning the Kurdish issue, he asserted that Ağca's act was not only aimed at the Pope but should be viewed within a broader historical context. He argued that, especially considering the past oppression of Kurds and Christian minorities, the assassination attempt on the Pope should be seen as a continuation of this historical persecution.

A Call to the Vatican and a Message of Peace

In the continuation of his letter, Öcalan expressed that the Vatican should adopt a more active stance against such events. Following his analysis of the assassination attempt and Ağca's background, he called on the Pope for a peaceful resolution and stated that he was ready to abandon armed struggle. At this point, he suggested that the Vatican should go beyond being merely a religious center and act as a political and cultural force.

The Significance of the Letter

Öcalan's letter to the Pope carries great political, diplomatic, and historical importance. Firstly, by putting forth new claims regarding the background of the assassination attempt on Pope John Paul II, he supports the view that the incident was not simply an individual attack. Secondly, the letter serves as a diplomatic appeal to the Vatican. Öcalan advocated that the Vatican take on a mediating role in the Kurdish issue and called for more active involvement from global actors.

Additionally, the letter represents an attempt by the PKK leader to strengthen his own political position and draw international public attention. The inclusion of peace messages supports Öcalan's narrative that he is seeking political solutions instead of armed struggle. Therefore, the letter is not merely a call—it can also be interpreted as an effort to position himself as a new actor on the international political stage.

By addressing the assassination attempt by Mehmet Ali Ağca in an international context, Öcalan's letter questions the political dynamics and intelligence links behind the event. Viewing the assassination not as an isolated act, Öcalan claims that the event unfolded in line with inter-state political interests. While prompting a renewed historical and political discussion about the Pope John Paul II assassination attempt, the letter is also recorded as a text inviting the Vatican to become a more active actor in the Kurdish issue. Furthermore, it can be seen as a strategic move by Öcalan to influence international public opinion.

Letters from Ağca to Apo

Mehmet Ali Ağca also made various statements about Abdullah Öcalan at different times. In 1998, while imprisoned in Italy, he criticized the Italian authorities' interest in Öcalan (who was then in Italy), stating through his lawyer Marina Magistrelli that two different standards were being applied when compared with his own case.[33]

In a 2015 statement, Ağca expressed that the Turkish government should not engage in any dialogue with Abdullah Öcalan and referred to him as a "psychopath and traitor."

Ağca Invites Apo to 'Kneel and Repent'

Ağca resurfaced in 2000 with a letter addressed to

---

33 Milliyet newspaper, "Ağca's Öcalan Rebellion", 129.11.1998

Abdullah Öcalan. This letter was filled with phrases such as "I invite you to kneel and repent" and slogans like "Down with the PKK, down with Armenian terrorism, down with Greek and Syrian betrayal gangs." In the letter, Ağca harshly criticized Öcalan's past actions and ideology, portraying himself as a nationalist and patriotic figure.

The letter was written a year after Abdullah Öcalan had been captured and brought to Turkey in 1999. At that time, Öcalan had been sentenced to life imprisonment and had made statements suggesting that the PKK should end its armed struggle. Ağca, who was extradited from Italy to Turkey in the same year, used the letter as a manifesto emphasizing his nationalist identity.

The phrase "Fate brought us together in Rome," found in Ağca's letter, is a notable historical reference. Ağca's connections to international organizations before the assassination attempt on the Pope in Europe were widely discussed for years. In this context, the statements in the letter indicate Ağca's tendency to view himself as both a national and international figure.

Mehmet Ali Ağca's letter to Abdullah Öcalan is significant not only as a personal message but also as a reflection of Ağca's ideological stance and his impact on public opinion. This letter can also be read as a reflection of the political and societal climate in Turkey in the early 2000s.

The Letter War Between Ağca and Öcalan

There have been direct or indirect written polemics between Mehmet Ali Ağca and Abdullah Öcalan, both of whom spent many years in prison. The letters exchanged between these two figures are important in revealing their views of each other and how they evaluated one another through their respective ideological lenses.

Ağca's Letters:
In his letters, Ağca accused Öcalan of being a pawn of major powers, while presenting himself as a victim of a global conspiracy because of the Vatican assassination attempt. He also claimed that Öcalan lacked leadership qualities and that the PKK was being used as a tool by foreign powers against Turkey.

Öcalan's Letters:
In his written statements interpreted as responses, Öcalan defined Ağca as a product of the system and a figure with deep state connections. According to Öcalan, Ağca concealed the truths behind his own case and played a role serving the interests of great powers.

Analysis of Mehmet Ali Ağca's Letters to Abdullah Öcalan

Ağca resurfaced in 2000 with a letter to Abdullah Öcalan, which reflects the continuation of his ideological stance. This letter was particularly filled with phrases like "I invite you to kneel and repent" and "Down with the PKK, down with Armenian terrorism, down with Greek and Syrian betrayal gangs." In it, Ağca harshly criticized Öcalan's past actions and ideology, portraying himself as a nationalist and patriotic figure. This indicates that during his years in prison, Ağca had adopted a certain mindset and wished to share these ideas with the public.

In his earlier letters, Ağca had described himself as a victim of international conspiracies, questioned the powers behind the assassination, and put forward various conspiracy theories about world order. His letter to Öcalan is a continuation of this narrative, this time directly targeting elements he viewed as supporters of the PKK.

The timing of the 2000 letter corresponds with the year following Öcalan's capture and sentencing to life imprisonment. During this period, Öcalan had called for the PKK to abandon armed struggle. Ağca's letter served as a nationalist manifesto during this time.

In his earlier writings, Ağca also portrayed himself as both a victim of international forces and a defender of Turkey and the Turkish nation. In the letter to Öcalan, he maintained this attitude, emphasizing his presence in Rome during the Pope assassination process and using the phrase "Fate brought us together in Rome." This can be interpreted as an effort to build a bridge between his past and present.

Ağca's letters were generally publicized through the media. The 2000 letter to Öcalan was reportedly given to his lawyer and made public, suggesting that Ağca's intent was not only to deliver a message to Öcalan but also to reach a wider audience. Similarly, his earlier letters also generated considerable public reaction when shared with the media.

Although Mehmet Ali Ağca and Abdullah Öcalan operated on vastly different ideological planes, both became focal points of global interest in the realms of international politics and diplomacy. Ağca's criticisms of Öcalan underscore sharp divisions born of ideological differences and strategic interests. On the other hand, Öcalan's efforts to establish relations with the Vatican can be interpreted as attempts to gain international legitimacy. The "letter war" between the two figures reveals their perspectives of one another and brings historical and ideological clashes to light. Their influence on global powers, media, and diplomacy has made them two of the most striking figures in modern political history.

The MHP and Alparslan Türkeş's Distant Stance Toward Mehmet Ali Ağca

Mehmet Ali Ağca became one of the most talked-about figures in Turkey following the 1979 assassination of journalist Abdi İpekçi. His escape after the assassination, his international connections, and his attempt on the life of Pope John Paul II turned him into a globally controversial figure. However, despite claims that Ağca had ties to the nationalist movement in the past, the Nationalist Movement Party (MHP) and its leader Alparslan Türkeş maintained a distant stance toward him and occasionally stated this openly.

In Turkey, following the İpekçi assassination, Ağca's name was frequently associated with the nationalist movement. However, these claims were explicitly rejected by MHP and Alparslan Türkeş. In his testimony during the MHP and Idealist Organizations trial after the September 12 military coup, Türkeş stated that no assassination was organized by the MHP and that Ağca was an individual actor.

Türkeş repeatedly emphasized that such actions did not align with the principles and values of the nationalist movement. He stated that Ağca had no ties to the MHP and committed the assassinations on his own initiative.

Ağca's Statements and Their Impact on the MHP
Mehmet Ali Ağca's statements about both the Abdi İpekçi and the Pope assassinations often changed, with

contradictory remarks that called his credibility into question. This weakened the claims linking Ağca to the MHP and further clarified that he was a figure operating outside the control of the nationalist movement. During this period, Türkeş and the MHP adopted a particularly cautious policy to avoid being associated with Ağca's actions. These inconsistencies in Ağca's statements reinforced the justification for the MHP's distance from him. In both Turkish and Italian courts, Ağca consistently denied any links between his actions and the MHP or nationalist organizations, presenting himself as a lone terrorist.

Türkeş and the MHP's Strategic Positioning

Alparslan Türkeş and the MHP took a clearly distant stance toward Ağca's actions and statements, seeking to preserve the discipline and ideological coherence of the nationalist movement. Under Türkeş's leadership, this posture contributed not only to viewing Ağca as an individual actor but also helped the nationalist movement maintain its identity as a disciplined political organization during the dark period of Turkey's left-right conflicts. Türkeş's reserved approach reflected efforts to protect the MHP's public image and ideological consistency during that era.

Ağca and the MHP: Damage or Divergence?

The allegations about Ağca's past ties to the nationalist movement and the association of his actions with the MHP put the Nationalist Movement Party and Alparslan Türkeş in a difficult position. So, did Mehmet Ali Ağca's actions actually damage the MHP? The answer to this question can be better understood by analyzing the political and societal context of that time.

The Disciplined Structure of the MHP and Türkeş

Under the leadership of Alparslan Türkeş, the MHP in the 1970s established an ideological framework as a right-wing political party and paid close attention to making the nationalist movement a disciplined organization. The MHP aimed to educate nationalist youth and make them part of an intellectual and political movement. In this process, individual actions and uncontrolled behaviors were seen as elements that could threaten the image and political goals of the movement.

Mehmet Ali Ağca's assassination of Abdi İpekçi and the subsequent developments posed a potential threat that could damage this disciplined structure of the MHP. However, Alparslan Türkeş tried to protect the MHP from such accusations by clearly rejecting Ağca and emphasizing that he had no connection with the movement. The association of Mehmet Ali Ağca with the nationalist movement negatively affected the public image of the MHP. The killing of a respected journalist like Abdi İpekçi triggered a strong reaction among large segments of society. Although attempts were made to associate this murder with the MHP, Türkeş's quick and clear response helped limit the damage to the party.

In Turkey, left-wing circles and political rivals targeted the MHP by linking Ağca's actions to the nationalist movement. Especially during this period, when left-right clashes were at their peak, existing criticisms of the MHP's youth organizations intensified with Ağca's actions. Mehmet Ali Ağca's individual acts raised the debate about how open the MHP was to uncontrollable behavior. The emergence of such uncontrolled individual actions within Türkeş's party was seen as a threat in terms of ideological unity and party discipline. Mehmet

Ali Ağca's individual acts created a potential threat that could negatively affect the MHP's public image. However, Alparslan Türkeş's leadership skills, clear statements, and the MHP's disciplined structure prevented the damage from growing. Türkeş continuously emphasized that they had no ideological or political connection with Ağca and tried to keep the party away from this negative perception.

Therefore, the damage Mehmet Ali Ağca caused to the MHP remained mostly limited to accusations by political opponents and did not seriously affect the party's ideological integrity. However, Ağca's name went down in history as a symbol frequently mentioned among the accusations the nationalist movement faced during the chaotic environment of Turkey's left-right conflict.

Did Mehmet Ali Ağca's Action Accelerate the Collapse of the Soviet Union?

Mehmet Ali Ağca's 1981 assassination attempt on Pope John Paul II not only targeted a religious leader but also turned into an international crisis. The theories that emerged after the assassination attempt pointed to the possibility that Soviet and Eastern Bloc intelligence agencies (especially the KGB through Bulgarian connections) may have been behind the act. However, Ağca's statements, actions, and the international political environment led to a broader evaluation of these theories.

After the assassination attempt, Mehmet Ali Ağca made constantly contradictory statements in his testimonies. Sometimes he implied that the Soviet Union and Bulgaria were behind the assassination attempt, while at other times he denied these connections. These contradictions made it difficult to uncover the truth behind the assassination. Ağca's confessions further increased the West's suspicions toward the Soviet Union but failed to provide solid proof.

The Pope assassination became a tool for the Western world to accuse the Soviet Union. Although the truths behind the assassination were never fully clarified, the incident served the West's efforts to portray the Soviet Union as the "source of global instability." Especially the United States and NATO used these claims as propaganda tools to further isolate the Soviet Union.

The Soviet Union's Defense and Propaganda

The Soviet Union and Bulgaria frequently stated that they had no involvement in the Pope assassination. Moscow argued that such accusations were part of the West's Cold War propaganda and that the facts behind the assassination were distorted by the West. However, these defenses failed to create a strong enough impact on the international public.

Mehmet Ali Ağca's assassination attempt on the Pope and the subsequent "Bulgarian Connection" theory caused the Soviet Union to suffer a serious loss of reputation internationally. This incident led the West to target the Soviet Union and the Eastern Bloc more aggressively. However, the true perpetrators of the assassination were never fully proven. This situation suggests that Mehmet Ali Ağca's actions were used as a tool with the potential to harm the Soviet Union.

In conclusion, although Mehmet Ali Ağca's actions did not directly target the Soviet Union, how the West used the incident imposed significant international costs on Moscow. The assassination attempt went down in history as one of the most striking examples of Cold War propaganda wars.

Mehmet Ali Ağca's 1981 assassination attempt on Pope John Paul II was a major event that deeply resonated in world politics and is considered to have had an indirect effect on the collapse of the Soviet Union. This incident was not just an assassination attempt, but a development that reshaped the balance in international relations amid the tense atmosphere of the Cold War.

Impact on the Outcome of the Cold War

Mehmet Ali Ağca's act and the Pope assassination accelerated the propaganda and ideological war of the Cold War. Especially the U.S. and Western Europe used this event to adopt a stronger stance against the Soviet Union. This situation placed the Soviet Union in an even more difficult position economically, politically, and ideologically.

Although the main factors that accelerated the collapse of the Soviet Union were economic collapse, popular movements in Eastern Europe, and ideological tensions, incidents like the Pope assassination indirectly influenced this process. The assassination attempt undermined confidence in the authority of the Eastern Bloc and boosted the morale of movements fighting against communist regimes.

A Spark That Accelerated the Collapse

While Mehmet Ali Ağca's act was not a direct factor in the collapse of the Soviet Union, it played an important indirect role. The assassination attempt on the Pope weakened the Soviet Union's influence in Eastern

Europe, strengthened propaganda against Moscow in the Western world, and accelerated the process of dissolution in the Eastern Bloc.

Although the collapse of the Soviet Union mainly stemmed from economic collapse, ideological conflicts, and popular movements, Ağca's act took its place in history as one of the events that triggered this process. The assassination attempt reshaped the dynamics of the Cold War and became one of the factors that accelerated the Soviet Union's dissolution.

Is Mehmet Ali Ağca a Hero?

From some perspectives, Mehmet Ali Ağca can be seen as a "positive" figure in world history, especially with the claim that he indirectly contributed to the collapse of the Soviet Union. Here are the grounds cited by those who defend this view:

Contribution to the Weakening of the Soviet Union: Ağca's assassination attempt on Pope John Paul II strengthened the propaganda portraying the Soviet Union as a more aggressive and oppressive power in the Western world. This accelerated the dissolution of the Eastern Bloc. If one views the collapse of the Soviet Union as a gain in terms of human rights, freedom, and the advancement of democracy, Ağca could be considered a hero due to his indirect impact. The attack on the Pope increased international support for the Solidarity Movement in Poland. This support contributed to the collapse of the Eastern Bloc and played a significant role in toppling authoritarian regimes. Some argue that Ağca was a pawn in international intelligence games and became part of a system beyond his control. From this perspective, Ağca can be seen as a tool that exposed the power plays in global politics.

According to Whom Is Mehmet Ali Ağca a Traitor?

From another perspective, Mehmet Ali Ağca's actions can be considered a betrayal to the world and to humanity. This view is based on the following reasons:

- **Violence Against Innocent People:** Mehmet Ali Ağca murdered Abdi İpekçi, a journalist who advocated peace and reconciliation, and later attempted to assassinate the Pope, a spiritual leader for millions. These acts can be viewed as violence against innocent people for individual or ideological reasons and thus as betrayal from the standpoint of universal values.

- **A Figure That Created Chaos and Turmoil:** Ağca's actions increased chaos in international politics and escalated tensions between countries. His actions can be seen as part of events that threatened world peace.

- **An Unreliable and Contradictory Personality:** Ağca's constantly changing statements and inconsistent explanations have made him an unreliable and manipulative figure to many. Allegations that he hid or distorted the truth about his actions strengthen the notion that any positive effect of his was purely coincidental.

Hero or Traitor? The Role of Ideological and Historical Perspective

The answer to this question largely depends on one's ideological and historical point of view:

- **Cold War Perspective:** If someone views the Cold War as the West's struggle for "freedom and democracy," and considers that Ağca's actions helped accelerate the dissolution of the Soviet Union, they may view him as a hero. However, if the same person considers that these acts were carried out by targeting an innocent religious leader, they may move away from the idea of heroism.

- **Humanitarian and Universal Values Perspective:** From a viewpoint that values human life and peace, Mehmet Ali Ağca's actions clearly involve violence and are seen as unacceptable. In this case, he is not a hero, but rather a figure who harmed humanity.

- **His Own Contradictions and Reality:** Ağca's contradictory statements and ever-changing narratives may be interpreted as an attempt not to serve an ideology or purpose, but to create mystery around himself and his actions. This makes it difficult to see him as either a hero or a traitor; instead, he may be viewed as a manipulated tool.

What Does Mehmet Ali Ağca Represent for Catholics?

Mehmet Ali Ağca's assassination attempt on Pope John Paul II on May 13, 1981, in the Vatican caused a deep trauma within the Catholic world, while also giving rise to a powerful spiritual message. This event was not only perceived as a physical attack on the Pope but also as an assault on the spiritual leader of the Catholic faith—and thus on all Catholics. Ağca became a figure who represented both a threat and a testament to the strength of faith and the forgiveness of their leader. In this context, what Ağca represents for Catholics can be examined under three main themes: trauma, forgiveness, and a spiritual message.

The assassination attempt created deep trauma in the Catholic world and simultaneously produced a spiritual message. The event became a test of faith and an opportunity for the Pope to reinforce Catholic values by demonstrating forgiveness. Additionally, the mysteries and conspiracy theories surrounding the incident ignited significant debate within the Catholic world. This article evaluates the meanings that Ağca holds for Catholics in the context of trauma, forgiveness, spiritual messages, and mysteries.

Secrets and Conspiracy Theories in the Catholic World

Ağca's attempt was not merely seen as an individual act but was also interpreted as being backed by hidden powers and secret agendas. This led to various conspiracy theories:

- **The Fatima Prophecy Connection:** Pope John Paul II believed his survival was linked to the Fatima Prophecy and viewed the event as a divine warning.
- **International Powers and KGB Links:** Some claimed that international powers like the Soviet Union and the KGB were behind Ağca's act.
- **Ağca's Contradictory Statements:** His inconsistent statements post-incident raised doubts about the real perpetrators.
- **Hidden Agendas within the Vatican:** Some

conspiracy theorists alleged that factions within the Vatican itself manipulated the event.

Ağca remains a complex figure—both as an assailant and part of a story of forgiveness. While his attack traumatized Catholics, the Pope's reaction turned the incident into a symbol of peace and hope. The enduring mysteries surrounding it continue to fuel debate. Therefore, what Ağca represents to Catholics is shaped by both his actions and the Pope's response, making him a central figure in historical, spiritual, and political discussions.

Trauma: An Attack on the Pope as an Attack on the Catholic World

Pope John Paul II was not only a religious leader but also a global ambassador for peace. His advocacy for human rights and freedoms—especially against communist regimes in Eastern Europe—made him a source of inspiration for Catholics. The assassination attempt at one of the holiest places of Catholicism caused trauma due to:

- **Targeting the Spiritual Leader:** The assault was seen as a direct attack on the heart of Catholic faith.

- **Violence in a Sacred Space:** The event's location—St. Peter's Square—deepened the spiritual impact.

- **A Provocation Against Catholic Beliefs:** Some Catholics saw it as a provocation and challenge to the Church's message of peace.

Forgiveness: The Pope's Spiritual Strength

One of the most significant meanings Ağca holds for Catholics stems from the Pope's act of forgiveness. Despite the attack, the Pope visited Ağca in prison in 1983 and publicly forgave him. This had a profound impact:

- **The Power of Forgiveness:** Forgiveness, representing God's love and human sanctity, is central to Catholic doctrine. The Pope's gesture became a powerful example of this value.

- **A Living Example of Christian Teaching:** The act illustrated the core Christian teaching: "forgive your enemies."

- **The Pope as a Symbol of Martyrdom and Resilience:** His survival was seen as a divine gift, reinforcing his spiritual leadership.

Spiritual Message: The Triumph of Faith

Beyond trauma, the event became a story of spiritual strength and religious values. The attack and the Pope's response conveyed messages such as:

- **Victory of Good over Evil:** The Pope's survival and act of forgiveness symbolized moral triumph.

- **Perceived Divine Intervention:** Some viewed his survival as miraculous, especially in connection with the Fatima Prophecy.

- **Power of Forgiveness and Peace:** His forgiveness turned the event into a symbol of reconciliation and the embodiment of Catholic values.

A Complex Figure for Catholics

Ağca represents a contradiction—both an aggressor and a component of a story of forgiveness. His actions and inconsistent statements contributed to a perception of him as manipulative and untrustworthy. While some Catholics saw him as a traitor to their faith, others believed his actions served a divine purpose. This complexity prevents a singular, clear interpretation of Ağca within Catholicism.

In essence, while his attempt inflicted a deep wound, the Pope's forgiveness transformed it into a story of hope and peace. Thus, Ağca's significance to Catholics is shaped as much by the Pope's response as by his own actions.

Conclusion:

Mehmet Ali Ağca remains a multifaceted figure for Catholics—an aggressor, a symbol of forgiveness, and a participant in a divine narrative. This complexity places him at the center of historical and spiritual debate.

Ağca's Role in Russian Orthodoxy and Vatican Relations

Russia has long been a center of Orthodox Christianity, and tensions between the Catholic and Orthodox churches have persisted historically.

- Pope John Paul II tried to strengthen dialogue between the two churches.
- A rivalry existed between the Vatican and the Russian Orthodox Church, especially in Eastern Europe over spiritual authority.

Ağca's attack did not weaken the Vatican but instead increased the Pope's spiritual power, making the Vatican even more influential in the Orthodox world.

- **Strengthened the Catholic Church:** The attempt reinforced the Pope's leadership and spiritual unity among Catholics.
- **The Orthodox Church's Defensive Stance:** The Russian Orthodox Church remained cautious of any Vatican influence, and Ağca's act indirectly advantaged the Vatican in this rivalry.

During the Cold War, Ağca's act was used ideologically by the West against Moscow, damaging the Soviet Union's global image.

- **Strengthened U.S. and NATO Anti-Soviet Policies:** The incident justified greater pressure on the USSR.
- **Energized Eastern European Anti-Soviet Movements:** Movements like Solidarity in Poland gained more Western support.
- **Weakened Soviet Influence in Eastern Europe:** Associating Moscow with the attack fueled resistance against the Soviets.

Thus, Ağca's act dealt a blow to Soviet and Orthodox Russian global influence.

- **For the USSR:** Ağca was seen as a tool used by the West to discredit them.
- **For the Russian Orthodox Church:** The act boosted Vatican's spiritual authority at their expense.
- **For the Russian Federation today:** The event is viewed as Cold War propaganda used against Moscow.

Ağca's significance to Russia stems from his role in

weakening the Orthodox world and the USSR. Even today, debates over the Pope assassination reflect the historical echoes of Russia's rivalry with the West.

What Does Mehmet Ali Ağca Represent for Turks and the Islamic World?

Due to the 1979 Abdi İpekçi assassination and the 1981 assassination attempt on the Pope, Ağca became a controversial figure in both Turkey and globally. While he is often labeled a "terrorist" in the West, reactions in Turkey and the Islamic world were mixed.

Perceptions of Ağca varied among nationalists, Islamists, and secularists. His contradictory statements over time made forming a clear opinion difficult.

Mehmet Ali Ağca from the Perspective of Turkish Nationalists

Ağca was associated with the nationalist movement in the 1970s, though MHP (Nationalist Movement Party) and its leader Alparslan Türkeş denied any organizational ties, distancing themselves for several reasons:

- **Conflict with MHP's Discipline:** The MHP was an ideologically disciplined movement; rogue actors like Ağca were seen as damaging.
- **Negative Fallout from İpekçi's Murder:** The assassination linked the MHP to political killings.
- **Pope Attempt Not a "Turkish Cause":** His international act lacked relevance to nationalist goals.

Thus, Turkish nationalists did not see him as a hero and rejected his association with their movement.

Ağca in Islamic Circles

Reactions in Islamic circles were also mixed.

- **Radical Elements:** Some viewed the attack as action against Christianity, framing Ağca as a kind of warrior against the West.
- **Mainstream Islamists:** Mainstream Islamic groups did not support him, emphasizing that Islam forbids killing innocents.

The Pope wasn't seen as an enemy to Muslims, and the Vatican promoted interfaith dialogue, further reducing sympathy for Ağca.

Mehmet Ali Ağca in Secular and Intellectual Sections

Secular Turks and intellectuals viewed Ağca negatively.

- **Seen as a Murderer:** The killing of prominent journalist Abdi İpekçi was a severe blow to press freedom.
- **Hitman Image:** Many believed Ağca had ties to shadowy elements and intelligence agencies.
- **Harmed Turkey's Image:** His actions and erratic behavior hurt Turkey's global reputation.

Ağca in the Islamic World

Perceptions of Ağca varied by region:

- **Arab World:** While the assassination attempt made waves, he was not considered a hero.
- **Iran:** Despite anti-West rhetoric post-revolution, Iran did not recognize him as an Islamic figure.

- **Pakistan and Afghanistan:** Neither militants nor radicals embraced him. In short, Ağca did not gain widespread support in the Islamic world.

The Third Secret of Fatima and Why It Was Not Understood in Turkey

The Third Secret of Fatima was a prophecy allegedly revealed by the Virgin Mary to three shepherd children in the town of Fatima, Portugal, in 1917. This secret, which resonated widely in the Christian world and was concealed by the Vatican for many years, has been the subject of various theories and speculations. However, interest in this topic in Turkey has remained limited, and it has not been widely understood by the masses. So why wasn't the Third Secret of Fatima sufficiently discussed and examined in-depth in Turkey in an academic sense? The reasons are as follows:

Being a Christianity-Based Prophecy

The Third Secret of Fatima is rooted in the Catholic belief system and is considered a prophecy of the Virgin Mary. Since the majority of Turkey's population is Muslim, it is natural that a subject related to Christian theology did not attract widespread interest. There are also mystical and prophecy-focused events in Islamic tradition; however, these are generally assessed within their own religious and historical context. Therefore, the Fatima prophecy remained from a different religious perspective in Turkey.

Being Seen as a Topic Specific to the Vatican and Catholic World

The Secrets of Fatima are largely perceived as an internal issue of the Vatican. The Vatican kept these prophecies secret for many years and only decided to reveal them at a specific time. The limited number of scholars and media in Turkey interested in the Catholic Church and the Vatican has been a factor preventing such topics from becoming popular. While in the Western world the Fatima Prophecy is often discussed alongside papal policies, in Turkey it remained a topic that does not directly affect daily life.

Lack of Interest from Turkish Media and Academia
Media in Turkey generally focuses more on local and political events. Although the Third Secret of Fatima has been reported from time to time, it has not undergone academic or historical analysis as it has in the West. At the academic level, studies focused on Ottoman history and Islam are more prevalent; therefore, a Vatican-centered prophecy has not entered the research agenda of scholars.

Different Religious and Cultural Priorities in Turkey
The religious and cultural sensitivities in Turkey are mostly based on Islamic tradition. Topics such as the Mahdi, Messiah, and Signs of the Day of Judgment attract more interest than the Fatima Prophecy. Additionally, the name "Fatima" being associated with the Prophet Muhammad's daughter Fatima has also led to some confusion. The Turkish public and media are more interested in political and religious developments in the Middle East rather than religious visions in the Christian world.

Being Overshadowed by Conspiracy Theories and Political Debates

The Third Secret of Fatima has occasionally been mentioned along with conspiracy theories, but these theories mostly remained at a speculative level. According to some claims, there are hidden messages related to Turkey within this prophecy. The assassination attempt on Pope John Paul II and the connection of Mehmet Ali Ağca to this event have been linked to the Fatima Prophecy. However, these connections have not been thoroughly examined through academic and official channels and have mostly remained speculative and media-centered narratives.

The Importance for Turkey of Understanding the Vatican, the Western World, and Western Belief Systems

Understanding the Vatican and Western beliefs is important for Turkey to grasp its relations with the Western world from an international political and historical perspective. Religious beliefs and prophecies in the West often influence political decision-making processes and carry strategic importance in international relations. Considering the historical tensions and religion-based politics between the Islamic world and the West, Turkey's understanding of the West's religious and political dynamics could enhance its foreign policy effectiveness and enable more conscious actions in regional balances.

Ağca's Influence on the Media

Following the assassination attempt, Ağca became a striking figure through the media. His statements to the press, behavior, and trial process led him to become a famous character. Ağca's remarks to the media were often provocative and attention-grabbing.

Manipulation of Media and Public Opinion

Ağca's relationship with the media was at times interpreted as a strategy aimed at manipulating public opinion. His various statements and behaviors in the media were intended to influence both the public and the authorities.

Media Reflections and Speculations

Speculations regarding the reasons behind the assassination and Ağca's motivations received extensive media coverage. Different news outlets presented various theories about Ağca's ideological and political connections.

Ağca's Media Relations During Imprisonment

Media interest in Ağca continued while he was in prison. Statements and interviews he gave from prison allowed him to maintain a presence in the public eye.

Perceptions Formed by the Media and Public

How the media portrayed Ağca significantly influenced public perception. The media's depiction of him shaped public opinion regarding the assassination and his behavior in the following years.

Mehmet Ali Ağca's relationship with the media contributed to his emergence as an internationally known figure and his extensive resonance with the public. News and analyses about him significantly influenced how the event and his personality were perceived.

Mehmet Ali Ağca and the Attempted Assassination of the Pope: Political Context, Theories, and Possible Realities

Mehmet Ali Ağca's attempted assassination of Pope

John Paul II on May 13, 1981, in the Vatican, became one of the biggest political events of the Cold War era. The motivations behind this event, possible actors involved, and global political dynamics remain subjects of debate. Ağca's identity, past, and connections raised the question of whether he was a lone assassin or part of a larger international conspiracy.

The Cold War and Turkey's Situation During Ağca's Upbringing

Ağca's youth coincided with one of the harshest periods of the Cold War. The 1970s were marked by intensifying ideological conflicts between right- and left-wing groups in Turkey. The power struggle between the U.S. and the Soviet Union had a significant impact on Turkey, leading to ideological polarization among youth. As a NATO member, Turkey was part of the Western Bloc and implemented strict policies within military and intelligence structures to prevent the spread of communism. Leftist movements were suppressed as being linked to the Soviet Union and the Eastern Bloc, while rightist movements became part of Western-backed anti-communist activities.

The military coup of September 12, 1980, was carried out to end the quasi-civil war between right and left factions but strengthened military tutelage in Turkey. Mehmet Ali Ağca was raised within the ultranationalist movement during this chaotic period and was trained along anti-communist lines.

Ağca and the ASALA Terror Organization Debates

It is now clear that Ağca had ties with right-wing nationalist groups during the 1970s. The late 1970s and early 1980s were a time when Turkish nationalists were in intense conflict with the Armenian terrorist organization ASALA. ASALA (Armenian Secret Army for the Liberation of Armenia) carried out assassinations and bombings targeting Turkish diplomats starting in 1975. Turkish nationalists responded with reciprocal operations both domestically and abroad. During this process, it was claimed that MIT (Turkish intelligence) and nationalist groups organized assassinations and operations against some ASALA members. While Ağca was not directly involved in fighting ASALA, he shared the same anti-terrorist rhetoric ideologically. Some claims suggest that being part of these anti-ASALA groups may have helped Ağca receive assassination training. However, there is no definitive evidence that Ağca engaged in direct conflict with ASALA.

Ağca, with a Turkish nationalist background, stood ideologically opposed to ASALA, a left-wing terrorist group that directly targeted the Turkish state. Therefore, it is unlikely he had any link with ASALA. ASALA's goal was to assassinate Turkish diplomats and officials to avenge the so-called Armenian genocide. For Ağca to collaborate with a group directly hostile to the Turkish state is not a plausible claim. The nationalist groups Ağca was involved with were in a state of war with ASALA. Thus, it is impossible for Ağca to have been supported or linked to ASALA. While ASALA received support from some Western European leftist groups and the Eastern Bloc, Ağca's connections were limited to anti-communist circles. ASALA operated through an organizational structure that carried out assassinations and bombings, whereas Ağca acted alone or with small groups.

ASALA never targeted the Vatican in its terror

campaign against Turkey. There is no concrete evidence showing that Ağca was trained by ASALA. During his initial interrogations by Italian authorities after the assassination attempt, Ağca claimed to be of Armenian descent. However, it is definitively known that he came from a Turkish and Muslim family. This statement is considered one of the many inconsistent claims he made during questioning and was not taken seriously in official investigations. These statements have been interpreted as part of a strategy to deliberately create confusion during interrogation.

There is no direct connection between Ağca and ASALA, and neither his intentions nor the background of the assassination align with ASALA's operations. Claims that ASALA was involved in the papal assassination are unrealistic and unsubstantiated speculations.

Ağca's Escape to Iran

After the assassination of journalist Abdi İpekçi, Ağca fled through Iran. In 1979, Iran had just undergone the Islamic Revolution and was undergoing a major political transformation. Ağca's escape to Iran has been interpreted as a strong sign that he was acting with the support of an international organization. Although the post-revolution Iranian government was accused of supporting some international groups due to its anti-Western rhetoric, there is no definitive evidence linking Iran to Ağca. Furthermore, Iran stood ideologically opposed to the nationalist-rightist circles to which Ağca belonged, suggesting that Iran was merely used as a transit route.

Ağca's Messianic Declarations

After the assassination attempt, Ağca used language

filled with threats against the Vatican and the Christian world. He declared himself the "Messiah" and developed religious-mystical rhetoric. He made contradictory statements at different times, blaming various individuals and groups.

Ağca frequently gave inconsistent and shifting statements in his testimonies after the assassination attempt. At times he blamed the KGB, the Vatican, and even the Illuminati and secret organizations. There were interviews in which he declared himself the Messiah. So, should these conflicting statements be seen as a sign of his psychological condition or as a strategy to obscure the truth?

Ağca's past raises the question of whether he was merely a hitman or a conscious actor in a larger scheme. His murder of Abdi İpekçi in 1979, subsequent escape, and eventual attempt on the Pope's life appear to be part of international power struggles rather than an isolated act of terror.

Conspiracy Theories and Realities

There are many conspiracy theories surrounding the papal assassination. Some argue it was planned by the KGB due to Soviet discomfort with a Polish Pope during the Cold War. Others believe internal factions within the Vatican used Ağca as a pawn in an internal power struggle.

Others claim that the Vatican used the Fatima prophecies as tools of political and religious manipulation. Was the Third Secret truly a prophecy about the assassination, or did the Vatican use this mystical narrative to legitimize events and strengthen its religious authority?

It is thought that Ağca first associated himself with the Third Secret of Fatima while in prison, during the process in which he was pardoned by the Pope. After the assassination attempt, the Vatican made statements linking the event to the Fatima prophecies, possibly prompting Ağca to discover this mystical narrative. The Vatican established a religious context by linking the assassination attempt to the Third Secret of Fatima. This created a narrative that the Pope was under divine protection, reinforcing the authority of the Catholic Church. From the perspective of Christian eschatology, the failed assassination was presented as evidence of divine intervention and became an argument supporting the sanctity of the Pope's mission.

Eschatology, Theology, Secrets, and the Vatican
When religion, politics, and mysteries are evaluated together in world history, many unknowns arise. Eschatology—the study of the end times and the afterlife—has been a topic of theological debate for centuries. In this context, the role of the Vatican, its effects on world politics, and figures like Mehmet Ali Ağca become topics of great curiosity.

Eschatology is a branch of theology dealing with how the end of the world will occur. The Book of Revelation in Christianity and hadiths about signs of the end in Islam offer clues about this topic. The views and interpretations of religious centers like the Vatican about eschatological events have sometimes echoed in world politics. From a theological standpoint, the Vatican's secret documents and its approach to prophecies are noteworthy. The Fatima Prophecies hold a significant place among the secrets the Vatican kept for years. How the Pope, as the leader of the Catholic world, approaches these prophecies points to the mystical side of the Vatican. The Vatican has evaluated these prophecies not only as a religious issue but also within the context of world politics. These secrets, often associated with anti-communist propaganda against the Soviet Union, helped increase the Vatican's political power.

The Vatican functions not only as a religious authority but also as a diplomatic and political power. The longstanding relationship between the Vatican and European politics from the Middle Ages to today demonstrates the global influence of the papacy.

Among the secrets the Vatican is alleged to have hidden are documents about the life of Jesus, the Fatima Prophecies, and secret correspondences in the Vatican archives. In particular, the attempted assassination of Pope John Paul II and how it was handled by the Vatican remain among the most discussed events.

Mehmet Ali Ağca and the Vatican

Questions such as which powers were behind Ağca's assassination attempt and whether this event was a message directed at the Vatican remained on the agenda for a long time. Ağca's connections, his contradictory statements following the attempt, and his claim that "I have a mission related to the Fatima Prophecies" made the event even more mysterious. Although the Vatican never fully clarified the background of the incident, Pope John Paul II's visit to Ağca in prison gave the assassination attempt a new dimension in the context of interfaith dialogue.

Contribution of the Assassination Attempt to Vatican State Policy

The assassination attempt against the Pope marked a critical turning point in the Vatican's state policy. First of all, following the incident, the Vatican significantly increased its security measures and made the Papal office a more controlled structure. Moreover, this event led the Vatican to take a more active role in global politics, particularly prompting a shift in its stance toward Eastern Bloc countries.

Pope John Paul II was known for his anti-communist stance, and the assassination attempt further strengthened his political position. His support for the Solidarity Movement in Poland notably contributed to the encouragement of anti-communist movements in Eastern Europe. Therefore, this event demonstrated that the Vatican was not just a religious authority but also an emerging geopolitical power.

Eschatology, theology, and the secrets of the Vatican have always aroused great curiosity throughout history. Mehmet Ali Ağca's attack on Pope John Paul II revealed the complex relationship between religion and politics. Even today, the full background of such events remains unclear, and the influence of religious authorities like the Vatican in political arenas continues.

On the other hand, major eschatological events in history, such as the Crusades, show how deeply intertwined religion and politics are and how religious motivations can drive global conflicts. Such major events continue to shape religious and political balances both in the past and today.

Some of the greatest mysteries of world history still await resolution, and the balance between religions and politics is constantly shifting. How eschatological beliefs and prophecies will shape future political events remains a subject of curiosity.

The Present-Day Significance of the Secrets and the Assassination

- **Political Perspective**: Today, the Third Secret of Fatima and the Papal assassination are viewed as important examples of how the relationship between religion and politics can be manipulated.
- **Religious Perspective**: For the Vatican, this incident became a narrative that reinforced the idea that Pope John Paul II was under divine protection.
- **Historical Perspective**: The assassination attempt is considered an event that demonstrates how deeply intertwined Cold War intelligence operations and church-state relations could be.
- **Modern Reflections**: Today, the event remains a subject of debate among conspiracy theorists and historians seeking to understand the Vatican's role in global politics.

The Impact of Mehmet Ali Ağca's 1981 Assassination Attempt on the Perception of Turks and Muslims in the West

During the Cold War, events such as the 1979 Iranian Revolution and the Soviet invasion of Afghanistan had already heightened Western concerns about the Islamic world. In this atmosphere, an assassination attempt by someone like Ağca—who had a Turkish and Muslim identity—against the leader of the Christian world added a particular sensitivity to the event. The attempt was widely covered in the Western media and approached from various narratives.

- **Perception of Muslim Terrorism**: After the assassination attempt, Ağca's identity was emphasized in the Western media, and the term "Muslim terrorist" began to spread. Publications like *The New York Times* and *Time* reported that Ağca had previously described the Pope as the "leader of the Crusades" and saw his action as an act of revenge. Notably, *Time* featured photos of Ağca and the Pope on its cover, presenting the event as a global crisis. Such portrayals created the impression in the West that the attack had religious motives.

- **Connection to the Soviet Union and Bulgaria**: In the American press, a theory emerged that the Soviet Union was behind the assassination attempt. Journalists such as Claire Sterling and Michael Ledeen claimed that the attempt was orchestrated by the Soviets via Bulgarian agents. This theory resonated widely in the West and remained a topic of discussion for a long time.

- **Clash of Civilizations Narrative**: In later years, the incident was cited as an early example of the Clash of Civilizations thesis. Especially after the September 11, 2001 attacks, as Islamophobic sentiment grew in the West, Ağca's assassination attempt was reinterpreted as an "Islamic attack on the West." It remained a significant turning point that fueled suspicion toward Muslims in the West.

- **Turkey's Role and Deep State Discussions**:

Some Western journalists interpreted Ağca's escape from prison and involvement in an international assassination plot as evidence of "deep state" structures in Turkey. Outlets like *Le Monde* and *Der Spiegel* highlighted connections between far-right groups in Turkey and certain elements within the state.

Impact on Turkey's Image

This event also caused serious damage to Turkey's image on the international stage.

- **Perception of Security**: Ağca's escape from prison in 1979 and his involvement in an international assassination attempt exposed weaknesses in Turkey's internal security. The Western media criticized the inadequacy of Turkish intelligence and prison systems.

- **Political and Diplomatic Effects**: In the aftermath, Turkey attempted to improve the negative perception in the West through diplomatic efforts. The military government at the time launched an investigation into Ağca's escape and sought to increase transparency in its relations with the West.

- **Relations with Europe**: The assassination attempt also harmed Turkey's relations with Europe. Prejudices against Turkey intensified, and the idea of a "Turkish threat" was revived in a historical context. During Turkey's EU accession process, events like these were frequently brought up as factors used against the country.

Mehmet Ali Ağca's 1981 assassination attempt deeply

affected Western perceptions of Muslims and Turks. The event has been examined from various perspectives including Cold War tensions, Islamophobia, and Turkey's international image, and it has remained a topic of debate for years. Within the framework of the Clash of Civilizations thesis, it became a symbol of tensions between the Western and Islamic worlds. The Pope's act of forgiveness and his meeting with Ağca went down in history as an important step toward easing these tensions.

Who Is Mehmet Ali Ağca?

Mehmet Ali Ağca is one of the most controversial figures on the stage of modern political history. His actions occurred under the influence of certain ideological and political dynamics, closely tied to the tensions in international relations of the time, the dual polarization created by the Cold War, and Turkey's internal political turmoil.

Picture 106. A family, a past, and an unknown future... Is this image the reflection of a simple life, or the beginning of a story hidden in the depths of history? The roots of an assassin... Were Mehmet Ali Ağca and his family standing in the shadow of an innocent past, or on the threshold of a destiny to erupt on the stage of history? Is this photograph the silent witness of a lost innocence and a bloody story to be written in the future?

Mehmet Ali Ağca is seen as an actor at the intersection of personal psychology, ideological tendencies, and the political atmosphere of the time. His actions should be analyzed not only as individual acts but also under the influence of inter-state relations, national security strategies, and political propaganda. Research shows that the motivations behind Ağca's actions stem from both personal psychological elements and broader political and social dynamics.

In this context, Mehmet Ali Ağca should not be seen merely as a hero or a victim but as a reflection of ideological conflicts and power struggles. His actions, reflecting the complex political environment of the time, radical ideological currents, and international political strategies, have secured their place in history as controversial and multi-dimensional events. He has been perceived as a shadow dancing with death, a name that pushed the boundaries of human reasoning, marking a historical era while disappearing into unknowns and mysteries.

Ağca was born in 1958 in the Taşbaşı neighborhood of Hekimhan district, Malatya. In his childhood, he attracted attention for his success in school and passion for reading. He completed his primary, middle, and high school education in Malatya with success and, during his youth, developed a strong habit of reading newspapers and books, forming a deep bond with literature. In middle and high school, he developed an interest in poetry. His poems, especially centered on themes of patriotism, appeared in local newspapers and were read as epic verses that touched the national sentiments of the time.

After spending his early childhood and youth in Malatya, he first studied at Ankara University's Faculty of Language and History, where he met nationalist youth leaders such as Abdullah Çatlı and Muhsin Yazıcıoğlu. Two years later, Ağca moved to Istanbul and continued his education at Istanbul University's Faculty of Economics.

His university years were a period that expanded his intellectual horizons and brought him into contact with various ideological groups. Influenced by the intellectual movements of the time, Ağca reflected the knowledge and critical thinking he gained during this period into later stages of his life. In Italian courts, Ağca was tried alongside Musa Serdar Çelebi, one of the nationalist leaders in Europe at the time, and Abdullah Çatlı was also called as a witness. Çatlı and Ağca were confronted in court. Ağca repeatedly emphasized in court that these individuals were not connected to the assassination and insisted his act was individual.

Known as a bookworm, Ağca read more than 1,500 books during his time in prison in Italy and regularly followed local and foreign press. This intense reading habit not only deepened his intellectual perspective but also enabled him to learn Italian and English to a very high level—so much so that he became proficient enough to write books in these languages.

Letters from Catholics to Mehmet Ali Ağca

In addition to being a globally controversial figure, Mehmet Ali Ağca has reached a wide audience through the books he authored. His works, published primarily in Turkey and various European countries, attracted readers' attention. His thoughts, especially on religious matters, resonated among different faith communities.

In particular, in the Catholic world, Ağca's name has become associated with the Fatima miracles. The Fatima miracle holds great importance for Catholics. Ağca's interest in these miracles and his references to them in his writings attracted special attention from Catholic Christian communities and generated particular interest in him.

As a result of this interest, Catholic Christians from around the world have sent letters to Ağca. A large portion of these letters expressed interest in his ideas and support for his views on the Fatima miracles. This interest even manifested on social media, where Catholic Christian groups formed to pray for Ağca. These groups operate on various social media platforms, praying for him and sharing his thoughts.

Mehmet Ali Ağca's life and actions have been featured in numerous films and documentaries in the West. His complex personality and his place in history have been the subject of varied interpretations. Most recently, the fourth episode of the Netflix documentary series *True Spy Stories*, titled *The Plot to Kill the Pope*, recounts Ağca's background and the political-intellectual atmosphere of his era through his own narratives and experiences.

Ağca's writings show that he is more than just a political or historical figure; he has also become a focal point in religious debates. His impact, especially in the Catholic world, has caused his name to be associated not only with past events but also with ongoing religious and philosophical discussions.

With his personal story, ideological quests, and continued relevance on the modern historical stage, Mehmet Ali Ağca presents a figure who combines multidimensional intellectual and cultural depth. Viewed from an objective perspective, he should not be regarded merely as an assassin or the actor of a dramatic event, but as a controversial and complex character who reflects the spirit of his time—where ideology and personal conflict intertwine.

In conclusion, Mehmet Ali Ağca has reached a wide readership through his interviews, books, and expressed thoughts, creating significant reverberations especially within the Catholic world. His interest in the Fatima miracles attracted the attention of Catholic communities, leading to the formation of prayer groups for him. This influence has positioned Ağca not just as a political figure in history, but also as a focal point of religious and philosophical debate.

A Figure in the Gray Zones of History

Mehmet Ali Ağca is a figure who can neither be fully defined as a hero nor entirely as a traitor. Although his actions have had great impacts on world history, whether these impacts were intentional or coincidental remains debatable. His roles in events like the assassination attempt on the Pope and the murder of journalist Abdi İpekçi reveal the power struggles shaping global politics, while also raising deep ethical and moral questions.

Ağca's identity is not limited to a single assassination attempt. His personal transformations and views on religion and ideology elevate him beyond the role of a mere perpetrator, turning him into a multifaceted character. Sometimes declaring himself as the Messiah, and at other times making striking claims about the global order, Ağca consistently presents a shifting identity.

Thus, the question of whether Mehmet Ali Ağca is a "hero or a traitor" finds its place in the gray areas of history and politics and is entirely subject to personal and ideological interpretations. One thing is certain: Ağca's actions and the mysteries surrounding them remain among the pivotal turning points of global politics.

www.ingramcontent.com/pod-product-compliance
Lightning Source LLC
Chambersburg PA
CBHW011126070526
44584CB00028B/3795